Michelet's Poetic Vision

Michelet, circa 1858

Michelet's Poetic Vision

A Romantic Philosophy of Nature, Man, & Woman

🐝

Edward K. Kaplan

🐝

University of Massachusetts Press
Amherst, 1977

Copyright © 1977 by
The University of Massachusetts Press
All rights reserved
Library of Congress Catalog Card Number 76-45050
ISBN 0-87023-236-3
Designed by Mary Mendell
Printed in the United States of America
Library of Congress Cataloging in Publication Data
appear on the last printed page of the book.
Frontispiece: Photograph of Michelet by Carjat, ca. 1858.
Reproduced by Jacques Buchholz.

*To Jeremy Joshua
and to those companions who taught me the power
of friendship*

Contents

Acknowledgments

It is a pleasure to recall with deep appreciation the people who accompanied me on the journey which has ended, provisionally, at the present book. My development as a person was decisively influenced by S. Ralph Harlow, Abraham J. Heschel, Albert J. Salvan, Howard Thurman, and my parents Emily and Kivie Kaplan.

Other people enriched *Michelet's Poetic Vision* more directly, by reading parts or all of the manuscript, by fruitful conversation and practical advice. I name them alphabetically and without titles. The book began as a Columbia University doctoral dissertation written under the inspiration of Michael Riffaterre; in addition I received precious counsel from Jean-Albert Bédé, Jack Bemporad, Bert Leefmans, Joseph A. Mazzeo, and Steven Marcus. That work was reconceived and vastly transformed, nourished by further research. The present study has reached its level because of the rigorous criticism and encouragement of Frank Paul Bowman, Jeffrey Carre, Donald Feitel, Jean Gaulmier, Oscar A. Haac, John Halsted, Alexandra Gilden Kaplan, Fred Russell Kramer, Margaret Mayne, Henri Peyre, Edward W. Said, Maurice Z. Shroder, Paul Viallaneix, and Seymour Weiner. The flaws that remain are my sole responsibility.

The invaluable technical assistance of Perry McIntosh and Judy Stark made my work much more pleasant. My research benefited from the efforts of Margaret Groesbeck and Floyd Merritt of the Amherst College Library and Jean Dérens and Véronique Laisné of the Bibliothèque historique de la Ville de Paris. The editors of *Europe, Nineteenth-Century French Studies,* and Les Presses Universitaires de Grenoble have graciously accorded permission to print here revisions of articles originally published in their pages in French. My Chronology is based on the one published by Paul Viallaneix in his thesis, *La Voie royale*. Amherst College helped finance work on the later stages of the present book, and Jennifer Campbell helped prepare the index. To these persons and institutions I express my gratitude.

Edward K. Kaplan

Introduction

The historian must not only observe his objects like the naturalist; he must preserve them. . . . In order to possess the world of culture we must incessantly reconquer it by historical recollection. But recollection does not mean merely the act of reproduction. It is a new intellectual synthesis—a constructive act.

Ernst Cassirer, An Essay on Man[1]

Jules Michelet has just begun to take his rightful place beside Victor Hugo and Honoré de Balzac as a luminary of French Romanticism. However, professional historians still distrust his most celebrated achievements—the seventeen-volume *History of France* (1833–1867) and the seven-volume *History of the French Revolution* (1847–1853)—because of Michelet's emotional style and the freedom with which he interprets documents. Nonspecialists tend to be unaware of the breadth of his accomplishments. French readers, for example, recall from their schooldays only such anthologized set-pieces as his passages about the taking of the Bastille or sublime moments in his story of Joan of Arc. English-speaking readers may know Edmund Wilson's brief but brilliant presentation of Michelet in *To the Finland Station* as the first socialist historian. Students of language—or art—may think of him only as the first to use the word *Renaissance* to label an entire civilization and body of attitudes: before Michelet it had designated only a mode of European painting. He is accepted today as a writer of passionately biased histories who possesses a genius for expression. Yet there is more to Michelet. He deserves a dignified place in the history of ideas as a lucid thinker who elaborated a philosophical system of remarkable coherence and breadth.[2]

Michelet was also a poet of history. He used facts to create an imaginative system with which he explained both the human and animate worlds. Like Hugo and Balzac he was first and foremost a creative writer who structured his existence through words. Many consider him the greatest lyrical prose writer of the French language because of his style's emotional intensity and pictorial concreteness, in his diaries[3] as well as in his more than fifty published volumes. When the second tome of the *History of France* appeared in 1834, Heinrich Heine congratulated Michelet: "You are the true historian, because you are at once a philosopher and a poet." [4] Michelet called himself an "artist-historian" (a term he explains in his *Preface* of 1869 to the *History*). He had a genius for penetrating the life of the past through empathy, or what the materialist philosopher Hippolyte Taine (1823–1893) called his "sympathetic imagination." Taine explained in his 1855 review of Michelet's *The Renaissance:* "I would not dare to say that he creates history; rather that it is created within him. The songs and thoughts of others, without him seeking them, form again on his lips and in his mind. He himself resembles that Universal being . . . who takes all forms, and who remains himself while becoming all things, and who brings along life and beauty wherever he penetrates." [5]

Michelet agreed with Taine that his empathic genius was the source of his creative method. He writes in *The People:* "I who have died many times, within myself and within history . . . God has given me the gift, through history, of being able to participate in all things." [6] The artist-historian identifies with the thoughts and emotions of personages he evokes in order to create an "integral resurrection of the past." Historians of ideas consider empathy the source of modern historical writing. Ernst Cassirer (1874–1945) insists that "it is the richness and variety, the depth and intensity, of his personal experience which is the distinctive mark of the great historian." [7] R. G. Collingwood (1889–1943) defines historical knowing as the reenactment of past experience in the historian's mind. These two great scholars fail to mention Michelet, although they recognize the importance of Michelet's two closest inspirers: Giambattista Vico and Johann Gottfried von Herder. It is surprising that they seem unaware that the author of the *History of France* best exemplifies "Herder's verb *einfühlen* [empathy] . . . the process whereby the organism of a culture is 'intuitively seen, inwardly experienced, grasped as a form or symbol and finally rendered into poetical and artistic conceptions.' " Here is how Michelet understood it: he dies to the present, lives with the dead, and finally resurrects them by describing himself.

Michelet studied the art, religion, literature, law, and folklore of the past, in addition to political events, as would an epic poet. His contemporaries recognized these qualities. Some anticipated modern criticism. After reading volume 5 of the *History of France* (Joan of Arc) Gasparin wrote to Michelet in January 1842:

> You are still an excellent narrator. . . . But at the same time you are a man of imagination, a man who excessively tries to put facts into a mythical system, one which not everyone can accept. That explains the controversies among your readers, many of whom still follow you only with suspicion. Fortunately, as you continue, the systematic part [of your work] becomes increasingly detached from the historical part. You no longer base one upon the other, you separate them. Some day it will be easy for you to give us your narration on the one hand, and, on the other, a very interesting work on the systematic progression and the mythical significance of history.[8]

Gasparin understood the two theoretically separable dimensions of Michelet's text: the story, and what Roland Barthes calls "Michelet's existential thematics," the recurring images underlying the historian's essentially petit-bourgeois ideology.[9] He appreciated the unity of Michelet's imagination but considered it subversive to factual objectivity. Gasparin did not trust Michelet's philosophical approach. I have embraced it. My study of *Michelet's Poetic Vision* attempts that "very interesting work on the systematic progression and the mythical significance of history." The voices of Michelet the poet, historian, and philosopher are one.

Michelet personifies the Romantic imagination. (Flaubert went so far as to call him the *only* French Romantic.) [10] Paul Viallaneix, author of the definitive study of Michelet's social thought and editor-in-chief of Michelet's *Oeuvres complètes,* does not exaggerate when he says that Michelet's works constitute an encyclopedia of Romanticism in the form of an epic poem.[11] The historian wrote the legend of the masses whose self-liberation his *Histories* celebrate. Joan of Arc, the Renaissance, the Revolution—and the all-inclusive myth of the People—were high points in a drama in which freedom progressed without end. The professor whom students at the Collège de France nicknamed "Monsieur Symbole" certainly illustrates René Wellek's definition of the Romantic vision: "Imagination for the view of poetry, [an organic conception of] nature for the view of the world, and symbol and myth for poetic style." [12]

Michelet's belief that writing was a means of social redemption corresponds to the Romantic image of the sacred artist or poet-teacher.

This myth continued the dream of Enlightenment intellectuals: the philosopher as universal legislator. Thinkers and writers after the Revolution discovered that history could mediate between past and future. Like his contemporaries Saint-Simon and Auguste Comte, Michelet's long-range goal was to replace Christianity with a religion of humanity. In the book which anticipates his entire production, *The People* (1846), he defined his vision of France as a religion.* The history of France, like the Bible, describes the path toward salvation: the two redemptions are the advent of Joan of Arc and the French Revolution. France imitates Christ the Redeemer, as he says: "France has given her life for the world." [13] The historian himself acts as the instrument of ultimate resurrection. Michelet's vision is Romantic for it reflects the hopes of leading poets, novelists, and political thinkers of the generation of 1830 such as Lamartine, Hugo, Saint-Simon, Fourier, Pierre Leroux, and George Sand.[14] Michelet's system, however, achieves full maturity later, during the Second Empire.

Michelet devoted his entire career to the revolutionary awakening of his nation. He was an historian with a moral mission who began as an exciting and controversial professor. Students responded enthusiastically to his impassioned and often theatrical lectures. He was slight of body and his hair had turned white by the time he was twenty-five. His pedagogy typified the tumultuous period preceding the February Revolution of 1848. Michelet gave provocative courses at the Collège de France with his lifelong friend Edgar Quinet (1803–1875) and the messianic Polish poet Adam Mickiewicz (1798–1855). Some claimed that the three were largely responsible for that national uprising.[15] The revolutionary journalist and novelist Jules Vallès (1832–1885) somewhat skeptically describes Michelet the prophetic orator:

> Sometimes when he spoke there were flashes of flame, like the heat of live coals, which passed into my mind. He would send light to me as a mirror would send the sun's rays directly into your face. But often, quite often, he would *poke the fire* excessively; he wanted to raise too many sparks.... What a beautiful head nevertheless, what a fiery eye! that bony and fine featured

* English-speaking readers unfamiliar with Michelet should start with *The People,* trans. John P. McKay (Urbana: University of Illinois, 1973). It is available in paperback as is Michelet's *History of the French Revolution,* updated trans. of John Cocks (Chicago: University of Chicago, 1967).

face, solid as a marble bust and as mobile as a woman's face, that hair in soldier style but of silver color, that modulated voice, such a modern phrasing; he had such a lively appearance!

Michelet defined his program to transform France and all Europe in his nonhistorical works. They are like pedagogical prefaces to the *Histories*.[16] The range of these more than twenty books is remarkable.* He conceived of them as vehicles of popular education which would instill in both middle-class and proletarian readers the principles of the French Revolution: freedom, justice, equality, and the family. As he continued teaching and writing learned histories he felt increasingly removed from his plebeian origins. He bemoaned his inability to communicate directly with those who could most benefit from his fervent democratic idealism. His educational books apply his republican ideology to such subjects as witchcraft, the history of religions, the social, sexual, and psychological dimensions of marriage, the French working class, and natural history. They all proposed a non-Christian but spiritualistic vision of the world. Even after the 1848 Revolution failed, Michelet expected his books to guide the transformation of a society of privilege into a democratic utopia.

He believed that education would liberate his fellow citizens' inherent powers. Two groups of nonhistorical works respond to that hope: studies of his society and naturalist books. The first series begins in 1845 with the publication of *Priest, Woman, and Family,* whose immediate goal was to save marriages by removing women from their confessor's authority. Love, he argued, was the instrument of social reconciliation and the family was its source. Since the woman was the foundation of the family, she was Michelet's representative. He develops his theory of marriage as an education in *Love* (1858) and its sequel *Woman* (1859). In *The Witch* (1862) he revises the negative image of women perpetrated by the medieval Church, and in his final educational book, *Our Sons* (1869), he details a program of what we call today "progressive education." France could be saved if children were led to realize their essentially good nature. These works extend the program he first sketched in *The People* (1846), the book seminal

---

* A complete chronological listing of Michelet's published works, with the editions and translations used in the present book, will be found in Part 1 of the Bibliography. In my exposition, I give only the English titles of works quoted with the date of the first French edition.

to his mission as moral guide. In it he dared to imagine that the antagonisms which divided his nation could be converted into friendship, love, and international harmony.

Michelet's best-informed and most fervent disciple, Paul Viallaneix, rightly places *The People* at the heart of the historian's career. In his encyclopedic thesis, *La Voie royale* (1959), Viallaneix describes how Michelet's concept of *peuple* encompasses sociological, historical, and philosophical realities. Exemplary is the historian's ambition to write a "religious philosophy of the people." Michelet celebrates the virtues of all humble beings, be they poor humans or silent animals; the deprived classes are vital sources of feeling, intuition, spiritual and moral energy. The nation must harness a "heroism of the mind"—the gigantic impulse which propelled the eighteenth century and produced the culmination of universal history, the French Revolution. Viallaneix accurately defines the philosophies of humanity and of nature derived from Michelet's republican ideology. My study explores its foundation: the historian's metaphysical and scientific interpretations of reality.

Michelet's natural history books are crucial since they justify scientifically and experientially the social inquiries and the *Histories*. This second group of nonhistorical works, almost completely neglected until now,[17] is the key to his program to transform humanity. His studies of *The Bird* (1856), *The Insect* (1857), *The Sea* (1861), and *The Mountain* (1868) demonstrate that both nature and mankind are infinitely creative. They bridge history and nature; they explain how the historian becomes educator, and then prophet.

These nature studies aimed to inspire those who opposed Napoleon III and his authoritarian regime. They responded to a pervasive anxiety and sense of meaninglessness. The Second Empire enacted stringent laws restricting freedom of the Press while French industrialism and its concomitant bourgeois materialism appeared to triumph. Many sensitive intellectuals—among them Victor Hugo and Edgar Quinet—chose self-imposed exile rather than implicitly support a government which cherished mediocrity. Politicians no longer promised utopias. Official Christianity was worse than dead; its reactionary character could no longer be ignored. Faith was absent. For Michelet religious and political faith were inseparable. His nature books join optimistic humanism and mystical religiosity. This was Michelet's manner of recognizing the repeated failures of the Romantic idealism which now appeared irrelevant. After 1848 Michelet's hopes became all the more compelling.

The literature of that period reflects a severe disenchantment with the social optimism of the Romantic period. From the British island of Jersey Victor Hugo attacked "Napoléon le Petit" in vitriolic satiric verse: *Les Châtiments* (1853). The Parnassian poet Leconte de Lisle, a former political activist, defined in the 1850s an approach to literature which abhorred personal or social content in favor of formal perfection. Even the intensely human sensitivity expressed in Charles Baudelaire's *Les Fleurs du mal* (1857) was considered by contemporaries as escapist and despairing. The humanitarian dreams of 1848 had almost vanished by 1856, the year that *Madame Bovary* appeared in the *Revue de Paris*. Flaubert's ironic masterpiece draws its substance (if not its style) from a relentless dissection of imaginative excesses in which the Romantic generation indulged. Yet the same year there appeared two lyrical expressions of an active and religious social idealism nurtured by that same Romantic inspiration: Hugo's *Les Contemplations* and Michelet's *L'Oiseau*.

Both masterpieces derive their unique force from the churning anxiety upon which they build. Their optimism seems excessive to us, but to the authors and their contemporaries it was frightening and frail. *Les Contemplations* and *L'Oiseau* both emerge from personal tragedy and political gloom. Hugo and Michelet completely identified with their nation. *Les Contemplations,* the summa of Hugo's poetic genius sent to France from exile, call for a renewal of hope beyond the tomb. *The Bird* also expresses a religious vision and inaugurates the inspirational mission which Michelet describes retrospectively in *The Mountain* (1868): "Living spirit of rebirth. True-heart cordial in these days of too general weakening. May this book, which strengthens us, steady others upon the slope, where, through weakness or chagrin, so many descend! If it need an epigraph, it shall be this word: *Ascend!* [*Remonter!*]." [18] This motto challenges the decadence of the new emperor's crumbling society and complements the positive themes of previous nature books: spiritual ascension in *The Bird,* personal immortality and social equality in *The Insect,* physical and mental renovation in *The Sea.* An important chapter title in the historian's final nature study states their ultimate goal: "Regeneration of the Human Race."

Michelet's Poetic Vision is based on his nonhistorical works, with special emphasis on his natural histories. For the latter describe Michelet's theory of animal evolution which underlies (and explains) his philosophy of history. Its two parts—"Nature" and "Humanity"—are theoretically convenient. Michelet himself was incapable of this exclusive distinction, since mankind, plants, animals—and even minerals—participated in the same scheme. In Part One, "Nature," I explore Michelet's theory of evolution in detail, relating it to his philosophy of humanity and to Romantic science. He was a sophisticated amateur who participated passionately in contemporary debates. Michelet's theories are ideologically motivated and respond to social ills. The nature books have a pragmatic, as well as intellectual function. Michelet's applications and solutions emerge in Part Two, "Humanity." His nature books extend the educational messages of social inquiries such as *The People, Love,* and *Our Sons.* Morality and theory were one.

Michelet was an original researcher in history. He became a superlative popularizer of knowledge when he harnessed his firm commitment to social change to his relentless encyclopedic curiosity. His educational works reflect the advanced thinking of his time on evolution, ecology, the social and psychological implications of sex roles, religious and poetic experience. They also demonstrate a sometimes comical naïveté. Feminists may or may not be amused by his profoundly unconscious ambivalence toward women. Hard-boiled scientists may smile at Michelet's descriptions of the evolutionary will to love, his beautiful developments on nightingale creativity, or the earth's yearning to contact the sun. A molecular biologist friend of mine roared with glee as he read of the jellyfish's desire for autonomy and the sea urchin's wish to become self-contained. But his laughter was neither harsh nor condescending. Sensitive to Michelet's enthusiasm and to his utter love for creation, the biologist sympathized with the moral passion of Michelet's naturalist thought. The modern researcher enjoyed the bold insights, and the limitations, of pre-Darwinian Romantic science.

With Michelet we enter the vital arena of nineteenth-century thought and imagination. His intriguing mixture of genius and manifest absurdity makes us wonder, but his extraordinary insights into the human mind endure. His pulsing and harmonious literary style sweeps us along. The imaginative dynamics which underlie Michelet's philosophy of nature and mankind allow us to discover the model of human perfection to which his theory of animal evolution points. Woman has a privileged place in creation, although the historian's limited conception of her social function prevented the full implications of his generous theory to emerge. His description of the ideal person, or man of genius, fulfills his educational mission. He intended that model to teach everyone how to formulate ideas, produce works of art, love and act with moral sensitivity. At the same time Michelet's poetic vision of mankind turns out to be his clearest self-portrait.

Note

Michelet's Poetic Vision is not a biography, but an itinerary of the historian's ideas and fantasies. The Chronology of Michelet's life and works which follows this Introduction provides all the background necessary. An English translation of his remarkable *Preface* of 1869 to the *History of France,* presented as an Appendix, will allow readers to test the implications of my study. Those unfamiliar with Michelet might read his *Preface* first, for it defines his unity for posterity, as he saw it at the end of a fulfilled lifetime. The *Preface* is an intellectual autobiography and a last testament; it still vibrates with the author's powerful presence.

I have attempted to retain the flavor of Michelet's exceptional French prose by quoting nineteenth-century English translations, which I have corrected when necessary. These Victorian translations capture much of the vitality of the French originals and should balance my primarily analytical approach. Perhaps this contact with Michelet's prose, limited as it is, will stimulate updated translations of these books, long out of print in both French and English. Michelet's survival as a major figure depends, I believe, on his works of popular education. Ellipses in quotations are indicated by spaced periods [. . .]; while the unspaced periods are the author's own *points de suspension,* meant to suggest a silent pause, often to provoke the reader's thoughts or daydreams.

Detailed endnotes which give sources and suggestions for further research are printed at the back of the book. Many of them are bibliographical and intentionally open-ended. Notes of immediate relevance to my exposition are printed at the bottom of the page.

Chronology

1798   On 21 August Jules Michelet was born in Paris in a deconsecrated convent chapel. His father, Jean Furcy Michelet, a native of Laon, ran a small printing shop. His mother, Angélique-Constance Millet, was born in Renwez of a peasant family in the Ardennes.

1800   The Michelet family took up residence on rue Montmartre, then rue du Jour (1801), then rue Française (1802).

1808   Michelet's father was imprisoned for debts at Sainte-Pélagie. He was freed the following year.

1809   Michelet learned to set type in his father's printing shop and began his studies in 1810 at the pension of M. Mélot, a grammarian and former Jacobin.

1812   Because of an official Napoleonic decree of February 1810 the number of Parisian printers was limited to sixty; Michelet's father lost his livelihood. In October Jules entered the Collège Charlemagne after some private tutoring.

1815   On 9 February Michelet's mother died after a long illness aggravated by the winter cold and malnutrition. His father moved to the nursing home at which he worked; Jules entered the Rhétorique class (the final year) at the Collège Charlemagne.

1817–19   Michelet earned his university degrees: *baccalauréat, licence, doctorat ès lettres* (theses on Plutarch and on Locke). In 1816 he had obtained the first prizes in French oratory and in Latin translation in the *Concours général*. He now made his living as a tutor. From 1820 on he kept a regular, almost daily private diary in which he noted his readings, projects for teaching and books, travels, intimate thoughts, etc.

1821   Michelet won third place in the newly established competitive examination, the *agrégation des lettres*. He was appointed professor at the Collège Charlemagne; and in 1822 at the Collège Sainte-Barbe.

1824   On 20 May Michelet married Pauline Rousseau in a religious ceremony. He was to have two children with her: Adèle (born 28 August 1824) and Charles. Encouraged by Victor Cousin, he undertook the translation of Vico's *Scienza nuova*.

1825   At the home of Victor Cousin, Michelet met Edgar Quinet (translator of Herder) and began a lifetime friendship. In June Michelet published his first book, a school manual, *Chronological Tableau of Modern History* (1453–1789).

1827   Michelet was appointed professor of history and philosophy at the Ecole Normale. In March he published the *Principles of Philosophy and History,* translated from Vico.

1828   He traveled in Germany from August to September. Upon his return to Paris he became tutor to the granddaughter of Charles X of France.

1829   He gave up his course of philosophy at the Ecole Normale. In November he devoted his teaching to Roman history. His son Charles was born.

1830   During the spring Michelet traveled in Italy. Following the Revolution of July he was chosen as private tutor to the Princess Clémentine, daughter of Louis-Philippe. In October Michelet was named head of the historical section of the Archives.

1831   In April his historical manifesto, the *Introduction to Universal History,* was published and in July his *Roman History.*

1833   On 21 November Michelet began to substitute for Guizot at the Sorbonne in the chair of modern history. Volumes 1 and 2 of the *History of France* (up to 1270) were published on 21 December. His lifetime was to be devoted to this *History,* which he called his life's "monument."

1834   From 5 August to 5 September he made a trip to England during which he discovered the industrial world.

1837   Volume 3 of the *History of France* (1270–1380) appeared in June, as did *The Origins of French Law*. Michelet traveled in Belgium and in Holland.

1838   Michelet began to teach at the Collège de France, occupying the chair of "History and Moral Philosophy." Trip to Venice.

1839   From 24 March to 7 April Michelet traveled to Lyons and Saint-Etienne, where he researched the conditions of the working classes. On 24 July his wife Pauline died from tuberculosis aggravated by alcoholism. Michelet experienced great remorse at having sacrificed his wife to his constant work.

1840   Volume 4 of the *History of France* (1380–1422) appeared in February. Around this time he began an ardent but chaste friendship with Madame Dumesnil, the mother of Alfred, an enthusiastic student of his at the Collège de France.

1841   Madame Dumesnil, suffering from cancer of the womb, moved into Michelet's apartment, rue des Postes. On 23 August volume 5 of the *History of France* (Joan of Arc) was published, showing evidence of his feelings for Madame Dumesnil.

1842   On 31 May Madame Dumesnil died after a long and agonizing illness. Accompanied by his children Charles and Adèle, and Alfred Dumesnil, Michelet traveled in Germany (19 June–30 July) in an effort to dispel his grief. During this period Michelet sought in natural science support for his belief in personal immortality.

1843   In July Michelet published courses he gave with Edgar Quinet at the Collège de France, entitled *The Jesuits*. In August, Alfred Dumesnil, the son of Michelet's deceased friend, married Adèle Michelet. Michelet then traveled to Switzerland with his son Charles. Volume 6 of the *History of France* published January 1844.

1845   *Priest, Woman, and Family* was published on 15 January and put on the Index in April. A violent clerical campaign ensued against the teachings of Michelet and Edgar Quinet.

1846   *The People,* the summa of Michelet's educational writings, was published on 20 January. His father died at seventy-six years of age.

1847   Michelet interrupted his monumental *History of France* to undertake the *History of the French Revolution,* for which he is now best known; volumes 1 and 2 appeared in February and in November. He also traveled to Holland, and wrote a letter to Frederick-William, the king of Prussia, soliciting money for Polish insurgents.

1848   On 2 January Michelet's course at the Collège de France was suspended by the government. In February the Revolution took place. In March Michelet and Quinet solemnly resumed their lectures in the Sorbonne amphitheatre. Michelet was recognized as one of the spiritual leaders of the restored Republic. In November he met for the first time, and immediately fell in love with, Athénaïs Mialaret, a young orphan (born 1821) who worked as a governess for the Cantacuzène family then living in Rumania.

1849   Volume 3 of the *History of the French Revolution* was published on 10 February. On 12 March he married Athénaïs in a civil ceremony. In his course at the Collège de France, he extolled the cause of love and of popular education.

1850   Volume 4 of the *History of the French Revolution* appeared on 10 February. On 2 July Athénaïs gave birth to their only child, Yves-Jean-Lazare, who died on 24 August.

1851   Michelet's course was suspended on 13 March because of noisy demonstrations by his students against Louis-Napoléon. There were many protests against this measure. Volume 5 of the *History of the French Revolution* was published in the spring. On 24 October Michelet refused the half-salary which the government offered him. In November he published part of *The Golden Legend* under the title *Poland and Russia: The Legend of Kosciusko.*

1852   Michelet refused the oath of allegiance to the Empire and was officially removed from the Collège de France and from the Archives. In June he withdrew in semi-exile to Nantes.

1853   Michelet fell ill in March. On 1 August volume 6 of the *History of the French Revolution* appeared. Michelet, exhausted and depressed, spent the winter at Nervi, Italy, near Genoa, recovering slowly.

1854   *Democratic Legends of the North* appeared on 21 January. *Women of the French Revolution* was published in the same month. Michelet sojourned at Genoa, Turin, and Acqui (5–30 June) where he underwent remarkable therapeutic mud baths. He formulated a philosophy of nature. He then returned to Paris.

1855   He published volume 7 of his *History of France,* the *The Renaissance,* on 1 February. Michelet began *The Bird* from 21 April to 2 July under the influence of Athénaïs. On 2 July volume 8 of the *History of France (The Reformation)* appeared. He traveled to Belgium and Holland. On 15 July his daughter, Adèle Dumesnil, died of tuberculosis. Michelet returned to Paris for the funeral.

1856   Volume 9 of the *History of France (The Wars of Religion)* appeared on 8 March. *The Bird,* Michelet's first nature book, was published on 12 March. From July to September Michelet traveled in Switzerland and on 10 November volume 10 of the *History of France (The League of Henri IV)* was put on sale.

1857   Volume 11 of the *History of France (Henri IV and Richelieu)* appeared on 27 May. The Michelets spent the summer in Fontainebleau where he wrote *The Insect,* published in October. In December the couple left for Hyères where they remained for several months.

1858   Volume 12 of the *History of France (Richelieu and the Fronde)* appeared in March. Summer visits to Granville and Pornic in France. On 17 November Michelet published *Love,* followed by *Woman* in November 1859.

1860   Volume 13 of the *History of France (Louis XIV and the Revocation of the Edict of Nantes)* was published in April. Michelet visited Rouen, Vascoeuil, and Etretat, where he finished *The Sea,* begun in April; it was published on 15 January 1861.

1862   Volume 14 of the *History of France (Louis XIV and the Duke of Burgundy)* appeared in February. Michelet's son Charles died on 16 April. On 7 November the publisher Hachette refused to sell *The Witch,* fearing a scandal and a seizure. The work was published by Dentu and Hetzel.

1864   Summer sojourn in Normandy. Michelet published *The Bible of Humanity* on 31 October. In November Michelet began an extensive reexamination of his past; he sorted notes from his private diary and, partly because of his wife, burned some of them.

1867   Sojourns in Veytaux and in Switzerland. The final volume of the *History of France* (*Louis XVI*), volume 17, appeared on 10 October, volume 16 (*Louis XV*) having been published in May 1866. *The Witch* and *The Bird* (in a new, illustrated edition) were reissued. On 1 February 1868, *The Mountain* was published.

1869   In January Michelet's *History of the French Revolution* was republished with a new preface. In September he completed a long and important autobiographical preface to the Lacroix edition of the *History of France*. On 12 November *Our Sons* appeared.

1870   Michelet began work on his *History of the Nineteenth Century*. On 5 August, following the declaration of war on Prussia, Michelet signed the manifesto for peace drawn up in London by Marx, Engels, and Louis Blanc. Michelet was at Montreux at the time of the defeat and the fall of the Empire. On 29 October, he went to Florence, where he remained for a while.

1871   Michelet wrote *France before Europe* with the hope of ending his country's moral isolation; it appeared on 25 January. He had his first stroke on 30 April. On 22 May, upon learning of the collapse of the Commune, he was stricken by a second attack. He momentarily lost his speech and the use of his right hand. He left for Switzerland on 20 June and returned to Hyères in October.

1872   Volume 1 of the *History of the Nineteenth Century* was published on 3 April. Michelet returned to Paris in May. In October his chest became inflamed and his right hand became half-paralyzed.

1873   Volume 2 of the *History of the Nineteenth Centry* appeared on 15 March. In the summer the Michelets vacationed in Switzerland, in the Alps, then at Hyères, where he finished volume 3 of his *History of the Nineteenth Century*.

1874   In January he drafted a preface for volume 3: the book was ready. On 9 February Michelet died of a heart attack.

One: Nature

Jules Michelet

Historian, Philosopher, Naturalist

A vast, all-embracing literary personality dominates Michelet's works: that of the author. This persona represents a model understanding of French history; it testifies to the research's validity and to its practical application. That is why Michelet systematically guides us through his numerous books by examining their common design. He defines his goals at various points in the texts, but reserves his most explicit statements for prefaces. We meet Michelet directly in his prefaces. The most suggestive of these autobiographical reflections span his lifetime: his introduction to *The People* of 1846 and his *Preface* to the 1869 edition of the *History of France.** They portray a reflective identity which develops with the progress of his nation. His method of seeing history in personal terms relates the past with the present so that his *History* becomes alive with the ideas and passions of his contemporaries. Michelet was the moral judge of France. He fully expected his insights to change his materialistic bourgeois readers into spiritualistic followers of the French Revolution. The nation should imitate her historian.

The autobiography which introduces the book seminal to Michelet's career, *The People,* conveys such a lesson. He presents there the two sources of his genius—spiritual intuition and historical insight— as paths to follow. The preface takes the form of a personal letter to his close friend Edgar Quinet and describes the childhood experiences of religion and history that inspired the career which brought him

---

* An English translation of his most famous preface, the one published at the head of *The History of France,* will be found in the Appendix. The *Preface* of 1869 is Michelet's comprehensive appraisal of his accomplishments.

from poverty to fame. Michelet captures your curiosity by telling about his non-Catholic upbringing and then dramatically explains how, at the age of twelve, he experienced a mystical insight:

> I had not yet imbibed any religious ideas... And yet in these pages [of the *Imitation of Christ*], I suddenly perceived, at the end of this sorrowful world, deliverance by death, another life and hope! Religion thus received, without human intervention, was very strong within me.... How shall I describe the dreamy state into which I was thrown by the first words of the *Imitation?* I did not read, I listened... It was as if this sweet and paternal voice was addressing me... I can still see the large and unfurnished room, cold and desolate; it appeared to me actually illuminated by a mysterious radiance... I could go no further in that book, not understanding Christ; but I felt God.[1]

Michelet asserts that God is accessible within the world, independent of any dogmatic system. This statement coincided with his violent controversy with the Jesuits and it typifies his individualistic approach to religion. His opposition to the Catholic church was definitive by 1846, yet he deems it indispensable to express his compelling sense of the spiritual. He believes that a modern faith in a living God originates in such intuition.

Michelet's account of the genesis of his historical imagination is also exemplary. He evokes a striking intuitive experience which demonstrates that insight and moral emotions cannot be separated:

> My strongest childhood impression, next to this [with the *Imitation*], is of the Museum of French Monuments, since so shamelessly destroyed. It was there, and there only, that I received my first vivid impression of history. I would fill those tombs with my imagination, I would sense the dead through the marble; and it was not without some terror that I would visit the vaults where slept Dagobert, Chilperic and Fredegonda.

Michelet's exceptional capacity to identify with historical figures is the basis of his artistic "resurrection of the integral life of the past"—his motto as an historian. He was able to empathize with the people described in dusty archives as he depicted in incandescent colors the struggles of forgotten souls. This historian's talent has ethical consequences: "The great historians of whom I speak were brilliant, judicious, profound. As for me, I loved more."[2]

Michelet was a socially committed writer, but his activism was not political. He considered his ideas, not his actions, as revolutionary. His *History* would provide examples for the common people and stimulate them to realize their potential for leadership. As he saw it, his mission was to convince his fellow citizens to use the rights and powers they inherited from 1789. In 1848, Michelet declined the invitation of Hippolyte Carnot (1801–1888), the education minister of Lamartine's provisional government, to serve on a commission on pedagogical reform. Michelet believed that it would be more beneficial for him to finish the *History of the French Revolution* which he had begun the year before. Instead of accepting temporary public involvement he dedicated himself to that work. It sustained him through the *coup d'état* of 2 December and, despite his severe physical and emotional exhaustion, he completed it in 1853.

Yet politics took its toll. Michelet was forced to transform his existence at the age of fifty-four. Like several other intellectuals (including Taine and Quinet), he refused to sign the 1852 oath of allegiance that Napoleon III required of his civil servants. The advent of the Second Empire abolished his sources of livelihood, his posts at the Collège de France and the National Archives. A succession of fervent dreams and disappointments had come to a bitter end. The "glorious days" of the July 1830 revolution, which had inspired the credo of his *Introduction to Universal History,* had vanished with the sobriety of Louis-Philippe's bourgeois monarchy. His hopes for French revolutionary ascendancy, culminating in the events of February 1848, were again crushed by the election of Louis-Napoléon and the reaction of 1849. Then came Michelet's destitution in 1852. On 19 May he sadly bade farewell to his home, though noting optimistically in his private journal: "I had with me also thoughts fortified with hope and renewal: to change habits, to shatter routines, is probably a step toward casting off the *old man,* toward making a new one, more fruitful perhaps, better, more useful?" [3] His influence was henceforth purely literary. In semi-exile from Paris he became one of Napoleon III's foremost opponents, as he continued to preach his lifetime ideal of a European democratic revolution. [4]

In the French countryside, and later in Italy, he discovered that natural history could provide a response to his personal needs and to those of his ailing nation. The profound anxiety of his demolished hopes stimulated a quest for nature's meaning. Its ideological aspect is most obvious. Michelet's attempt to penetrate nature's mysteries extends his mission as an historian equally interested in the past and in contemporary affairs. In the autobiographical preface to his first naturalist study, *The Bird* (1856), he connects the democratic ideology he celebrated in *The People* with his present interest in ornithology: "Thus, all Natural History had appeared to me [in 1846] as a branch of politics. All living species would arrive, according to their humble right, and knock at the door seeking entrance into the bosom of Democracy." [5] Though many of his contemporaries were amazed that the historian could stoop to such a trivial diversion (and blamed his wife), others, among them Hippolyte Taine, recognized that *"The Bird* [was] merely a chapter added to *The People*. The author has not abandoned his [moral] career, but has enlarged it." [6] The nature books, in fact, become the "scientific" justification of his historical ideology.

Michelet's biographers agree that his second marriage at the age of fifty to Athénaïs Mialaret (1821–1899), a young, orphaned governess, decisively influenced the rest of his life and works. He first met this intensely cerebral but pale and sickly woman in Paris in November 1848, after she had read *Priest, Woman, and Family* and had written to ask if he would become her mentor. They immediately fell in love and were married in March 1849. From that time on she became his constant companion and literary helper. It was she who induced him to study nature, and his preoccupation with the vicissitudes of their intimate relations (detailed in his diary) led him to write treatises on women and love. In 1852 he broke the pattern of almost fifty years of study and controversy in Paris and left the capital with the intention of discovering the joys of country living in Nantes. He was disappointed but went on to rural Italy. His tenacious young wife inspired Michelet to overcome what might have become an insurmountable depression. Because of her, his second marriage was an emotional rebirth. In Italy he restored his physical strength at a health spa in Acqui, through a regimen of baths of mineral water and hot mud. These therapeutic baths of June 1854 consolidated his belief that nature was life's eternal source.

Michelet scholars have harbored much hostility and suspicion toward the second Madame Michelet. There are indeed good reasons to doubt her assertion that she had a major influence over her husband's later writings. After his death she published texts under his name which she altered to fit her notion of the historian's style.[7] According to some contemporaries she was jealously possessive of her husband's time and kept many people away. His diary reveals her frigidity and how she blackmailed her new husband, withholding her sexual favors unless he allowed her to "collaborate" with him as writer. (Michelet did encourage this neurotic behavior to satisfy his needs.) She claimed in public to have created large parts of the nature books in particular, and the excessive lyricism and sentimentality they sometimes display have led some critics to take her at her word. The evidence suggests, however, that the influence of Athénaïs on the conception and textual elaboration of the nature books was minimal. She only catalyzed his imagination.

The origin of the nature series can be traced to the autumn of 1855, when Athénaïs became fascinated with ornithology under the influence of Toussenel's *Le Monde des oiseaux.** At night she would read to her husband from the writings of travelers and naturalists, associating him closely with her new enthusiasm. Michelet at first encouraged his wife's efforts to write a book on birds, and later absorbed it into his own creative program. Instead of helping her complete the fragmentary chapters she had started, he simply took her notes and began a new—and personal—endeavor. On 21 June 1855 he jotted the following laconic and trenchant note in his journal: "Began to recast my love's book." [8] The diary then records wide reading, speculations on natural philosophy, and progress in the composition of specific chapters of *The Bird,* soon published under his name. While the historian-turned-naturalist gallantly insisted that his wife was his active "collaborator"—in his last will and testament he repeated this, thanking her for their financial success[9]—both internal and external evidence establish that her role was not that of creator, but rather that of a loving, but limited, research assistant.

The manuscripts of the nature books are written almost exclusively in the historian's firm hand.[10] Passages of Madame Michelet's prose always appear in quotation marks in the manuscripts and the published text and are sometimes corrected in the final version by the master; while research notes and citations from secondary sources are

* Journalist Alphonse Toussenel (1803–1885), friend and former secretary of the historian, wrote a series of nature studies inspired by theories of his master, Charles Fourier: *L'Esprit des bêtes* (1847), *Le Monde des oiseaux: Ornithologie passionnelle* (3 vols., 1853–1855).

in her thinner, arabesque script. An unpublished letter (dated 26 September 1856) from Eugène Noël,* friend and confidant of both Michelet and his wife, to his best friend, Alfred Dumesnil, the historian's son-in-law, records Athénaïs' displeasure at having her contributions to the book chopped up and digested by her overpowering husband:

> The desire to laugh came back even more violently [writes Noël] when she said: "I hope that he will go back to his *History of the XVIth Century*. Once involved in it he will no longer think of anything else. I will take charge of correcting the proofs of our book on birds and I will try to restore everything that he has taken away from it. But, Sir, that will no longer be easy, because he has torn up all the passages of mine which he has replaced with his. But certainly I will not leave his if I can remove them and retrieve mine.". . .[1]

Fortunately she did not succeed. And yet many years later, the "abusive widow" took more and more credit for the creation of all four nature studies, claiming that Michelet had put into them only "the golden powder of his style." If this external evidence is not enough, the rigor with which the nature books complete Michelet's theory of mankind makes obvious how integral they are to the historian's vision.

Indeed, long before his relation with Athénaïs, Michelet had acquired an intense interest in nature. An important event in his private life reveals this and explains why he had so little trouble consuming the naturalist research of his second wife. In 1840 he began to share a deeply intellectual friendship with the mother of his most devoted student, Alfred Dumesnil, who soon became his son-in-law.† Madame Dumesnil (born 1799) was a sensitive and devout woman who at the

---

* A writer and a gentleman farmer, Eugène Noël (1816–1899) lived in the country near Rouen with his mother, corresponded almost daily with his friend Alfred Dumesnil, authored books on Béranger, Rabelais, and Voltaire, and *J. Michelet et ses enfants* (1878), based on his own and Dumesnil's correspondence with the historian. A nature enthusiast, Noël introduced the Michelets to Felix-Archimède Pouchet (1800–1872), director of the Rouen Natural History Museum and staunch defender of spontaneous generation.

† In 1843 Alfred Dumesnil (1821–1894) married Adèle, who died of tuberculosis in 1855. For many years he did the bulk of Michelet's administrative work, including correction of proofs, became Lamartine's secretary in 1853, and edited Edgar Quinet's *Oeuvres complètes*. Among his own works are *La Foi nouvelle cherchée dans l'art* (1850), *Livre de consolation* (1855), *L'Immortalité* (1861).

age of seventeen married a banker from Rouen with whom she was unable to share her rich inner life. Michelet, whose first wife Pauline had died the previous year, discovered with Adèle Dumesnil a spiritual companionship he had enjoyed with no other woman. When Madame Dumesnil became dangerously ill with what was diagnosed as a malignant uterine tumor, she and her son moved into Michelet's apartment with the permission of her husband. The historian took charge of his dying friend, whose belief in personal immortality he shared. He remained tolerant of her Catholic faith despite the fact that he was engaged in a ferocious battle against the Jesuits. It was at his friend's deathbed that Michelet became aware of the indissoluble link in his mind between love, religious hope, and the life sciences.

During Madame Dumesnil's most painful agony he would read to her, not from the Bible, but from books on natural history, especially from those of his friend, Etienne Geoffroy Saint-Hilaire (1772–1844). Michelet himself drew inspiration from these readings. He reinforced them by inviting the naturalist and his colleague, the physiologist Antoine Serres (1786–1868) to his home. The historian's diary records his reactions on 20 May 1842, the day before Madame Dumesnil's death:

> In the midst of that death, slow and without horror, I persisted in seeking new reasons to live.... I delved into the source of all life, nature; I read the articles *Animal, Whales* [*Cétacés*].* The latter touched me deeply. A poem should be written on those poor creatures, generally sweet and intelligent, judging by their brain and family habits, but condemned by the contradiction of their physical organization.
>
> Last Saturday, I had Serres and Geoffroy Saint-Hilaire come here from the Institute. I admired how that bold mind will not accept the category of reptiles, classing some of them with the fish, others with the birds....
>
> [Etienne Geoffroy Saint-Hilaire] reminds me of one of those primitive barbarians who had so much life and blood in them that, even if they were killed, they would fight on; he reminds

---

* These articles appeared in the *Encyclopédie nouvelle* (8 vols., 1836–1841) edited by Pierre Leroux and Jean Reynaud. Reynaud (1806–1863) was a Saint-Simonian socialist, philosopher, and personal friend of Michelet. His book of religious philosophy, *Terre et ciel* (1854), defended metempsychosis and immortality and deeply impressed the historian. Our chapter 4 on *The Insect* discusses Michelet's belief in survival after death.

me of a barbarian who, without ceasing to be one, has invaded
modern science, shattering it like the vain threads of all our
classifications.[12]

Here already is an anticipation of *The Sea,* the nature book which
almost twenty years later summarizes Michelet's theory of evolution.
The essence of these reflections, however, appears in the homage to
Geoffroy Saint-Hilaire with which they end. For it was Geoffroy who
at that time represented Michelet's vision of nature's unity. Fifteen
years before his first naturalist study, the historian attempted to penetrate the enigma of death and sensed that nature held the secret of
eternal life.

Heroism of the Spirit: Michelet's
Philosophy of Nature and Humanity

There is no separation between Michelet's internal turmoils and
his public program. His task was always to affirm human freedom.
The theater of history was humanity's relationship with nature. He
applied Vico's principle of the *mens heroïca,* the heroism of the mind,
to describe history as a battle between matter and spirit, represented
by nature and humanity respectively. From the very start of his career,
his study of human events had one basic aim: to investigate the relation of freedom to determinism. As time passed he modified his understanding of the natural world; yet he consistently followed the
philosophical program he set forth with youthful passion in his *Introduction to Universal History* in 1831: "With the beginning of the
world commenced a war which will end only with the world, and
not before; that of man against nature, of spirit against matter, of
freedom against necessity [*la fatalité*]. History is nothing other than
the account of this interminable struggle." [13] In this view nature is
dominated by matter and seems to be the irreducible enemy of spirit—
spirit being pure freedom. The deeper meaning of this opposition,
however, appears on the same page of Michelet's manifesto when he
defines his optimistic concept of history as "the eternal protest . . . , the
progressive triumph of freedom."

Michelet's concept of nature changes during his lifetime, but the
principle that spirit seeks liberation from material necessity remains
firm. The absolute dualism of nature and spirit implied by the 1831

Introduction gives way to a more affirmative view of the animate world. The historian defines his mature understanding of nature in the 1869 *Preface* to the *History of France* in which he describes the Promethean creativity of humanity as the fulfillment of nature's inherent potential, its "sublime" power: "The sublime is not at all outside nature; it is, on the contrary, the point at which nature is most herself, in her natural height and depth." [14] He now viewed nature as a source of vitality which humanity could exploit because of its intellectual powers.

Michelet believed that as an historian he could contribute to humanity's self-creation by defining its nature. What is the essence of mankind as he saw it? He first rejected materialism which considers people to be products of their milieu and argued in favor of both free will and a universal moral sense. In *Our Sons* (1869), he characterized "the moral sense as a primitive [human] instinct" [15] rather than as a product of social acquisition, thus opposing his "illustrious and dear neighbor" Emile Littré (1801–1881), editor of the famous historical dictionary and the leading spokesman for Positivism. The historian traces this Kantian theory to Rousseau's *Profession of Faith of a Savoyard Vicar* (1762) which stated that "God and the moral law [*Dieu et Droit*] are identical." [16] Sensing the historical influence exercised by Rousseau on Kant, whom he dubbed the "stoic of Koenigsberg," Michelet used both to dignify his belief that the essence of mankind was freedom.

Michelet's role was to raise his contemporaries' historical consciousness so that they could lucidly and systematically exploit their inherent freedom. He compares humanity with nature in order to remind the former to utilize self-awareness and to rise above deterministic forces such as climate, race, and culture. Human beings, moreover, can create a "second nature." Michelet characterizes civilization as a second nature because the process of human invention is analogous to God's creation of the world. The historian's naturalist books simply extend his view of the Enlightenment. The eighteenth century, according to Michelet, initiated mankind's enduring self-liberation:

> From the day that action returned to the world, not only a prodigious creation of sciences, of arts, of industries, of powers, of mechanical forces were the result,—but also a new moral force.
>
> Action is moralizing. Productive action, the pleasure of creating, are such a great attraction, that serious workers easily dominate

every tiny personal passion. To create is to be God. [*Créer, c'est être Dieu.*] [17]

This declaration of faith from Michelet's last educational book, *Our Sons,* was published in 1869 just before the fall of the Second Empire. The theory taught by the book was timely, for its optimism was sorely needed. Michelet believed that despite overwhelming historical circumstances humanity remained capable of fulfilling its essential nature—through action.

Scientific creativity and moral action were always possible, in this view, because they utilize divine energy. Human invention requires that one consciously control the determinism of passions. Hence, humanity can create itself in both the inner and outer worlds. In other words civilization is another nature, parallel to, but not on the same plane with, God's creation.[18] Michelet joins the Romantic generation of apostles of progress such as Proudhon, Saint-Simon, Pierre Leroux, Victor Hugo, and many others, and persists in seeing creative passion and freedom as the measure of mankind.[19]

Michelet dedicated his life to the hope that mankind, powerful within its limits, would imitate God's freedom *within the world.* The religious dimension of his thought is thus essential and in no way contradicts his dedication to the community. All his books, both historical and educational, seek to liberate humanity by imparting knowledge which people could systematically utilize. A prose poem on the theme of action from *Our Sons* summarizes the single goal of Michelet the historian and Michelet the naturalist:

> "Enlarge God!" Did Diderot, who spoke these sublime words, know their depth, their diverse, admirable and fertile meanings?
>
> Those words mean: Enough temples. The Milky Way for temple, the infinite of Newton. They mean: Enough dogmas. God stifles in those tiny prisons!
>
> But "Enlarge God" especially means: Let us emancipate the divine life. It inhabits human energy; it ferments there; it hastens to pour forth as living creations. The divine life is in nature, seethes in it, wants to flow out in torrents.
>
> Don't you see that the earth wants to produce, to enrich you, to give forth springs and fruits, to create new races, healthier and more lasting, to create without limit peoples and harvests?
>
> Let us be intelligent. Let us close the books a little, open again the great book of life. Let us work! Off with our coats! Let us

release the fecund spirit which seeks to go forth, open its gates.
Thrust aside the obstacles, the fetters. Let us enlarge God! [20]

Michelet inspires us to confront life by arguing that both humanity and
nature are infinitely powerful. Human thought continuously liberates
and increases "the divine life" within the world. Michelet's natural
religion completes his religion of humanity. The heroism of the mind
harnesses natural forces and with them transforms mankind. Michelet
lays the groundwork of a personal faith in opposition to authoritarian
Christianity. His Bible is "the great book of life," of nature and
human action. The historian forgets his initial view of nature as the
enemy of freedom as he discovers in the animate world the sources
of human energy.

Romantic Science and Philosophies of Nature

Michelet replaces Revelation with natural science. He defends the
cause of freedom against materialistic determinism, and against Biblical
fundamentalists who believed nature to be lifeless without God. In
fact, Michelet's theory of nature and humanity develops a philosophy
and type of imagination widespread at the turn of the century. His
naturalist polemics continue the controversy which came to a head in
1830 at the Paris Academy of Science. It consisted of a debate between
the two leading natural scientists of France, Michelet's friend Etienne
Geoffroy Saint-Hilaire, and the paleontologist Georges Cuvier (1769–
1832). This event was a watershed for all pre-Darwinian thought
relating to the structure of the animal world, problems of scientific
method, and what was later called theory of evolution.* Like Balzac
in his 1845 *Avant-propos* to the *Comédie Humaine,* Michelet staunchly
defended Geoffroy Saint-Hilaire's vision of nature, a view which
helped prepare the ground for a truly scientific study of evolution in
France. He shared with Geoffroy and his supporters their nonbiblical,
transformist view of nature and their belief in its unity. The sources
of Michelet's philosophy of nature emerge from the history of that
debate.

---

* Charles Darwin's *Origin of Species* (1859) was not published in French
translation until 1862 and not fully accepted in France until after Michelet's death.
The historian's theory of evolution was well established long before the Darwinian
revolution. More on Michelet's reactions to Charles Darwin in chapter 3.

The fact that Geoffroy Saint-Hilaire and Michelet were among their century's first evolutionists is perhaps due to the deep influence on them of Lamarck. Jean-Baptiste Monet, Chevalier de Lamarck (1744–1829) was Darwin's major French precursor, although at the end of his career he suffered from severe neglect and poverty.[21] Buffon (1707–1788), the leading naturalist of the eighteenth century, invited Lamarck to the Academy of Sciences to study botany. When the Museum of Natural History was reorganized in 1793, Lamarck was given the chair of zoology devoted to "white-blooded animals," which he later named "invertebrates." At the same time Etienne Geoffroy Saint-Hilaire was transferred from the study of mineralogy to invertebrate zoology and soon became sympathetic to Lamarck's theories. Lamarck stated his central position in his *Philosophical Zoology* of 1809. He believed in spontaneous generation and in the gradual, progressive transition of animals from one form to another in increasing complexity of organization. He argued that new organs were produced by physical needs and consolidated by habitual use. These views led to the disputed doctrine of the inheritance of acquired characteristics. By the 1820s, Lamarck's theories had not taken hold, in large part because of Cuvier's opposition to transformist views, and because of the latter's authoritative position in the Academy of Sciences.

Cuvier came to Paris in 1794 "to fill the place of Linnaeus, to become another legislator of natural history," as Geoffroy Saint-Hilaire put it. These two leaders reflected the fundamental conflicts of Romantic science although they remained collaborators for many years and created French zoology, paleontology, and comparative anatomy. Cuvier, closer in perspective to Geoffroy's master Daubenton, thought that science should subordinate reasoning and speculation to the collection and classification of data; Cuvier also believed in the preexistence of germs* and in their indefinite *emboîtement,* an encasing of miniature organisms one within the other up to the point of an original divine creation. Geoffroy, for his part, rejected this notion; he stood closer to Buffon in his belief in the variability of species and was convinced that "as a result of successive changes arising from the material conditions of the globe, in the course of centuries, certain animal forms

---

* This is my translation of the French *germe,* denoting a seedlike entity which gives rise eventually to a fully developed organism. In this context, germ, or germen, has no relation to the modern word for bacteria.

have been imperceptibly replaced by others." [22] Cuvier's opposition to his colleague's transformism was clearly motivated by a theory of creation based on a literal interpretation of the Bible.

The thinking of Michelet's generation was permeated with the ideas and methods that clashed at the Paris Academy of Sciences in 1830.[23] On 15 February Geoffroy presented a memoir by Laurencet and Meyranx which demonstrated an analogy in anatomical structure shared by cephalopods (octopus, squid, cuttlefish, and so on) and vertebrates. It furnished direct evidence for Geoffroy's favorite idea, a single pattern for all animals, which he named rather imprecisely the law of the "unity of plan and composition" [*l'unité de plan et de composition*]. This meant that all animals exhibited a single structural plan, that of the vertebrates. Cuvier, by then the recognized "dictator of biology" because of his remarkable discoveries in paleontology and comparative anatomy, believed that transitions between four distinct plans of organization were impossible and insisted that the species were immutable. What really outraged Cuvier, however, was a statement which the young authors directed against his method: "Today science is pursuing a goal different from that of former times; then it was necessary to construct Zoology, now we are seeking to understand the philosophical resemblance of beings." [24] At the insistence of Cuvier, the classifier *par excellence* of his time, Geoffroy made them remove that fatal sentence from their memoir. But the battle had already started.

Cuvier's counterattack was presented on 22 February in a memoir comparing cephalopods and molluscs, the true goal of which was to "pulverize [Geoffroy's] principle of analogy" and "the unity of composition and plan." Cuvier revealed his underlying fears in a paper he delivered on 5 April: "There is, at least vaguely, behind that theory of analogies, another theory, quite ancient and long since refuted, but which some Germans have reproduced to support the pantheist system called nature philosophy, which asserts the production of all species by the successive development of primitively identical germs." [25] Cuvier's key word is *pantheism;* it represented for him a materialistic doctrine of transformism, one which precluded an original divine creation. Cuvier's biblical orthodoxy conditioned his science.

The debates at the Paris Academy ended inconclusively on 5 April but their significance did not escape the public. Michelet took sides in the worldwide controversy they provoked. In *The Insect* he defends the position of André-Marie Ampère (1775–1836), known today as a father of electricity, who supported Geoffroy. In 1832 Ampère gave lectures at the Collège de France on "successive and progressive creations," in opposition to Cuvier.[26] Ampère taught that "when an animal changes its conditions of existence, all that is essential to its organism subsists, while new formations appear in relation to the new environment."

Michelet was especially sensitive to the philosophical implications of the controversy, as was Cuvier. That is why in *The Bird* and *The Insect* he cites a popular anecdote about Goethe, whose defense of Geoffroy Saint-Hilaire was published in the *Annales des sciences naturelles* in 1831. The views of the author of *The Metamorphosis of Plants* symbolize Michelet's interpretation of the event. The news of the Revolution of 1830 had reached Weimar. Eckermann became upset and ran to Goethe's house where the aged philosopher inquired as to what he thought of the "great event": "The volcano has erupted; everything is in flames, and we no longer have a transaction behind closed doors!" When Eckermann excitedly began to recount the fall of the Bourbons, Goethe replied that he had misunderstood his question, that Goethe was speaking, not of politics, but of the scientific revolution, occasioned by the open breach between Cuvier and Geoffroy Saint-Hilaire. Eckerman preserves Goethe's philosophical appraisal:

> "The matter is of the highest importance," continued Goethe, "and you can form no conception of what I felt upon learning of the meeting of the 19th of July [*sic*]. We now have in Geoffroy Saint-Hilaire a powerful and permanent ally.... The best of it is, that the synthetic manner of treating nature, introduced by Geoffroy into France, cannot be kept back any more.... From the present time in France as well [as in Germany], mind [or spirit] will rule over matter in the study of nature. There will be glances into the great laws of creation, into the mysterious laboratory of God! Besides, what is all intercourse with nature, if, by the analytical method, we merely occupy ourselves with individual material parts, and do not feel the breath of the Spirit, which prescribes to every part its direction, and orders every deviation by means of an inherent law!" [27]

It may appear absurdly anachronistic for Michelet to promote Goethe's vision of spiritual unity twenty-five years after the fact.

Hadn't the deterministic world-view of Positivism rendered the French historian's defense of Lamarck and Geoffroy Saint-Hilaire irrelevant? Quite the contrary. Professional scientists writing when Michelet's nature books were being published argued the same issues.

Isidore Geoffroy Saint-Hilaire (1805–1861), the son and biographer of the great Etienne, illustrates the problems confronting natural science in the 1850s and 1860s. I have chosen Isidore Geoffroy not only because he was an influential savant in his own right. (Charles Darwin, in the historical sketch preceding the sixth edition of the *Origin of Species,* cites him as one of his leading precursors.) He was also a lifelong friend of Michelet. Isidore Geoffroy wrote Michelet letters dating from 1841 to 1860 which closely guided the historian's scientific reading and thinking.[28] In a book published in 1854 which Michelet read, Isidore Geoffroy defines the dilemma facing thinkers of the Second Empire. First he traces the history of zoology from antiquity to the present. Then he describes the methods of three men who represent three schools of thought: Cuvier, or the Elementary School; Schelling, or the Transcendental School; and Etienne Geoffroy Saint-Hilaire, or the Scientific School—a reconciliation of the first two.[29] Isidore's summary of their differences explains the positions taken by Michelet in his nature books.

Isidore Geoffroy Saint-Hilaire states that in the mid-nineteenth century it was common to praise Cuvier without reserve while mocking Lamarck's *Philosophical Zoology.* (First published in 1809, its second edition did not appear until 1873.) Cuvier, he writes, eschewed philosophizing and preferred to devote his energies to perfecting a system of classification. Yet, he supported his biblical notion of creation by affirming the preformation of germs. He believed in successive creations which followed a series of universal catastrophes.

Isidore Geoffroy's example of the opposite way of studying nature is the German Friedrich Schelling (1775–1854), whose philosophy of nature was expressed between 1797 and 1799.[30] Schelling represents the German Romantic "Philosophy of Nature" which impregnated European thought at that period, along with Goethe, Kielmeyer, and the philosophies of Lorenz Oken (1779–1851) and of Schelling's former pupil, Georg Wilhelm Hegel (1770–1831). Schelling and Oken, according to Wilhelm Windelband, used Goethe's findings on comparative morphology "to exhibit the *unity of the plan* which Nature follows in the succession of animate beings, yet this connected system was not . . . properly a causal genesis in time . . . . It is not their point to ask whether one species has arisen from another; they only wish to show that one is the preliminary stage for that which the other accomplished. Their teleology describes the upward struggle of material manifestations of forces, up to the organism in which it comes to consciousness." [31] These German philosophers of nature were not evolutionists as we understand the term; they described a theory which was later demonstrated by the empirical studies of others.

Michelet's theory of evolution and his naturalist method have much in common with the German Romantic imagination. Yet he refused any parentage with Schelling or Hegel, despite the striking resemblances between their ideas. The French historian considered them pantheists in whose eyes events are determined by forces other than free will. His lifelong fidelity to certain imaginative structures also suggests that the question of direct derivation is of limited relevance. The fact is that he absorbed into his personal system ideas that were "in the air" during his youth.

The parallels between Michelet's and Schelling's views on nature, however, do illuminate the former's system. Schelling was more appreciated during his lifetime in France than in his native land. Isidore Geoffroy stresses Schelling's importance to French naturalists and philosophers and summarizes his doctrine in a way that reflects Michelet's views.[32] According to Schelling, "Nature is the manifestation of God; it is God's thought realized, and where he *contemplates himself.* [Italics are Isidore Geoffroy's way of quoting Schelling's actual expressions.][33] The *creation of the universe* or the *evolution of the absolute* is an *eternal act of knowledge;* and the system of nature is the *expression of the universal spirit within matter,* the *revelation of the infinite in the finite.*" Put differently, nature is the form of God, it is the embodiment of his thought.

Schelling's and Michelet's "scientific" methods presuppose that nature and mind follow the same laws; that is, nature follows the laws of the human mind. In Schelling's words: "Nature is but the visible organization of our mind." Hence, in exploring the human mind one discovers at the same time nature's laws. *A priori* rationalism is Schelling's scientific method, as Isidore Geoffroy puts it: "Instead of rising from facts to their laws, one descends from laws to facts."

Schelling goes even further, according to Isidore Geoffroy's exposition:

For Schelling, the activity of the mind can thus be assimilated into the activity of nature, or better, to the activity of God himself, which is *realized* in nature. We think in the same manner as God has created. Our thought is almost an interior creation. From this comes the proposition, which has become so famous, and so admired by the nature philosophers, even though they have found it excessively ambitious: "To philosophize on nature is to create nature."

Schelling's bold doctrine suggests Michelet's own view of nature as a vehicle of divine activity, as well as the latter's view of human civilization as a creation parallel to nature. Yet even the highly imaginative historian who respected fervently the documents of the past did not identify thought and physical existence so closely.

Isidore Geoffroy's picture of his father Etienne's presumed resolution of the methodological crisis applies even more directly to Michelet. Isidore states that his father established a new direction for science, "characterized by the intimate alliance of *reasoning* with *observation,* of *synthesis* with *analysis.*" [34] Etienne represents for him the model which scientists of the nineteenth century should emulate:

The author of *Philosophical Anatomy* thought, as did Cuvier, that science's first need is certainty; from this the necessity of observation. But he also believed, as did Schelling, that observation can give but an imperfect idea of the whole; that reasoning, thought alone, can perceive that admirable network of relations and harmony which so magnificently unites all the works of the Creator.

Isidore's lyrical ending to this text on the history of science is typical of the esthetic, poetic approach to zoology of Michelet's generation.

A more objective contemporary scientist, Henri Milne-Edwards (1800–1885), judges the state of natural history a little differently. In his government report, *Recent Progress of Zoological Sciences in France* (1867), Milne-Edwards writes critically of what he calls Etienne Geoffroy's "philosophical" approach: "Similar to those substances which intoxicate when imbibed too freely, and which fortify in moderation, the principles inspiring those naturalists became a powerful aid to those prudent observers who could apply them within reasonable limits." [35] The writer obviously favors lots of data with a little theory. Milne-Edwards praises Cuvier as the model of empirical scientific method, although he recognizes Etienne Geoffroy's considerable influence in the late 1820s and the importance of theoretical generalizing inspired by his efforts. Even by 1867 French natural history was uncertain about method and still questioned Charles Darwin's theories.

Michelet was not alone in his struggle to harmonize his *a priori* philosophical system with science. He studied nature in order to challenge those who understood life in exclusively deterministic categories. In *The Bird, The Insect, The Sea,* and *The Mountain* he utilized their methods of observation and collection of facts as he elaborated his epic of the animate world. But he added to material evidence a sense of the spirit within nature which his sympathetic imagination revealed. It was then that he discovered in evolution the pattern he saw in history, that of a "progressive triumph of freedom."

2

Evolution

The Constant Metamorphosis

Nature and history act out the same striving toward freedom. Michelet's account unswervingly traces their identical teleology. This confluence would not surprise the reader of the *Tableau of France* (1833). Michelet's geographical portrait of the nation introduces volume 2 of the *History of France*. There he states two principles which remained unchanged throughout his life. First, he understands history in terms of physiology; the significance of geography and culture emerges through organic metaphors:

> France is a person . . . nations can be classified as animals. The common pleasure of a great number of its parts, the internal solidarity of those parts, their reciprocal functions and influences, —that is social superiority. That is the superiority of France, in all the world the country in which nationality, national personality, approaches most closely to the individual [human] personality.[1]

Michelet's zoology is clearly preevolutionary, his history anthropomorphic. The development of physical organisms coincides with mental progress; a nation evolves according to the increasing coordination of its various cultures and regions.

Michelet's second constant is a philosophical view closely linked with his *Introduction to Universal History* published two years before. The *Tableau of France* summarizes all French history as the progressive liberation of peoples from racial and environmental determinism. Michelet defines this struggle in terms of basic antitheses. The goal is to achieve a harmonious, collective, cooperative existence:

Society and freedom have conquered nature, history has effaced geography. In that marvellous transformation, mind [or spirit: *esprit*] has triumphed over matter, the general over the particular, and the idea over the real. The individual man is materialist, he willingly submits to local and private interest; human society is spiritualist, it tends ceaselessly to free itself from the miseries of local life, and to attain the lofty and abstract unity of the nation [*la patrie*].

Michelet's materialist/spiritualist opposition is not final. He confesses his commitment to foster, in all realms, the life of spirit, of freedom. Ideology and philosophy are completely interdependent. Individual autonomy, first of body, then of mind, guides his account of the human and animate worlds. Evolution completes the evidence of history as it confirms the spiritual aspiration of all life forms.

The nature books trace "that marvellous transformation." Natural science is another language which solidifies Michelet's metaphysical intuition. In *The Sea,* the book which depicts evolution, he associates his natural philosophy with Lamarckian transformism. He even features the author of *Zoological Philosophy* as a martyr to that cause. Lamarck's very career, his switch from botanical research to zoology in his work at the Jardin des Plantes, illustrates for Michelet the dynamic unity of all realms:

The genius of metamorphosis had just been emancipated by botany and chemistry. It was a bold but fortunate stroke to remove Lamarck from the botanical pursuits which had occupied his life, and to impose upon him teaching about animals. This fervent genius, accustomed to miracles by the transformations of plants—full of faith in the oneness of all life—evoked the animal creation, and that great animal, the globe, from the petrification in which they had previously lain. He re-established from form to form the circulation of spirit [*l'esprit*].[2]

Metamorphosis bridges nature's differences. Michelet's references elsewhere to Goethe, author of *The Metamorphosis of Plants,* reinforce this statement of Lamarck's putative spiritualism. So does his defense of Geoffroy Saint-Hilaire's doctrine of the animal world's "unity of plan and composition." Michelet's fundamental idea is that separate sciences discover the same universal life force. The image of the world as a single animal renders this theory of nature useful by justifying his reasoning by analogy. Everything points to spiritual unity.

Michelet views nature as a form of spirit, as his interpretation of Lamarckian metamorphosis demonstrates. We can clarify the historian's "reading" of nature as a language of God by using terminology which describes the metaphorical structure of human language—while keeping in mind that Michelet believed literally that divine forces inhabit nature. Existence has two dimensions: spirit and matter. Each can be interpreted in terms of the other. For Michelet these realities were interchangeable. Our present analysis will consider them only as separable realms susceptible to symbolic interpretation.

For Michelet, then, various "forms" in the physical world—birds, fish, plants—are, to use the terms of I. A. Richards, "vehicles," concrete images of spirit, for they all manifest an analogous vital direction.[3] (For Schelling too, as we have seen, nature is the exteriorization of the divine Mind.) God, the abstract or absent reality which the "vehicle" suggests—in Richards' terms the "tenor" of the metaphor—is the ultimate origin of life. The common "ground" of spirit and substance in the preceding quotation is the movement of life, "the *circulation* of spirit." The cooperation of spirit and matter produces the *élan vital*. Michelet's theory of evolution thus translates a mystery: earthly life reveals spiritual intention. The historian-naturalist translates these symbols literally. That fact is the key to his system. His understanding of nature as a *form* of spirit gives theoretical unity to his doctrine of evolution and is the foundation of his natural religion.

Nature's pattern becomes visible in the Paris Museum of Natural History, which symbolizes the evolutionary process. The museum, accessible in experience or imagination to Michelet's public, represents the *organized* microcosm of nature's hierarchy. Its vertical structure follows the ascension of species:

> Our Museum of Natural History, in its too narrow confines, is a palace of enchantment. The genius of metamorphoses, of Lamarck and Geoffroy Saint-Hilaire, seems to pervade the entire edifice. In the dark halls below, the madrepores silently lay the foundation of that increasingly living world which is rising above them. At a higher level, the people of the seas, having attained its complete energy of organization in their higher animals, prepares the way for terrestrial organisms. At the top of all are the

mammals. —Over whom the divine tribe of the birds unfurl their wings and seem still to sing.

Michelet's admiration for Lamarck and Geoffroy Saint-Hilaire puts him squarely in the camp of contemporary transformism. The historian's term *metamorphosis* is approximately equivalent to what we understand today as *evolution*. He symbolizes advancing development as an ascension toward increasing light. Marine life steps above the collective life of madrepores and presses toward the individuation and mobility of fish. According to Michelet's teleological view of the animal kingdom, marine life "prepares" earthly forms. Mammals are higher in this system than sea creatures, because they enjoy independence from the environmental determinism of water. He qualifies birds as "divine" since their flight frees them almost completely from material necessity. The metamorphoses of living forms reveal the same progressive self-liberation that Michelet explores in history.

The notion of metamorphosis indeed guides us through Michelet's labyrinth of nature. A whole cluster of synonyms will form around this term, allowing Michelet to identify the development of mineral, vegetable, and animal with a single spiritual process. As a technical term, in his day as now, metamorphosis does not normally denote evolution in its modern sense; it means "the succession of forms which an animate being [usually an insect] traverses to arrive at its adult state." [4] Yet it was common in the mid-nineteenth century to use "metamorphosis" to express a transformist—as opposed to fixist— interpretation of species development. The historian probably derives his use of "metamorphosis" to suggest transformations from species to species from Geoffroy Saint-Hilaire's famous principle of the "unity of plan and composition," which supposes that the entire animal realm can be seen as a single organism.[5] Michelet adds spirit to Geoffroy's notion of physical unity.

Michelet was not negligent in avoiding the word *evolution* in the books on nature he wrote from 1856 to 1868. As late as 1870, the naturalist and anthropologist A. de Quatrefages (1810–1892), in a book on Charles Darwin and his French precursors, rejected it in favor of *transformism:* "The idea of simple *evolution,* perfectly in agreement with the manner in which [René] Réaumur [1683–1757], and [Charles] Bonnet [of Geneva, 1720–1793] and their contemporaries understood the development of preexisting germs, seems to me to tally very little with the rather considerable changes necessary for meta-morphosing [*pour métamorphoser*] radiata or molluscs into verte-brates, infusoria into birds or mammals." [6] Note that Quatrefages suggests transformist doctrine by the verb "to metamorphose." The semantic association of "evolution" with the unfolding of preexisting germs created at one time by God (the very opposite of modern evo-lutionary theory) was so strong that Darwin himself avoided it in the first five editions of the *Origin of Species*.[7] Michelet follows his most well-informed contemporaries when he uses the term *metamorphosis* to suggest the unity of nature and its thrust toward perfection.

The historian, much like Schelling and Geoffroy Saint-Hilaire, justifies his hypothesis by claiming that the notion of metamorphosis is an *a priori* of the mind. In a note to *The Sea,* he cleverly invokes Cuvier's authority to favor an approach which the paleontologist would have found antagonistic to his own:

> In ascending throughout these pages to the higher life, I have taken as my guiding clue the hypothesis of metamorphosis, with-out seriously wishing to construct a *chain of beings.* The idea of an ascending metamorphosis is natural to the mind, and, to a certain degree, is imposed upon us by necessity. Cuvier himself confesses (toward the end of the Introduction to his book on *The Fish*) that if this theory has no historic value, "it has at least a logical basis." [8]

Michelet is cautious about accepting the concept of a *chain of beings* because for him it implies an unchanging hierarchy established by a single divine creation.[9] This static eighteenth-century view of the ani-mal kingdom (codified in Linnaeus' system of classification) is con-sonant with Cuvier's known bias against transformism. Michelet's use of the great classifier to prove an opposite theory is indeed curious. Cuvier's uncharacteristic sympathy for a purely logical theory (in contrast to an empirically demonstrated hypothesis) is the clincher to our historian's rhetorical argument. The purpose of natural ascension is metamorphosis. The notion of universal metamorphosis also reveals by analogy the same processes throughout all the realms.

The Organic Mineral

The first principle of metamorphosis is vitalism. Michelet's view that life can be explained by some substance (or force) inherent to the inert world and not exclusively by chemistry or physics allows him to find emerging energy even in rocks.[10] Vitalists believe that matter possesses potential life, an *élan vital*. Michelet follows this path and employs the notion of metamorphosis to discover the transition between inorganic mineral and organic substance. An exceptional biographical event had confirmed that idea: Michelet's therapeutic mud baths at Acqui, Italy, in which he apparently experienced earth's energy-giving properties.* He interpreted this event in 1854 before he became aware of the possibility of writing natural histories. These were the immersions which gave birth to a full-fledged "scientific" theory described eighteen years later in *The Mountain*. Hot mud treatments had given new vitality to the historian's tired body. His description of the emergence of life from inert minerals flows from that telluric intuition.

In *The Mountain* he first recounts the details of these baths; then in an important analytical development he follows the path from his feelings of rejuvenation to its technical justification. This text exemplifies his essentially philosophical approach to science:

> Such was the Earth for me in her bounty at Acqui: thus did I see her rise in vapor and liquid through the divine mud which saved me; thus, I thought, did she act in the numerous strata which compose her enormous density.
>
> Her life is *expansion;* expansion which, from her deeply lying furnaces, across her solid mass, works, and transforms, and electrifies her elements, when exalted by the heat, liquified and aerated, and raises them to the surface, so that they may be completely vivified and animalized.[11]

The word *expansion* replaces *metamorphosis* in this intuition of mineral vitality. Michelet's objective explanation hinges on the transformations of solids to liquid gas. This purely physical process appears to produce organic substance through the influence of electricity and heat. He rationalizes this passage from mineral to animal life by evoking material causes.

Further discussion explains more fully how minerals become or-

* He describes his immediate reactions to the treatments in *Journal II* (7–28 June 1854), pp. 263–74. See below chapter 6, section "Is Michelet a Pantheist?" for a detailed analysis of his literary exploitation of the experience.

ganic while revealing the author's polemic intent: to absorb contemporary materialism into his spiritual vision. His vitalism aims to
discredit the mechanistic view of creation that he attributes to orthodox
Christianity: "This fact [of the successive animalization of minerals]
could not be comprehended so long as earth remained inert, petrified
by Genesis, by Biblical tradition." Michelet's "scientific" evidence thus
disposes of the biblical conception of earth as "inert" and "petrified";
he uses these terms to attack antivitalistic views as well as to describe
matter inanimate without divine intervention. For Michelet, biblical
geology is mechanistic, it excludes any possibility of spiritual force
inherent to matter.

Michelet's earth, on the other hand, possesses "an expanding and
burning soul," a molten mineral core endowed with a will to become
living. We must get used to the historian-naturalist's admixture of
poetic and experimental discourse. He has done research (a lot from
secondary sources, it is true), has consulted scientist friends, and sincerely believes that he expresses their latest findings. Yet the broader
assumptions which shape his information are essential.

Michelet's demonstration indeed concludes with a gigantic metaphor, one which summarizes his science in a way consonant with his
philosophy. The key word *metamorphosis* discloses the vitalistic message in his mechanical-chemical "proofs":

> The mechanical processes, the chemical combinations, filtration,
> trituration, expansion, eruption, fermentations far exceeding the
> capacity of the mineral, [the earth] accomplishes all, even the
> impossible. She succeeds in mounting upwards. Augmented in
> power, she ascends. For life grows by life, obstacles, and friction.
> Enriched with unknown electricities, [the earth's] soul arrives at
> its goal. What a voyage! What changes she has undergone on her
> way! If her nucleus possesses a greater density than steel (as
> *Thompson* says), if it is loadstone (as *Poisson* asserts), the *meta
> morphosis* [my italics] must be immense in order to draw from
> that steel, that iron, or from granite almost equally hard as iron,
> so many ductile materials—to mobilize, shatter, liquefy, and va
> porize—and from vapors, reduced to the condition of boiling
> waters, to bring to the surface for our benefit, these potent elixirs
> of life. It is liquid animality. Only the organs are wanting. But it
> mingles with ours, and is easily converted into our blood. Why
> not? Is it not perfectly natural? It is the blood of our Mother,
> who opens her veins for us.

All geological-chemical descriptions end at this: Earth is an animal, a mother. The organic metaphor at the foundation of Michelet's thinking has again surfaced. At this crucial point in his exposition, vitalism suggests the even more fundamental metaphor of Woman. Yet here Michelet contains himself. Chemical change can explain the passage from mineral to animal, for material forces cause life to advance at this primitive level of evolution. Michelet blends spiritualism and materialism as he discovers the link between inorganic and organic matter: "We have found in fermentation and electricity the passages in which inert matter rises to an organic state. The eternal barrier that has been assumed between them has lowered and disappeared. . . . Everything is future or present life. Everything slips incessantly from one form of life to another." [12] The processes supporting the views of his materialist contemporaries demonstrate to the author of *The Mountain* an active striving toward higher existence inherent to matter.

Earth's Marine Womb

The Earth-Mother who directs Michelet's geology guides us as well through marine evolution—the naturalist foundation of his theory of mankind. His account reveals that female needs ultimately direct morphological progress. Michelet's theory substitutes metaphors for facts in a way which parallels his explanation of the metamorphosis of inert mineral into fluid organic substance. But recent research may render his thinking less fantastic. The author of *The Sea* anticipates the aquatic theory of evolution proposed by Sir Alister Hardy in 1960, and popularized in the fascinating book by Elaine Morgan, *The Descent of Woman* (Stein and Day, 1972). Both theories trace basic human characteristics to those of female aquatic mammals and their need to protect infants in a marine environment. Both displace the focus of evolutionary theory from man the aggressive inventor of weapons to woman the nurturant mother. The main difference is that Michelet is not bothered by the origins of humanity. His evolutionism concerns rather the moral and religious significance of life in general.

Michelet conjectures on the origin of animal life in a strange and beautiful chapter in *The Sea,* "The Sea of Milk." Its title refers both to the mucous consistency of sea-water thickened with reproductive matter at spawning and to amniotic fluid in the uterus. Advanced life emerges from the womb of Mother Earth, the sea: "Her children, for the most part, seem like foetuses in the gelatinous state, which absorb and produce the mucuslike matter, overwhelming the waters with it, endowing them with the fertile softness of an infinite womb, where newborn children incessantly swim as in a warm milk." [13]

Sea-water contains an organic mucus which becomes vitalized by chemicals and electricity like the Acqui mud. Michelet shares with Lamarck and the German nature philosopher, Oken, the belief that a universal mucus is life's basic substance. He explains the origin of life in the sea by a spontaneous generation in which volcanic heat stimulates the emergence of primitive organisms:

> In the first ages of the world, countless volcanoes exercised a far more powerful submarine action than they do today. Their fissures and intermediary valleys permitted the marine mucus to accumulate in places, and electrify itself in the currents. There, without doubt, the gelatine took hold, consolidated itself, grew strong, worked and fermented in all its nascent power.
>
> The yeast, or leaven, was the attraction of substance for itself. Creative elements, innately dissolved in the sea, formed combinations—I almost said marriages. Elementary organisms appeared, at first to dissolve and die. Others, enriched by their débris, endured, as preparatory beings, as slow and patient creators, which, thenceforth, commenced beneath the waters the eternal toil of fabrication, and even now continue it before our eyes.

Michelet's "scientific" explanation is couched as a reverie on the past impregnated with Lamarckian hypotheses. As Stephen Mason explains them, "Lamarck thought that minerals, plants, and animals, had all developed from a common source. In the beginning, he held, there were gelatinous and mucilaginous particles, together with the exciting forces of heat and electricity. Such forces had led to the development of animals from the gelatinous particles and plants from the mucilaginous, whilst the same forces had turned the waste animal and plant products into mineral matter. At first, in the simple organisms, the supply of heat and electricity required to sustain them and drive them towards higher forms derived entirely from the environment. But as the scale of creatures ascended, organisms began to generate their own heat and electricity, so that they sustained themselves and provided their own evolutionary force." [14] Michelet's theory follows this pattern exactly. His tautological explanation—"the attraction of substance for itself" and the "creative elements innately dissolved in the sea"—

underlines the self-formation of life in matter. In his view, creation
is continuous, eternal, reaching into the present.

Michelet conscientiously follows the rise of marine organisms
through all their transitional phases. His vision of the sea as a womb
personalizes his biological hypotheses. The continuation of the above
passage clearly reveals the author's fascination with the mysteries of
human birth. Once he finishes the task of explaining the origin of
elementary organisms, he describes how such creatures as madrepores
and polyps create a milieu which favors the emergence of animals:

> The sea, which nourished them all, distributed to each what
> would benefit it in its own manner, and to its own advantage. . . .
> Their débris [of madrepores, etc.], and their constructions, clothed
> the dark nakedness of the virgin rocks, daughters of fire, which
> had plucked them from the planetary center, and hurled them
> forth sterile and burning.
>
> Quartz, basalts, and porphyries, and half-vitrified pebbles, all
> received from our little creators a less inhuman envelope of the
> soft and fertile elements which these derive from the maternal milk
> (as I call the sea mucus), which they carefully elaborated and
> deposited, and by which they rendered the earth inhabitable. In
> these more favorable milieux could be accomplished the improve-
> ment and ascension of the primitive species.
>
> These works must have developed at first among the volcanic
> islands, at the bottom of their archipelagoes; in those sinuous
> mazes, those peaceful labyrinths, where the waves penetrate only
> with discrete gentleness, which formed such warm cradles for the
> newborn.[15]

The end of this passage is worthy of psychoanalytical study, for it
suggests the desire for a return to the womb.[16] Yet Michelet is not
diverted from his exploration of life's advance in the sea. A cycle in
which calcified organisms die and then nourish new generations prepares this evolutionary rise.[17] Organic waste nourishes more independent beings.

Michelet has imperceptibly passed from a predominantly materialistic (though vitalistic) explanation of life to a spiritualistic one
which defines life in terms of volition. Michelet pictures an almost
conscious purpose in a drop of water in which the first living creature
is born. First he observes under the microscope a small cloud of gelatinous and fleecy matter; suddenly he sees a group of fine hairlike

filaments form and exclaims: "Behold the first attempt of life *which wants to organize itself* [my italics]. These confervae, as they are called, are found everywhere in fresh water, and in salt water when it is at rest. They begin the double series—of plants of marine origin, and of those which became terrestrial after the earth emerged." [18]

The origin of marine and terrestrial vegetation, then, is this inherent desire to progress:

> Who can foresee or divine the history of this drop of water?— Plant-animal, animal-plant, which shall first emerge from it? Shall there issue from that drop the infusoria, the primitive *monad,* which, by the constant agitation and vibratory motion, shall soon develop into a *vibrion?* which, ascending step by step, polyp, coral, or pearl, shall perhaps arrive in ten thousand years at the dignity of the insect?

Michelet firmly opposes Cuvier and his school of catastrophists (who believed the globe to be only six thousand years old) when he asserts the fact of nature's slowness. More basic, though, is his description of an immanent development from simple to more complex and mobile forms of life.

At this point in his account of plant development the author of *The Sea* begins to announce that evolution of mind is nature's ultimate purpose. In a passage that becomes increasingly lyrical, he describes the prefiguration of thought within the animate world; this he finds in the luminous colors of marine vegetation. The sensitivity of certain plants implies some voluntary independence from their environment:

> These plants have their motions; these shrubs are sensitive; these flowers tremble with a nascent sensibility, from which will shall be born [*où va poindre la volonté*].
>
> An oscillation which is full of charm, a completely gracious equivocation. On the borders of the two kingdoms, mind [*esprit*], under these floating likenesses of a spectacular enchantment, witnesses its first awakening. It is a dawn, it is an aurora. Its dazzling colors, its mother-of-pearl lights, proclaim the dream of the night and the thought of the coming day.
>
> Thought! Do we dare use the word? No; it is still a dream, still a reverie, but one which gradually becomes clearer, like the dreams of morning.

Michelet's description of the origins of consciousness involves a definite hierarchy of mental processes. His exposition translates this formation of primitive thought by one metaphor: awakening from sleep. Night refers to sleep, a state in which consciousness remains one with its contents: the dreamer cannot, by an act of free volition, awaken to separate himself from his dream. In the language of evolution, night is the state in which vegetables remain fully dependent upon milieu, hence the terms *dream* and *reverie* which Michelet uses to characterize the impersonal will of sea plants. Daytime, on the other hand, brings forth light, which represents mental freedom; just as thought emerges, "like the dreams of morning," so self-conscious will awakens.[19]

The evolution of thought corresponds, on a higher plane, to the physical independence of an organism from its surroundings. Waking consciousness can be tested by a voluntary separation of the I from its perceptions. This voluntary awareness requires a differentiated ego. Self-consciousness must emerge before an autonomous ego may be freely exercised. Awareness of self steps above the mobility which defines animal as opposed to vegetable existence. The physically sensitive reactions and movements of the marine plants just described manifest, in Michelet's view, a rudimentary form of will. Free will explains the superiority of animals and ultimately of human beings over the rest of creation. These plants advance when their sensitivity surpasses mere reflex.

The quest for personal autonomy henceforth defines marine evolution. The same desire that directs minerals toward organic existence impels the medusa (jellyfish) to separate itself from the security of collective life. Michelet explains the spiritual significance of the process in this apostrophe to the sea:

> Every polyp is not resigned to remain a polyp. In your republic some restless creatures exist, who assert that even the perfection of this vegetative life is not life. They dream of a separate existence: to go forth and navigate alone; to see the unknown, the boundless world; to create themselves, at the risk of shipwreck; it is a certain thing which shall dawn in them, and remains obscure in you:
> I mean, the soul.[20]

The "soul" of the impersonal life force reappears as a thrust toward individuation. Yet the jellyfish still resembles the polyp (that is, hydra, sea anemone, coral) which remains anchored to a colony; according to Michelet the unfortunate creature liberated itself before its body could develop as far as its soul: "The embryo was sent out too soon from the womb of the common mother, torn from its solid base, from the association which insures the security of the polyp."

Michelet then insists upon the essential philosophical implications of this episode. Although the jellyfish failed to realize its material goals, it took a firm spiritual stride. As an individual it asserted its freedom over physical determinism (in French, *fatalité*):

> It is the first and pathetic outburst of the new soul, which has broken forth, though still without defense, from the safeguards of the common life, trying to be itself, to act and suffer on its own account—this soft vague sketch [*ébauche*] of free nature— this embryo of freedom!
>
> To be one's self, to be in one's own self a complete little world, ah! the temptation is great for everyone! Universal seduction! Yet this fine madness is the secret of all the effort and all the progress of the world. But in these first attempts, there seems so little to justify it! One might say that the jellyfish was created on purpose to capsize.

The French word *ébauche* (denoting an artist's preliminary sketch, or in biology, a rudimentary stage of organ development) recalls Michelet's teleological view of natural "metamorphosis." Each evolutionary plateau is merely another push toward a predetermined goal. The jellyfish's embryonic freedom from milieu incarnates the emergent soul in nature. The relative failure of the jellyfish reminds us that physical independence, individuality, and motion are necessary preconditions of spiritual autonomy.

The consolidation of individuality in the marine vertebrate kingdom is marked by the passage from the jellyfish, "that gracious theme of nascent freedom," to the sea urchin. Michelet argues that physical need still determined this transformation. He imagines the sea urchin's deepest desire as one for security: "Oh mother sea! I want but one thing, *to be* ... to be one, without exterior and compromising appendages, —to be compact, strong in myself, and rounded, for that is the form which will give the fewest exposed points, —to be centralized." [21] The sea urchin, however, enjoys only a primitive self-sufficiency. The higher realm of animal individuality is what Michelet calls "personality" or *person-ness*.

Animal Individuality and Feminine Morality

The sea urchin, a developmental end-point, reaches nevertheless a dead end because its progress is primarily one of form. Perfectly round, it embodies a complete unity. These conclusions of 1861 simply extend the observations of the physiologist Dugès quoted in Michelet's early *Tableau of France:* " 'As one advances the scale of animal life, one sees that segments join more intimately with each other, and the individuality of the whole becomes more pronounced. Individuality in composite animals consists not only in the amalgamation of all the organisms, but more so in the common pleasure of a number of parts; a number which increases as one approaches higher levels. Centralization becomes more complete as the animals ascend the scale.' " [22] But in *The Sea* Michelet goes beyond this and the text from the *Tableau* quoted at the beginning of this chapter. *The Sea* defends the ideology of *The People:* cooperation between individuals is superior to mere individualism. *Union* is the step above *unity.** Society, or the nation, is the highest evolutionary stage. The sea urchin illustrates this stance: "His perfected isolation had sequestered him, put him apart from the rest, deprived him of all association which is essential to progress." [23]

The possibility of cooperation between selves leads to an enhancement of personality which in turn prepares the realization of moral values. Michelet's theory presupposes that spiritual values within the animal world must be rooted in physical powers. Only then can an individual's will be realized. Fish dramatically represent the quest for spiritual fulfillment that accompanies physical independence. They are the freest of sea creatures because of their centralized nervous system and extraordinary mobility:

> The free element, the sea, must sooner or later create for us a being closely resembling it—a being eminently free, sliding, undulating, fluid, flowing like the waves, but deriving its marvellous mobility from the internal miracle, still grander, of a central organism, subtle and strong, and very elastic, such as hitherto no other creature has in any way approximated.

Henceforth, *The Sea* focuses upon the inner life of its actors. Security of body should prepare autonomy of soul. True spiritual prog-

* This problem has been clarified by Jean-Marie Borzeix, "L'Unité et l'Union, du *Peuple* à la *Bible de l'Humanité,*" *Romantisme,* nos. 1–2 (1971), pp. 111–16.

ress depends upon self-consciousness, a quality which marine creatures at this level do not possess. The reproductive process furnishes an apt means of evaluation. (The author of *Love* and *Woman* will dwell on it at every level of life.) The individuality of fish is perfected, but their personalities remain constrained. Their loving, their procreation are quantitatively impressive but unfortunately stay anonymous:

> It saddens one to think of the billions and billions of the in-habitants of the sea whose only love is still vague, elementary, impersonal. Those species which in due succession ascend in pil-grimage toward happiness and light, yield up to the waters, to unknown chance, the best part of themselves, their being. They love, and they will never know the beloved object in which their dream and their desire were incarnate. They give birth to their progeny without ever enjoying that felicity of rejuvenescence which we find in our posterity.[24]

Michelet is distressed by the absence of an advanced spiritual need: the conscious incarnation of one's dream, that is, a continuation, or realization, in children, of the creation of one's mind. Love among the fishes is "vague, elementary, impersonal," for they lack self-awareness in spawning: eggs and sperm are simply released into the sea while the donors swim off to their respective haunts. Evolution's next stage sees the flowering of individual identity within the family. The new standard-bearers of nature's progress become conjugal, and especially maternal devotion.

Moral values appear in the marine world with the evolution of aquatic mammals. For this is the species in which the female, according to Michelet, controls the destiny of her race. The prototype of this new series of beings—and the word *ébauche* insists upon Michelet's teleological view—is the whale. The female whale prefigures the family love practiced by mankind. This massive beast illustrates the most ambitious aspirations and limits of sea animals, and provides the author with a transition between aquatic and terrestrial evolution. The historian evokes this ascension in another apostrophe to the sea:

> Great mother, who began life, you cannot guide it to the end. Permit your daughter the Earth to continue the unfinished work. You see that in your very bosom, at the sacred moment, your children dream of Earth and her fixedness; they approach her threshold, and render her homage.

It is for you to begin again the series of new creations by an unexpected prodigy, a majestic prototype [*ébauche*] of that warm amorous life, of blood, of milk, of tenderness, which shall find its full development in the terrestrial races.

Michelet clearly believes that Mother is the Alpha and Omega of evolution. Evolution uses higher physical capacities such as warm blood and lactation to prepare moral development. Michelet values whales for their tenderness and considers that warm blood produces moral sensitivity. He thus traces the evolution of human love and its extension, compassion, to their origin in female animals.

Whales also exemplify the tragic condition of all nature, for their exceptional gifts are ultimately inhibited. Whales represent spiritual advance contrained and eventually crushed by physical necessity:

Let us speak plainly. From the grandiose creation of the gigantic mammal issued nothing but an impossible being, the first poetic gush of the creative force, which, originally aiming at the sublime, descended, by degrees, to the possible and permanent. The admirable animal was endowed with every requirement, stature and strength, warm blood, sweet milk, kindness. It lacked nothing but the means to live. It had been made without reference to the general proportions of the globe, without regard to the imperious law of weight.[25]

The Romantic historian reveals the basic polarity of his imagination as he identifies with the creative impulse of God. The dialectic of the sublime and the balanced suggests that God himself, the freest creator of all, must recognize the authority of material laws. The author of *The Sea* states this naturalist observation in esthetic terms: "The first poetic gush of the creative force" (that is, nature's limitless evolutionary energy) can exist only in harmony with "the general proportions of the globe." Michelet's dithyramb on the whale leads to this conclusion: the grand idea, the sublime effort of transcendence, the ethic of the demiurge must answer the practical demands of life.

It is only when amphibious mammals emerge from the sea that moral evolution is consolidated and begins to be realized. Whales cannot fulfill their potential for love because their huge size makes the quest for food overwhelming. Other amphibians approach closer the human ideal of love. The dugong and the walrus are two whale-like creatures that inhabit earth peacefully, primarily because vegetable sustenance is available. They demonstrate how moral development comes to the fore once physical preconditions are satisfied. The moral theme of Michelet's description of evolution—that of the harmonious development of physical and spiritual capacities—is demonstrated most fully by the female of the species of seals, sea cows, and so forth: "The permanency of family ties, deeply felt tenderness, increasing daily in intensity (nay more, Society itself), —all these grand realities began when the infant first slept upon its mother's breast."

Spiritual needs produce physical change. Seallike mothers illustrate the single force behind evolution. Michelet's explanation of how they developed hands is strikingly concrete and produces one of the most (unintentionally) hilarious moments in his writings. (At best his theory demonstrates the pitfalls of uncritical metaphorical thinking.) He argues that an idea (an *idée fixe*) caused the development of the hand in the female sea cow (the French *lamentin* is far more euphonious). In other words, this morphological advance was provoked by an almost conscious application of will by the animal. The "hand" of the sea cow mother literally embodies its desire to love:

> This extreme tenderness, which is peculiar to the Lamentins, is expressed in their organization by a well-defined physical progress. In the seal, a great swimmer, and in the unwieldly sea elephant, the arm remains a flapper. It is held close-set to the body, and cannot disengage itself. At length the female lamentin, a gentle amphibious woman, *mama di l'eau* [*sic*], or water-mother, as our natives call her, accomplishes the miracle. By a continual effort her arm succeeds in releasing itself. Nature is stirred to invention by the ever-present idea [*l'idée fixe*] of caressing her infant and clasping it close. The ligaments yield and stretch, and allow the forearm to go forward, and from this arm radiates a palmated limb.
> —It is the hand.[26]

Michelet's scientific explanation may appear thoroughly idiosyncratic, yet it is nothing more than an extension of Lamarck's famous doctrine (itself much ridiculed by others) of the creation of new organs by "effort," those transformations then being consolidated by habit.[27] On the moral level of the historian's theory, this example of maternal tenderness exemplifies the evolutionary force which seeks incarnation. A person analyzing the author's imagination would say that these transformations concretize his *idea* of love, in the same way as his image of ascending metamorphoses symbolizes a spiritual system. Hands permit tender care of amphibious children, and in superior animals they enable mastery of the environment.[28] This extraordinary genesis of the sea cow's hands demonstrates that the higher one ascends in the process of evolution, the more effective one's will becomes in controlling one's destiny.

Michelet draws parallels between terrestrial and marine evolution. He explores the theory advanced by Benoît de Maillet (1656–1738), that certain species of sea people (called tritons, sirens, or mermen) emerged from the dugong and sea-cow family. Maillet argued that land animals descended from their marine counterparts. He thus furnished an object of mockery for many generations. However he does enjoy the historical distinction of having expressed one of the "first fumbling attempts to link cosmic to biological evolution." [29] Michelet rejects Maillet's theory of the origin of the human race mainly because he is satisfied to give the sea its own significance:

> All life, undoubtedly, originated in the sea. But it is not from the highest animals of the ocean that the parallel series of terrestrial forms—of which man is the crowning achievement—took its start. They were already too rigidly established, too specialized, to furnish the beginning [*ébauche*] of a nature so entirely different.[30]

Sea mammals were too precisely adapted to their environment to change and produce humanlike mermen and land creatures. Michelet thus avoids the controversy of humanity's emergence from beasts which would detract from his main purpose: to demonstrate a moral and physical development common to both. He does this to encourage readers to emulate the best of the animal world.

Freedom from Gravity: The Bird

Michelet's account of bird evolution is also directed by the principle that moral advance depends upon the liberation from milieu. Birds are the most mobile and freest of creatures since they have conquered gravity itself. Michelet had illustrated the physical superiority of birds by the image of ascending floors in the Paris Museum of Natural History. Bird development thus follows a teleological pattern of wing and flight perfection. Nature's will and purposefulness are revealed at transitional moments of evolution:

Let us pause a few moments at the solemn passages where life, uncertain, seems still to oscillate, where nature appears to question herself, to examine her volition. *"Shall I be fish or mammal?"* says the creature. It falters, and remains a fish, but warmblooded, belonging to the mild race of lamentins and seals. *"Shall I be bird or quadruped?"* A great question, a perplexed hesitancy, a prolonged and changeful struggle. All its various phases are discussed, the diverse solutions of the problems naïvely suggested and realized by weird beings like the ornithorhynchus [duck-billed platypus], which has nothing of the bird but the beak; like the poor bat, a tender and innocent animal in its family nest, but whose undefined form makes it grim-looking and unfortunate. You perceive that nature has sought in it the wing, and found only a hideous fuzzy membrane, which nevertheless performs a wing's function.[31]

The author of *The Bird* defends the hypothesis that "nature seeks wings," that it seeks maximum freedom. He discusses quickly the awkward flightless penguins while dwelling upon the gliding and soaring "king of the tempest," the frigate bird: "We have reached the end of the series begun by the bird without wings. Here is the bird which is nothing but wing." Michelet elaborates the theme of flight as liberation from necessity in almost as schematic a manner as the present account and reveals its philosophical significance in a hymn to the frigate bird:

> May you take me upon your wings, O king of the air, fearless and unwearied master of space, whose wondrously swift flight annihilates time! Who more than you is raised above the base fatalities of existence?

The step beyond wing evolution is moral evolution. The higher development of the avian species hinges upon its freedom from material forces. Michelet draws a harsh picture of primeval times and describes how giant birds of prey destroyed lower forms (for example, enormous reptiles) which polluted the earth. He interprets these violent wars as a purification of life by the death of inferior species after which another level of evolution emerges: "Thus nature gravitates toward a less violent order. Does this mean that death will ever diminish? Death, no; but certainly pain." [32] A moral value based on the primacy of the inner life defines this advance. For pain is a sense of anguish as much mental as physical. Smaller, creative birds can flourish when they are released from the fear of painful struggle; a peaceful environment allows them to enhance their inner powers: "To arrive at the higher orders, the heroes of the winged race, the great and impassioned artists, we must reduce the bird in size, in order to glorify the mental and moral development."

What explains Michelet's facile identification of birds with mankind's highest qualities, intelligence and morality? Did his adoration of his wife produce his passion for ornithology? Perhaps the picture of the human mind which underlies his celebration of flight accounts for his enthusiasm for that race. The answers become clear when Michelet considers the bird's power of *sight* as an image of his ultimate goal:

> Behold, yonder, him who flies above, who hovers, who dominates the world, who swims in a sunbeam; he enjoys the ineffable delight of embracing in one glance an infinity of things which yesterday he could see only one by one. Obscure enigma of detail, suddenly made luminous to him who perceives its unity! To see the world below oneself, to embrace and to love it! How divine, how sublime a dream!...

No dream was more compelling to the young professor who in 1831 had dared to embrace a universal history. He attempted nothing less in the *Bible of Humanity* he created thirty-three years later. As an historian flying in thought above the centuries, Michelet could grasp in a single glance the progress of civilizations. The luminous vision which birds attain symbolizes for him a perfect understanding of the world.

Yet birds conquer only space, not time. The upward movement of their flight represents the aim of animal metamorphosis: light and freedom. But light is not only physical; it is also perceptual and mental. The bird's physical freedom endows it with an ideal vision of the world which is a model of human understanding. Put philosophically, physical autonomy is necessary in order to unfetter an animal's *mediating functions* based on free choice.[33] Inner life then appears: will, thought, and moral values. Bird sight represents for Michelet a form of perception which is *symbolic of the mind's own development*. Birds demonstrate that thought and creativity are the end-points of nature's spiritual quest.

3

A Spiritual Interpretation
of Evolutionary Theory

Michelet accompanies his account of evolution with criticism of various theories still under debate in his day. He avidly read encyclopedias and periodicals concerned with natural history and, aided by his wife's research, he kept in touch with his scientist colleagues' and friends' professional discussions. In his nature books, he tackles adversaries by citing authorities to support his conclusions. His use of the opinions of scientists may sometimes seem more rhetorical than historically accurate, since he often borrows only a single aspect of their thought. Nevertheless, there is a serious and mostly successful attempt on Michelet's part to place the reader squarely in the intellectual arena. The historian's gift for evoking human passions awakens a sense of the trials and uncertainties of nineteenth-century science.

Michelet begins and ends his presentation with one assumption. His information is meant to teach the public his spiritual vision of evolution. From the beginning of his nature series, in *The Bird,* he affirms his belief in nature's unity of purpose, in its quest for harmony and progress. This unquestioned view remains firm despite the possibility that nature's direction may depend upon geographical influences: "Why is that happy spectacle of alliance and harmony, *which is the goal of nature* [my italics], present only in the climates of our temperate zone?" [1] His question asserts the teleology of concord which underlies his doctrine of evolution.

Nature as a School of Peace

Michelet's fidelity to this single view clearly emerges from his confrontation with Charles Darwin's celebrated principle of a "struggle for life," which contemporaries interpreted as a violent process. For our purposes, let us distinguish two Darwins: the Darwin of the *Beagle* voyage (1831–1836) who published observations on the gradual building of reefs and atolls by coral animals (*Structure and Distribution of Coral Reefs,* 1842), and the more influential, mature Darwin of the *Origin of Species,* published in England in 1859, but not translated into French until 1862.* In an important note to *The Insect* (1857), Michelet cites the first Darwin to support his own opposition to a theory which explained the rise of land from the sea by sudden cataclysms and catastrophes:

> See Darwin (summarized with genius by Lyell) for an account of that prodigious manufacture of calcium, claimed alternately by fish and polyps, who use it to construct islands, and will soon build continents. . . . The grand theories of crises, the epochs of nature, the revolutions of the earth, lose therefore some of their importance. We know now that everything is crisis and constant revolution.[2]

Michelet rejects Buffon's "epochs of nature" (the title of his final and perhaps grandest book, 1778) and other catastrophic theories in favor of doctrines of peaceful and slow transformation.

It is only eleven years later that he meets Darwin's theory of evolution head-on in *The Mountain* (1868)—well after the consolidation of both his and the English naturalist's ideas. When faced with a warlike interpretation of the Darwinian principle of natural competition, Michelet gracefully reinterprets prevailing opinion:

> "The struggle for existence!" (Darwin.) This grand and simple formula will inaugurate a new era in natural history. It expresses with wonderful force the violent competition which prevails among myriads of beings (plants and animals), all interested in living; cruel and yet innocent; killing others to preserve themselves.

* *De l'origine des espèces, ou des Lois du progrès chez les êtres organisés,* translated from Darwin's third edition by Mlle Clémence Royer (1830–1902), an eminent philosopher in her own right and author of several books. Her translation contains an extensive introduction defending Darwin's views. Michelet read this translation immediately after publication (his diary states on 13 August 1862) and began to correspond with the translator. Michelet's brief correspondence with Darwin is of little consequence.

A struggle, say I, and an innocent struggle; which, inasmuch as it secures the equilibrium and harmony of Nature—therefore *her internal peace* [*sa paix d'elle à elle*]—is not in truth a struggle;—but rather an exchange, a rotation [*roulement*]. In the Tropics, the movement is accelerated, and becomes infinitely rapid.[3]

Michelet escapes from the moral predicament raised by animal cruelty and violence by concentrating on nature's total context, the furtherance of overall harmony. His "social Darwinism" is of the pacifistic sort. A positive *value* allows Michelet to integrate and reinterpret seemingly antithetical explanations of nature's life and death cycles.

He devotes the main body of *The Mountain* to a precise history of geology intended to justify an intuition of nature's gentleness. The way in which Michelet elaborates his double agenda of scientific and ideological debate is exemplified in a lengthy passage in which he confronts various schools of geological thought. In it he cites scientific authorities in both an historical and moral framework. Very astute hints of how political and social values can condition scientific discoveries emerge from what appears as a morass in which more names are produced than explanations. The cumulative effect of Michelet's popularized history of geology is to instill moral principles almost subliminally and without recourse to a forbiddingly technical exposition.

The historian starts by discussing the innovative geological theory of upheavals (*soulèvements*), a mountain-building process caused by the sudden cracking of the earth's hard and solid crust; the subsequent cooling of the surface causes contractions of the liquid interior, which in turn produce mountains:

> This daring "revolution of upheavals" was directed, we must not forget, not only against the Bible and the Flood, etc., but against the Popes of the age, by von Buch against his master Werner, by Elie de Beaumont against his master Cuvier. It was not the less approved by high authorities; by the Aragos, the Ritters, the Alexander von Humboldts. Only one voice dared to contradict it, —that of Constant Prévost.
>
> . . . [The English are] rigidly attentive, and in appearance phlegmatic; anxious to see only reality in itself; they looked at Nature with eyes on whose retina was already impressed their own England, the idea of industrial creation. At the climax of our upheavals, toward 1830, when von Buch and Elie de Beaumont

seemed securely enthroned, a grave voice arose, the geology of [Sir Charles] Lyell. In his powerful and ingenious treatise, earth for the first time figured as a worker [*une ouvrière*] who, with calm, incessant, and regular labor, manufactures herself.

Lamarck, as early as 1800, had asserted that the slow gentleness of the processes of Nature, —that the influence of the milieux in which she wrought, and the infinite time allowed to her work, —would suffice to explain everything without supposing any acts of violence, any *coups d'état* of creation or destruction. Who would have believed that England, a country so Biblical and so long behind in scientific research, would have resumed the tradition of Lamarck, when neglected and almost forgotten by France herself? The result was admirable. The voyages of Darwin revealed to us in the Southern Seas the silent toil of the innumerable polyps engaged in creating the future earth; on whose surface, perhaps, man shall hereafter reside. And at the same time the German, Ehrenberg, demonstrated that the enormous rising of the Andes and other mountains is nothing but the buried ruins of a microscopical world—of shells, silex, and organized limestone— which has softly and gradually risen there, layer upon layer, during millions of years.

These, then, are the two schools: the school of war, the school of peace. The latter is gaining ground. The principle of "peace at any price" which, through Cobden's exertions, prevails in the political relations of his country, seems to animate Lyell, and Darwin. They suppress *struggle* in nature [my italics], and decree that the earth shall perform all her operations without violent excesses; that imperceptibly, through millions of centuries, she shall modify and transform herself.[4]

The ideological lesson of this geological history is obvious. Michelet fully exploits the ambiguity of the word "upheaval"—it refers to both politics and to mountains—as he builds a case for a peaceful version of creation. His theory of knowledge implies that science and politics can reveal the same reality.

Let us untangle this highly condensed and tendentious view of the history of science. Though Michelet is often guilty of oversimplification and a biased use of sources, his analysis is remarkably accurate for an amateur in the midst of controversy. At the end of the eighteenth century, two people represented the predominant catastrophic view of creation which was a compromise between biblical literalism and the discovery of stratifications and fossils in the earth. The German geologist Abraham Werner (1749–1817) is associated with the "Neptunist" account "for the stratification of the earth's crust [which assumed] that all the layers of rock had been precipitated out of a turbid universal sea which had once covered the entire planet." [5] Georges Cuvier represented a second catastrophic view: in his effort to provide scientific support for orthodox Christian beliefs, Cuvier affirmed that the earth's strata were produced by "a multiple series of creations taking place successively in distinct geological epochs." Michelet also presents an accurate account of Leopold von Buch (1774–1852), who turned against his teacher, Werner, with a view similar to that of Elie de Beaumont (1798–1874), a friend of Michelet and professor at the Paris School of Mines. Elie de Beaumont "suggested in 1829 the Vulcanist view that geological catastrophes were caused by a sudden cracking of the earth's solid crust, due to the cooling and contraction of the liquid interior." [6] However, as Stephen Mason points out, "neither [Werner] nor Beaumont could accept the idea of a slow and gradual geological evolution of the earth which became associated with the Vulcanist view in Britain." The period between 1790 and 1820, "the Heroic Age of Geology," represented by Werner and Cuvier on one side, and by von Buch and Beaumont on the other, has thus been both dramatically and precisely evoked by our historian.

Other names provide a backdrop for the main protagonists. Michelet presents François Arago (1786–1853), Professor of Geodesics at the Paris Ecole Polytechnique and the Observatoire, and the German geographer Karl Ritter (1779–1859) as part of the same conspiracy against nonviolent geology. The celebrated authority of Alexander von Humboldt (1769–1859),* author of the widely read *Kosmos,* a physical description of the world, completes that of his collaborator, Ritter. Michelet reserves his *coup de théâtre,* however, for Constant Prévost (1787–1856) who since 1809 had opposed Cuvier's catastrophic explanations with one similar to Sir Charles Lyell's theory of gradual geological "evolution." [7]

Sir Charles Lyell (1797–1875) occupies a special place in the

---

* Humboldt's published accounts of his geographical explorations had a deep impact on the young Darwin, influencing his *Naturalist's Voyage around the World.* One of the last of the great travelers, Alexander von Humboldt contributed significantly to the "religion of science" which dominated much of nineteenth-century thought. See Loren Eiseley, *Darwin's Century,* pp. 153–56.

histories of both geology and zoology. Michelet's early views on evolution were profoundly formed by Lyell's masterwork, *The Principles of Geology: being an attempt to explain the former changes of the earth's surface by reference to causes now in operation,* published in 1830–1833 and translated into French in 1843–1848. Lyell's view, termed Uniformitarianism, affirmed a constant evolutionary pattern in the development of earth. (The term *evolution* in its modern sense was first used in discussions of geology.) It is Lyell who with Lamarck mediated between Michelet and the real founder of modern evolutionary theory. Loren Eiseley, in his award-winning study of Darwin and his precursors, *Darwin's Century* (1958), demonstrates how crucial Lyell's influence was on the future author of the *Origin of Species.* On the *Beagle* voyage, with little else to do other than read and observe nature, Darwin became aware of uniformitarian geology while studying the first volume of Lyell's *Principles of Geology;* in November 1832 he received the second volume, which contained Lyell's views on animal life and a summary of Lamarck's theories. "It is no wonder," writes Eiseley, "that Darwin, years after, expressed agreement with Judd that without the *Principles of Geology* the *Origin of Species* would not have been written." [8] Without going into the details of Michelet's excellent treatment of Lyell and Darwin, let us give him credit for recognizing, despite the inevitable incompleteness of his perspective, the historical contribution of geology to modern zoological theory.

Michelet's use of political and social terms to describe evolutionary theory clarifies the relevance of his naturalist studies to contemporary disputes. For him nature and history illumine each other. Lyell extends his knowledge of English industrialism when he characterizes the earth as "a worker who, with calm, incessant, and regular labor, manufactures herself." His social situation opened his mind to scientific truth. Michelet rises above his militant anglophobia (never having forgiven Britain for Napoleon's defeat at Waterloo) as he recognizes the significance of the English industrial revolution, its politically "peaceful" orderliness, and its economically progressive effects. He promotes the ideology of the radical English economist, Richard Cobden (1804–1865), whose political career was devoted to the furtherance of free trade and international disarmament. Cobden was also mainly responsible for the 1860 commercial treaty between France and England, which he hoped would dispel their mutual jealousy. Michelet's *History of the French Revolution* notwithstanding, he shared Cobden's pacifistic and bourgeois liberal predispositions. Violence could not explain either political or natural creativity.

Michelet concludes by insisting that his principle of gentle evolution is but an outgrowth of Lyell's "geology of peaceful transformations." Names which have now become familiar complete his analysis of the inception of the modern theory of evolution. The end of this text is especially intriguing because of the author's method of combining scientific chronicle, rational argument, and poetic imagination:

> This geological theory of peaceful transformations is supported by the fraternal assistance of the eminent masters of metamorphosis, as our [Etienne] Geoffroy Saint-Hilaire, Goethe, Oken, Owen, and Darwin; who show how the animal, under the varied influence of milieux, and by that instinctive impulse which leads it to *choose* [Michelet's italics] what is best for it, is made and modified. The new geology is, in truth, a branch of the great whole of natural history; it is the investigation of the movements and changes undergone by *that beautiful animal, the Earth* [my italics]. We study it as we do the elephant or the whale. Only— and the difference is great—the Earth is as slow and laggard in movement as it is colossal in size. It does not change, except by the action of ages. What need has it to hurry? It seems to know that it owns time and has all eternity before it.
>
> The reaction in favor of this new school is taking place legitimately, I believe, but not without injustice to its predecessors. Is it easy to put aside the crises, the upheavals, which all men but yesterday admitted to be facts, in concurrence with Ritter and Humboldt? Numerous mountains bear evidence of having undergone violent convulsions; such is our conclusion on first examining them. We must resort to many rationalizations before we can dismiss it, and believe in a slow and peaceful action.
>
> Even in the animal life best regulated in its functions crises will occur, sometimes of a morbid, sometimes of a natural character. Is it to be supposed that the *Earth-animal* [Michelet's italics] has not undergone analogous cataclysms, that in its prolonged life it has had no abrupt and violent intervals? [9]

The historian justifies his vitalistic imagery by invoking the ubiquity of "will" in nature. This universal volition begins with chemical striving in minerals for organic life; on the animal level it appears as a "choice" of the individual over against its environment. The principle that the evolutionary impulse is spiritual binds geology and zoology into a single science. Michelet strictly believes the earth to be a single organism. He complements the "scientific" level of his exposition by expressing his emotional appreciation of the proof. At the same time, by a careful rhetorical procedure, he leads the reader from an appositive ("that beautiful animal, the Earth"), which could function as a mere comparison, to a new verbal creation, a composite word ("the *Earth-animal*") which literalizes the previous analogy. Michelet's demonstration is rigorously structured, down to its most minute stylistic elements.

The hodge-podge of names used to support this poetic intuition is historically significant. Michelet's main heroes are of course Etienne Geoffroy Saint-Hilaire and Goethe, inextricably associated by their mutual aid in the 1830 debates against Cuvier, and by their common vision of natural and spiritual unity. Goethe most clearly asserted that "all nature's children must have been modeled upon one basic pattern, which might be called the prototype," and "that individuality is always a metamorphic variation of an original type [prototype] or interindividual pattern." [10]

The name of Lorenz Oken (1779–1851), buried rather unobtrusively in the list, explicitly associates Michelet's evolutionism with that of the German Romantics. Oken established a symmetrical cone or pyramid of beings, and by 1809, "elaborated [the idea of Kielmeyer] that in the course of its development, every animal passes through all stages of the animal kingdom, and that the foetus is a representation of all animal classes in time." [11] Stephen Mason associates Schelling with Oken, principally the latter's *Elements of Physio-Philosophy* (1810). Both "suggested that man was a complete microcosm because he was the final product of the world and summed up within himself all aspects of the previous development of nature." [12] We recall the striking resemblance of this system (as summarized by Isidore Geoffroy Saint-Hilaire) and that of Michelet: for both consider humanity and nature to be analogous. The passage from *The Mountain* under consideration only hints at these parallels while stressing the idea of nature's unity in a universal transformation.

The presence of the biologist Richard Owen (1804–1892) in this list of partisans of "metamorphosis" exemplifies Michelet's elliptical and sometimes indiscriminate use of scientific authorities.[13] Known as the "English Cuvier," Owen was the chief exponent of the theory that the skull consisted of parts homologous with vertebrae; he also described other structural analogies. He would have appealed to Michelet as well because of his work on parthenogenesis, a process of sexual reproduction that involves self-fertilization of the egg. (Parthenogenesis might have reminded Michelet of his cherished doctrine of spontaneous generation.) Yet despite these congenial views, Richard Owen was not a defender of evolution. In June 1860 he joined forces with Bishop Wilberforce in a brash attack against Darwin's *Origin of Species,* rejecting it on religious grounds. Obviously Michelet evokes only a partial aspect of Owen by mentioning his work on comparative anatomy which may be said to accept unity as a methodological hypothesis; Owen joins the ranks of those who demonstrate the structural continuity of "metamorphoses."

Michelet evokes Darwin's name to support the notion of "choice." The historian distorts this principle which probably refers to the evolutionary factor of sexual selection (that is, the choice of mates by the stronger; the other two essential factors are variability and competition). The author of *The Descent of Man* would have been surprised to find himself in the company of these fundamentally adverse predecessors and colleagues.

This passage from *The Mountain* also demonstrates a shrewd reasoning procedure. The author's attempt to understand the violence of mountain cataclysms in terms of an animal analogy is perhaps not so far-fetched: upheavals are, like sicknesses, exceptional adjustments to a normally balanced life pattern. Geological evolution is an almost eternally slow and consistent process. The discovery of the earth's true age by nineteenth-century geologists and paleontologists was in fact decisive in neutralizing the influence of scriptural literalism which had inhibited scientific progress.[14] Michelet's accommodation of Darwin's "struggle for life" with a view more congenial to his idea of nature's maternal love may also be closer to Darwin's intent. Michelet, despite his compliance to an imaginative construct and his incomplete information, keenly anticipates today's understanding of evolution.

Choosing a Theory of Maternal Creation

Michelet's geological theories combine sentiment and ideology. At stake is the dignity of nature in itself and by implication of mankind, as opposed to the denigration of both by Christian doctrine. Michelet's view was that nineteenth-century science had to come to grips with biblical literalism. The American sea captain and geographer of the sea, Lieutenant Matthew Fontaine Maury (1806–1873) represents Michelet's approach. Maury is the "learned poet of the sea" who penetrates nature through intuition and identification:

> [Maury's] book [*Physical Geography of the Sea,* 1855], so thoroughly honest and truthful, permits us easily to detect the internal struggle taking place between two states of mind: *Biblical literalism,* which represents the sea as a thing created by God at one moment, a machine revolving under His hand;—and the modern sentiment, *sympathy with nature,* which looks upon the sea as living, as a vital force, as almost a person, where the living soul of the world is engaged in a perpetual work of creation.
>
> ... Like Swammerdam, Bonnet, and many other illustrious scientists of devout spirit, [Maury] fears lest, by explaining Nature too much by itself, he should be unjust to God. An unreasonable timidity! The more we demonstrate everywhere the existence of life, the more we make known to man the great Soul, the adorable unity of all beings, through whom they beget and create themselves. Where, then, will be the peril if we discover that the sea, in its continuous aspiration after an organized existence, is the most energetic form of the eternal Desire which, in the past, called this globe out of chaos and is ever giving rise to life within it? [15]

Michelet fights to dissolve the theological impasse which stopped Cuvier and many others: the apparent contradiction between the concept of an utterly transcendent God removed from the world but imposing laws upon it, and the idea of a creative force immanent to nature. The real issue is the primacy of life within physical existence, whether or not nature can progress independent of arbitrary control. Michelet's presentation of Maury asserts that nature is spiritually free.

Michelet does not reject the possibility of an originally transcendent, or "supernatural," source of earthly life despite his affirmation of God's presence within nature. God is "the eternal Desire which, in the past [*jadis*], called this globe out of chaos." But the historian is more occupied with what is still in motion. His doctrine of a constant divine involvement in nature, his belief in life's self-formation, depend upon proof of a continuous creation. Natural evolution and human progress are vehicles of that eternal force.

The natural historian's quest for the earth's origin reveals most clearly his religious perspective. His reflexions are again directed by the idea of divine love.[16] In a far-reaching theoretical note to *The Mountain,* Michelet rejects two catastrophic or mechanistic views of creation and emphasizes the earth's slow organic processes. His guiding metaphor is appropriately one of animal incubation and maternal care:

> I am horrified by the two hypotheses of creation without love.
>
> *First,* The hypothesis of chance. Can anyone suppose "that the attraction of a wandering star, passing near the earth, to the north of the Equator, can have diminished the general pressure, stirred up a tide in the interior fluids of our globe, and by this movement have elevated those mountains which we call Old and New Continents"! (Poulett Scrope.)
>
> Here, indeed, is a fine stroke of chance! But common sense rejects it. Who can believe that a simple shock has created so admirable and so felicitously combined a system of the universe?
>
> *Second,* The hypothesis of an all-powerful mechanic, who, elaborating and equipping the inert machine, by a stroke of skill and force, a plain miracle, has suddenly urged into life this world —without any mutuality of feeling or communion of love [*sans mutualité ni correspondance d'amour*]—has mounted it on wheels, has set it going, and said to it: "Onward!" This is not worthy of God.
>
> The divine idea implies the gentle processes of life—tender incubation and maternal envelopment—above all, the patient succession and infinity of time.
>
> Violent shocks, thunder and lightning, that barbarous apparatus which barbarians supposed to have produced the world, are invariably (as everyone may observe) the cause of abortive births.[17]

Michelet's argument appeals to his reader's less rational faculties, to "common sense," that is, to prejudice and feeling. The same may be said of the author's own judgment. His scientific proofs, many of which are sound, are deduced from the principle of love; even Mother Earth herself was created through a maternal instinct within God the Creator.

Evolutionary Emergence of Love

Love is the key to Michelet's natural histories. His philosophical explanations of nature's progress reveal one reciprocal relation: the

Creator's maternal benevolence and the ceaseless desire of all life to reach the divine. Michelet's model is mankind, the image of God. Each form of life speaks of this quest. The historian's task is to translate.

Various languages express the emergence of spirit. Analogies from realm to realm reveal to the naturalist-historian its genealogy. Michelet uses the famous words of the dying Goethe to establish one basic metaphor in a passage originally published in *The People*:

> "Light! more light!" Such were the last words of Goethe. This utterance of expiring genius is the general cry of nature, and reechoes from world to world. What was said by that man of power—one of the eldest sons of God—is said by His humblest children, the least advanced in [the scale of] animal life, the molluscs in the depths of the ocean; they will not dwell where light never penetrates. The flower seeks the light, turns toward it, and without it languishes. Our fellow-workers, the animals, rejoice like us, or mourn like us, according as it comes or goes. My grandson, but two months old, bursts into tears when the day declines.[18]

All life shares the aspiration of the most elementary mineral. In *The Bird* Michelet uses another metaphor to describe nature's immanent force: "It is the cry of the whole earth, of the world and of all life; it is uttered by all species of animals or plants in a hundred diverse tongues—the voice which issues from the very rock and the inorganic world: 'Wings! we seek wings, and the power of flight and motion!' " We have only to read the languages of nature to discover the same spiritual quest.

Michelet's history of universal consciousness does not neglect vegetable tropism, considered today as a chemical process. He pictures a spirea tree almost voluntarily stretching toward light: "By the configuration of its branches you may plainly perceive how they strive after air and light. You see that it yearns and aspires. Its appearance is like that of a moving person." [19] Despite the obviously rhetorical comparison at the end of his description Michelet literally attributes to this plant impulses common to self-aware humans.

Michelet goes so far as to endow plants with a "soul," synonym in his language for a force analogous to human thought. He argues that vegetable instinct for self-preservation and growth, which could be considered simply physical, prefigures consciousness:

The ancients never doubted that the tree possessed a soul—dim and imperfect, perhaps—but a soul like that of every other animated being. It was the creed of humanity for ten thousand years, until the Scholastic Age transformed Nature into stone. The arrogant conception that man alone can feel and think, that so many creatures are but things, is a modern paradox of the Middle Ages. Science today teaches a contrary lesson, and approximates very closely the creed of antiquity. Every being, it tells us, even the most rudimentary organism, possesses the gift of labor and effort; the knowledge that it may insure and augment its life; the power (to use Darwin's phrase) of *selection* [*le choix,* underlined by Michelet]; and the sometimes highly skillful use of means which lead to this result. Each one is endowed with a personal *art* of being and growing, and continuously renewing its existence [*se créer sans cesse*].

The tree's "dim and imperfect soul" is its impersonal vital force. Michelet extends his vocabulary into a more personalized realm by equating instinct with an elementary form of free will, hence his interpretation of Darwin's theory of sexual selection as a "choice." Michelet uses these voluntaristic terms to abolish the usual notion of vegetable existence as utterly subordinate to milieu. Vegetables no longer exemplify complete passivity. The "personal *art*" and a self-creation of plants suggest their spiritual freedom. Michelet considers tropism as a primitive but conscious quest for transcendence of matter, the purpose of evolution.

Michelet's relentless anthropomorphism is far from being a sheer stylistic quirk; rather it points to the divine impulse shared by humanity and nature. Even the outpouring of the earth's liquid center expresses an almost conscious desire to contact the sun, as a woman would reach out for a man (in Michelet's male-oriented world) :

[The earth is] the tireless worker, born to toil and struggle. It is better so perhaps. She appears enthralled with the light of her father [the sun], that, in the strife and struggle against obstacles, love would perhaps make her forget self-love, and destroy her internal balance. She would rise out of herself.[20]

Michelet's personification of the earth's bubbling upward in terms of emotion suggests that consciousness can emerge even at this brute level. Everywhere love acts to transcend itself. This geological ethics is apparently justified by the earth's surrender of its secure immobility to risk a more noble purpose.[21]

Animal evolution, too, is guided by love. Michelet defines this universal ascent as a sentimental progression:

> The smaller existences, in order to reproduce themselves, are gifted with an obscure instinct, like an attraction, an interior gravitation, which is *love*. First comes the love of self for self (to use Geoffroy Saint-Hilaire's expression). They love themselves, and seek their own good. All this is the origin of the development of every being, its taste, its choice, its preference (*Darwin*), for all the good it has for itself, for all that ought to save and augment it, —make its little fortune, perhaps transform it, and raise it to a higher condition.
>
> Such is the ordinary process of life, which we are ready enough to admit today insofar as it relates to the world of the little, the minor existences of animals. But why should it be otherwise with the grander life of the Earth? [22]

This general description of evolution gathers many of Michelet's synonyms of the vital thrust. First it appears as a mechanical "attraction, an interior gavitation," then as an innate awareness, "an obscure instinct" which is impersonal, volitionally passive. The freer aspects of evolutionary will are love, taste, choice and preference, all of which require acts of will. Evolution is a living child of spirit and substance who lives by love.

Michelet's "scientific" proof for this metaphysical evolutionism lies in his analysis of sexuality. For at the "sacred moment" of intercourse a creature's will to transcend its given nature knows its greatest intensity:

> Love is the effort of life to rise above its being and to possess a might beyond the power natural to it. We see it in the fireflies and other little creatures which excite themselves to the point of flame; and not the less do we see it in plants, in the conjungarae, the algae, which, at the sacred moment, issue out of their vegetable life, usurping a higher one, striving to become animals.[23]

Reproduction reveals a quest for individuation. Sexuality involves a desire to transcend the self and to challenge what is. Michelet imagines what he pleases in the minds of copulating creatures and discovers there dreams of transcendence where others may merely see physical necessity.

Michelet goes further and seeks to verify his spiritualistic assertions experimentally. A true child of the Positivist era, the author of *The Mountain* welcomes the help of analytical science. He calls to his aid two professionals (now forgotten) whose studies of the physiology of plant reproduction confirm his philosophical hypothesis. Nature's spiritual identity can be demonstrated in the "sacred moment" (sacred because spirit is present) of vegetation:

> Morren has discovered in marshes some plants which, in the warm light, become animals for four hours daily, and then, when the day declines, resume a vegetable existence. But the equality of the two lives, the vegetative and the animal, is most plainly seen, —is, in fact, complete, —at the divine moment of love. Such flowers rise to the level of the highest animals, equal to the mammals, having the same seed. (See L. Lortet, on the *Preissia,* pub. in 1867.)
>
> In a word, through fermentation, the stone creates itself spirit [alcohol?]. Through love, the plant makes itself man.[24]

Michelet equates chemical fermentation and sexual reproduction. His bold and highly symbolic assertion that stone can metamorphose into spirit probably refers to the production of alcohol (spirit) by fermentation effected by tartaric acid crystals (stone),* while the apparent physiological identity of human semen and plant seed proves "scientifically" that all evolution is impelled by love. He remembers his use of Lamarck's analogies between botany and zoology when he fits these doubtful observations quite neatly into his moral scheme.

This ideological approach to experimental science explains why evolution appears to follow a spiritual hierarchy: by reproducing, nature adapts itself to a vision of love. To take a familiar case, fish yearn for a more stable condition, for land where families can be raised and enjoyed. Other examples recall the principle that morality precedes (and can effect) morphological change. The harsh love-making of sharks leads Michelet to suggest that a radical transformation may have emerged because of that species' aspirations:

---

* Louis Pasteur explored this process of fermentation in several monographs during Michelet's time. My thanks to Michel Serres for elucidating what was to me an exceptionally obscure reference.

If the life of the sea has a dream, a wish, a vague desire, it is that of fixity. The violent and tyrannical conduct of the shark, its iron grasp, its hook to the female, the fury of their union, give one the idea of a love cherished by the despairing. Who knows, in fact, if in other species of milder character and more inclined to family life, who knows if this incapacity of union, this endless fluctuation of an eternal but aimless voyage, may not be a cause of melancholy? They become, these children of the sea, entirely in love with the earth.[25]

Fish "metamorphose" into amphibians when they desire spiritual as well as physical freedom. Sharks are free to move but the agony of their intercourse demonstrates a need for relationships controlled by volition. Michelet has used the same terms in this context as when he described vegetable yearning as "a dream, a wish, a vague desire." This very sequence of words imitates the emergence of self-consciousness from necessity.

Michelet's democratic ideology is fully supported by his philosophy of nature. He argues for the spiritual and physical equality of the traditionally separate realms of animal, vegetable, and mineral. Animals are not superior to rocks since they both aspire toward a higher existence. The God of evolution is not one who chooses his elect but one whose love is unconditional:

It is love, then, love, which secures the *universal equality* between things and species. Let there be no more pride. The same law prevails from the greatest to the least, in the star as in the flower. There is no high, no low, —neither in the heavens, nor in love, —which moreover is heaven itself.[26]

Michelet attacks the pride of those corrupted by the idea of nature's social hierarchy. His fellowship with the animate world goes beyond mere pity for his inferiors. More basic is nature's right to develop its own moral system (and by extension, that of an individual to construct a religious interpretation of existence independent of the Church). Nature replaces the ecclesiastical establishment, not God. Michelet's democratic natural philosophy does not reduce humanity's status. It stresses rather the spiritual potential of all life.

Now that we have broken Michelet's code, can we find the basis of this moral evolutionism? Or, to be more precise, what is the common denominator of the various "languages" of evolution? The quest for freer movement is one of those languages, reaching toward more light is another. The vital force is thus an elementary form of will which becomes increasingly personalized and aware of itself, in the same way that the "World Spirit" of German philosophy becomes self-conscious within nature. For Michelet evolution reaches its Omega point when the physical world attempts to imitate the divine. *The Bird* again states categorically the author's religious vision:

> The tendency of every being—a tendency wholly natural, not arrogant, nor impious—is to liken itself to the great Mother, to fashion itself after her image, to crave a share in the unwearied wings with which eternal Love broods over the world. Human tradition is fixed in this direction. Man does not wish to be a man, but an angel, a winged deity.[27]

Mankind expresses its dreams in mythological images. Michelet follows this principle which he had learned from Vico and interprets angelic beings as an image of a desire to be released from gravity, from the necessities of material, earthly existence. For Michelet these dreams are not only symbolic. He describes them as intrinsic to nature. All creatures yearn to refine their spiritual potential.

Michelet criticizes theories of evolution primarily for their moral implications. His theory defends the notion of a peaceful creation and evolution, governed by a maternal divine action in the world. Consequently his picture of evolution displays an increase in moral values. The philosophy he derives from nature is egalitarian and religious, for he characterizes humanity's wish to be like God as "natural, and not impious." All beings seek independence from deterministic forces. The historian-naturalist's further exploration of the inner lives of animals and mankind shows how well they have succeeded.

4

The Inner Universe

Emergence of Creativity in Nature and Humanity

Michelet seeks ultimately to abolish any essential distinction between nature and humanity. The "metamorphosis" of desire and will culminates in mental and artistic creativity in the animal and human worlds. The "divine tribe" of birds reaches this evolutionary pinnacle when it creates songs. Michelet's "scientific" examination of bird instinct remains true to his philosophy of the liberation of spirit from matter. The independence from determinism required by creative imagination is parallel though superior to the liberation of organisms from their environment. Michelet argues even more clearly here that some animals possess the rudiments of human thought. He begins by portraying the mind in nature and then describes the mental progress of civilization; he calls civilization a "second nature" because it also reflects spiritual activity. Michelet's philosophy of humanity is thus completed logically though not chronologically by his philosophy of nature.

The Reason-Instinct Debate

The question as to whether or not intelligence is separable from mechanical instinct is "the foundation of all the philosophical and scientific controversies of the [nineteeth] century," wrote the Catholic professor of philosophy Henri Joly (1839–1925) in 1877.[1] At the bottom of that debate was a clash between the materialistic view that considers all thought as a modality of movement, to be explained by physiology (the view of, for example, Taine) and the spiritualistic view of mental creativity as spontaneous and independent of physical determinism. Henri Joly testifies to the importance of that problem to the Church of Michelet's time.

The philosophical ramifications of this question were essential. In his still authoritative government report on nineteenth-century French philosophy, Félix Ravaisson* saw the study of instinct as a key to the problems of mind vs. matter and of freedom vs. determinism. Ravaisson was an outstanding philosopher in his own right and willingly placed the author of *The Bird* and *The Insect* in a list of eminent scientists who "have sought to determine, with more precision than ever before, the differences and resemblances between instinct and intelligence." [2] These included Frédéric Cuvier (1773–1838), brother of Georges; Pierre Flourens (1794–1867), leading expert on instinct; the early anthropologist and evolutionist, A. de Quatrefages (1810–1892); the versatile yet solid scholar Alfred Maury (1817–1892); and a medical expert on the physiology of the nervous system, Alfred Vulpian (1826–1887). Although Ravaisson's friendship with Michelet explains in part the inclusion of the amateur naturalist among these distinguished professionals, the fact that he did so validates Michelet's claim to have written books of serious scientific import.

Michelet's position in the reason-instinct controversy typifies his spiritualistic view of nature. His refusal to be satisfied with explanations of animal behavior as instinctual and automatic parallels his horror of mechanistic accounts of creation. In his view the will emerges with bodily autonomy and differentiates itself as consciousness. Will finally metamorphoses into what Michelet calls the "soul" of animals: "Preconceived ideas and dogmatic theories apart, you cannot offend God by restoring a soul to the beast. How much grander is his work if he has created persons, souls, and wills, than if he had constructed machines!" [3] His equation of "persons, souls, wills" intimates that animal and human creativity have a common foundation. However, this part of the argument just soothes the timid reader whose opinions reflect the Cartesian dualism of nature and spirit accepted by many

---

* Jean-Gaspard-Félix Ravaisson-Mollien (1813–1900) was a secretary to Michelet between 1830 and 1838, doing research in German philosophy for the rapidly ascending historian; he remained a lifelong friend. Inspirer of Lachelier, Boutroux, and Henri Bergson, the author of *La Philosophie en France au XIXe siècle* (1867) could be said to represent a sophisticated version of Michelet's understanding of reality. Ravaisson's highly readable book, written for the 1867 Universal Exposition, presents the best account of French philosophy of that period.

nineteenth-century French theologians. Michelet reassuringly proposes that spiritualization of the animal kingdom exalts rather than debases the Creator.

His argumentation is primarily rhetorical. In general he uses the criterion of autonomous consciousness to differentiate reason from instinct. Reason involves the action of a *personal* will, not just mechanical responses to milieu. Michelet develops his polemic against the Cartesian view of animals as automata in *The Bird,* for he wants to define from the outset the presuppositions of his naturalist studies. He attacks his opponents' position by describing it in an ironic manner:

> Beasts are only machines, mechanical automata; or if we think we can detect in them some glimmering rays of sensitivity and reason, those are solely the effect of *instinct*. But what is instinct? A mysterious sixth sense which is indefinable, which has been implanted in them, not acquired by themselves—a blind force which acts, constructs, and makes a thousand ingenious things, without their being conscious of them, without their personal activity counting for anything.
>
> If this is so, this instinct would be invariable, and its works immovably regular, which neither time nor circumstances would ever change.[4]

Michelet first refines the view of animals as automata. Their "sensitivity" (*la sensibilité*) ties them to the physical apparatus of the five senses; but their "reason" is more than a blind force since it is part of a spiritual system. The book demonstrates how birds acquire their talents through the exercise of free will and individual choice. By stressing the irregularity and variability of animal intelligence, Michelet relates it to creative imagination and thought in human beings. He clinches this commonsense argument with the example of his canary Jonquille: Born in captivity it was unable to build a nest until taught to do so by its master.

Michelet's theoretical distinctions become more complex, and more faulty. In an extensive note to *The Bird* he seeks to authenticate bird "personality" with the same case of variability in nest building. There he uses the Italian word *ingegno* (genius or talent) to express artistic potential. The word is especially ambiguous when applied to birds, for the two modern denotations of "genius" refer either to an innate skill (or instinct) or to creative imagination:[5]

In those works which appear identical to inexperienced eyes, a Wilson and an Audubon have detected the diversities of a very variable art—according to means and places, according to the characters and talents of the artists—in an infinite spontaneity. Thus is extended the realm of freedom, fancy, and *ingegno....*

If these boundless diversities do not result from unrestrained activity and personal spontaneity, if you wish to refer them all to an identical instinct, you must, to support so miraculous a theory, make us believe another miracle: that this instinct, although identical, possesses the singular elasticity of accommodating and proportioning itself to a variety of circumstances which are incessantly changing, to an infinity of chances.[6]

The flaw in Michelet's reasoning is that he neglects the possibility that adaptation to changing conditions, as diverse and amazing as the results may be, does not *necessarily* imply absolutely free, spontaneous creativity. For the sake of his argument he adopts too rigid a definition of instinct, that of a force invariably producing identical objects regardless of circumstances. Indeed, Alfred Maury, in his contemporary study of instinct and mind, *Le Sommeil et les rêves* (1861), uses the same example of complex nest building to distinguish between pure automatism and free adaptation to conditions by a *relative* choice. Maury presents the nuanced view that physical conditions delimit a locus of personal action.[7] Whatever the validity of Michelet's rationalizations, the presence of familiar key words makes his defense of the independence of mind from matter obvious. His mission is to enlarge "the realm of freedom, fancy, and *ingegno.*"

Nature's Artistic Creativity

Michelet's speculations about animal imagination follow a theory which allows him to apply human categories to the natural system. To begin with, nature is composed of matter and spirit as is mankind. Furthermore, creation seems to seek the human mind. The intelligence of birds summarizes that development. Michelet's implicit comparison with humanity directs his exploration of the animal kingdom. How much truer of his study of artistic birds?

What are [birds]? embryo souls [*âmes ébauchées*], souls still specialized for certain functions of existence, candidates for the more general and more widely harmonic life to which the human soul has attained.

When will they arrive there? and how? God has reserved for himself these mysteries.

All that we know is this: that he summons them, them also, to ascend even higher.

They are, without metaphor, the little children of nature, the nurselings of Providence, aspiring toward the light in order to act and think; stumbling now, they by degrees shall advance much further.[8]

Michelet asserts "without metaphor" that lower animals possess aspects of mature human intelligence. This is reminiscent of the German Romantic view of Oken and Schelling which describes the human mind as a final unfolding of nature's previous development. The differences between the animal and human souls lie in their extensiveness. The animal soul is limited by its specialization, its relative enslavement to material determinism. The soul of mankind, in Michelet's view, synthesizes the particularized faculties of lower nature and controls them consciously through reason. That is how human beings master the diverse gifts of their animal brethren.

The author of *The Bird* shares with many writers of his period the view that human progress culminates in the artist. In his excellent *Icarus* (1961), an analysis of the Romantic image of the artist, Maurice Z. Shroder writes: "The belief that the artist is an ideal type, a full realization of the human potential, lay at the heart of the Romantic ethic." [9] The natural world also has its creators, and Michelet uses the nightingale to illustrate the creative soul of animals. He takes this literary symbol quite literally.[10] It was customary at the time to blind and cage such birds for their song. Michelet's nightingale is thus limited to its inner cosmos; unrestrained by its senses it can elaborate its innate powers:

Although his eyes were closed, I did not the less read within him. I perceived there the artist's soul, all tenderness and light, without rancor and without harshness against the barbarity of the world and the ferocity of fate. And it was through this that he lived, through this that he did not die, because he found within himself, in his great sorrow, the all-powerful cordial inherent to his nature: *internal light, song*. These two words mean the same thing in nightingale language.[11]

Michelet's sympathetic imagination penetrates this bird's dream and translates its secret poetry. He uses the image of light to describe the bird's inward aspiration, for it is another case of nature's striving. The fact that the creature is sightless underlines its independence from the determinism of its environment.

The paradox of a blind artist is merely apparent. The nightingale appears restricted only if imitation of the outside world remains the principle of creativity. Its blindness actually prepares free, open-ended imagination. The imprisoned singer is the very image of autonomous (or ideal) creativity and exemplifies the power of spirit over physical constraints: "In utter darkness, he sees with his soul and with love; from time to time, he can see, it seems, even beyond individual love, he can see in harmony with the ocean of infinite Love." [12]

Michelet insists that his description of the nightingale is literal. He goes so far as to present its behavior as typical of a "temperamental artist." [13] The captive nightingale is a supersensitive model of its fellow birds like the quasi-mythical "suffering poet" popularized by Alfred de Musset:

> Such a nightingale, born in freedom, which alone is the true nightingale, bears a very different value from one born in a cage: it sings quite differently, having known freedom and nature, and regretting the absence of both. The better part of the genius of a great artist is suffering. . . .
>
> *Artist!* I have said the word, and I will not take it back. This is not an analogy, a comparison of things having a resemblance: no, it is the thing itself.
>
> The nightingale, in my opinion, is not the chief, but the only one of the winged people to which this name can be justly given.
>
> And why? He alone is a creator; he alone varies, enriches, amplifies his song, and augments it by new strains. He alone is fertile and diverse in himself; other birds are so by instruction and imitation. He alone summarizes, contains almost all: each of them, of the most brilliant, suggests a couplet to the nightingale.[14]

Michelet's esthetics of avian creativity corresponds exactly to his theory of evolution. Artistic creation requires freedom; in the present instance the bird's physical mobility in forests first frees its imagination. Its subsequent enslavement is a corollary of freedom, because the anguish which it provokes stimulates the Romantic poet.* Furthermore, the creator is free from mechanical or academic formulas when separated from the passivity of simple perception; his inspiration is autonomous. Michelet rejects in this manner the imitation of nature, the Classical tenet which views the artist as a sort of mirror, almost an automaton. The Romantic artist creates a new synthesis of which lesser creatures are incapable: "He alone summarizes them all," and then rises above totality itself to produce something entirely original, a radically personal expression.[15]

Artistic imagination is the closest analogue of God's creation of the world. Imagination leads the infinite progress of civilization envisaged by the author of the *Introduction to Universal History*. Like history and evolution the nightingale's creativity continues divine love:

> Thus love and light are undoubtedly his point of departure; but art itself, love of the beautiful, confusedly seen in glimpses, and very keenly felt, are a second aliment, which sustains his soul, and supplies it with a new inspiration. And this is boundless—a day opened on the infinite.[16]

This element of boundlessness is the dynamic foundation of Michelet's thought. A quest for the infinite nourishes the constant effort of both animal and human invention: "The true greatness of the artist consists in overshooting his mark, in doing more than he wills, and something completely different, in passing beyond the goal, in crossing the limits of the possible, and of seeing even beyond the beyond."

Michelet appears to plunge entirely into these dreams. At the same time he remains thoroughly committed to his goal of improving daily existence. The true function of these sublime strivings is not to transcend nature entirely; they are rather a powerful goad toward intellectual and social progress. Reveries of the absolute are mainly inspira-

* This Romantic commonplace harks back to Jean-Jacques Rousseau's *Rêveries du promeneur solitaire* (5ᵉ Promenade), in which he observes: "I have often thought that in the Bastille, and even in a dungeon where I could see nothing, I would still be able to daydream pleasantly"—perhaps more pleasantly than in nature, he implies, because of the freedom given to memory and imagination. The Romantics favored such images as Tasso in the madhouse and Cervantes in prison as examples of the caged genius, singing all the more beautifully because he is enslaved.

tional. Spirit's ultimate goal is *incarnation*. Spirit (or in the present case, creative mind) transcends matter for the purpose of transforming the world. This process produced the hand in the sea cow; a loving act of will reshaped its flippers to hold the child to its breast. Michelet's underlying belief is that nature rises above itself in order to exercise its spiritual quest more freely.

The metaphorical aspect of Michelet's thinking explains his principle that spirit incarnates itself. His historical and evolutionary frescoes are images of his philosophical system. This creative process becomes vividly evident in his description of the mating behavior of nightingales. The example which has no basis in reality as we know it pictures creativity as not only independent of determinism, but also as capable of transmuting matter itself. His metaphor of artistic production develops the common nineteenth-century image of the conception of a child; it illustrates as well the action of a divine male principle on Mother Nature. The male bird's influence on the egg continues his fertilization of the female, as he literally incarnates his *idea* in the child. The male's mating song effects this postphysical influence:

> I have never heard him at that solemn moment without believing that not only should he touch her heart, but that he could transform, ennoble, and exalt her, transmit to her a lofty ideal, place within her the enchanted dream of a sublime nightingale who would be born from their love.
>
> It is his form of incubation; he broods over the genius of his lover, fertilizing her with poetry, aiding her to create for herself in her thought the child she will soon conceive. Every seed [*germe*] is first an idea.[17]

This episode is paradigmatic of Michelet's theory of nature. The bird child realizes the union of spirit and matter; it embodies the Idea since it is "a *sublime* nightingale." The fecund energy is inherent to the female; Michelet calls it "the lover's genius" and it corresponds to the vitality of all matter. However, the first impulse of creation is male; it is divine will seeking incarnation, mind seeking form.

The author summarizes his understanding of the evolutionary process in this symbol of a male divinity and a female nature. The song of the male bird reveals the structure of God's involvement with the world:

Thence spring the nest, the egg, the child. All these are an embodied and living song. And this is the reason that he does not leave her for a moment during the sacred labor of incubation. He does not remain in the nest, but on a neighboring branch, slightly elevated above it. He knows marvelously well that his voice is more potent at a distance. From this exalted position, the all-powerful magician continues to fascinate and to fertilize the nest; he cooperates in the great mystery, and with his song, heart, breath, tenderness and will, engenders still.

The male nightingale, separated physically from his fertile mate, is an image of a transcendent God who is at the same time immanent to a continuously creative globe. The "magician's" *idea* continues to guide natural growth though it is essentially nonphysical. He "continues to *fascinate* and to *fertilize* the nest." Michelet evokes the notion of a magical (or supernatural) power by the traditional meaning of the Latin *fascinare,* whereas he describes the mental process with the precise nineteenth-century meaning of "to fascinate": to hypnotize, to mesmerize, to control by the physical influence of one's "will power" the body and mind of another person. Will becomes incarnated in the loving relationship just described. Hence the child is a "form" of this spirit; it is "an embodied and living song." God's love has, in its natural evolution, passed from instinctive physical reproduction to lucid, voluntary creativity.

Human Instinct's Evolution toward Pure Reason

Michelet's studies of nature parallel his historical works while, reciprocally, his evolutionary theory elucidates the pattern of mankind. His contention that all love is divine abolishes the gulf between humanity and its supposedly inferior brethren. A loving God is both the source and the goal of human and animal development. Civilization depends upon an evolution of the mind which reflects divine creation; society and art are aspects of a *second nature* within a human context. Michelet applies his philosophy of nature to society most clearly in *Love* which he wrote in 1858 after *The Insect*:

Human art has no other processes of its own, no power but to imitate divine art [that is, evolution]. What has the latter done, what is it doing? From the great torrent of life, Love creates generations, the whole ascending progress of species [*des espèces*]. And with a concentrated drop of this torrent, it has created, and still creates, the world of invention and all intellectual progress.[18]

He defines the metamorphosis of humanity by the growth of instinct into pure reason. Humanity liberates itself from material determinism through thought and creativity, as do the animal species. Humanity's struggle is on a higher plane because it exercises its self-consciousness more freely. Yet its free will also arises from instinct, from automatic, emotional reactions to the world. The mind cannot progress if it simply responds to reality. Perception of the concrete world, even if it is self-conscious and systematic, is mostly passive. One refines thinking when one applies external perception to the inside world of the mind. Human thought becomes freest when it reflects upon thought itself. Mankind's capacity to examine the reasoning process is the end-point of spirit's self-realization within nature. This leads to pure reason and to an even greater freedom for creative imagination.

Michelet defines history by imposing an evolutionary frame of reference on civilizations. He elaborates in *Woman* (1859), the sequel to *Love,* a natural history of the mind which traces the emergence of free will from the determinism of instinct. In both these books he is as attentive to the thinking process in general as he is to woman's social role.[19] He transfers his theory of female and male cognition, that is, poetic intuition and rationality respectively,* to the history of Eastern and Western cultures. His account of their development follows the ascending scale of human reason:

> Poetic and prophetic intuition [or instinct], that Oriental process, so sublime in the Jewish writings, followed a no less thorny path, full of mists and mirages. It was determined [*fatale*], besides, depending on the wholly involuntary chance of inspiration.
>
> For that obscure process, Greece substituted a virile art of seeking and finding, of coming with certainty into the open day, by ways known to all, where one may pass and repass, and make a thorough verification. Man thus becomes his own architect and the builder of his own destiny. No particular man, but any man whatsoever—not the elect, nor the prophet, nor the special favorite of God. With the arts of reasoning, Athens gave to all the world an instrument of equality.

* See below chapter 7, "The Two Sexes of the Mind," for a detailed account of Michelet's analysis of "male" and "female" thought processes.

Until then there had been no connecting links. There were blind bursts of emotion, and attempts at reflection, but that speedily came to naught. All was unconnected and fortuitous—nothing systematic.

Until then all progress was by fits and starts. No true history of the movement of the human race was possible. Asia possesses little of the historical element; her scanty annals afford but isolated facts, from which one can draw no conclusions. Indeed, what conclusion can we draw from events ordered by fate, and uncontrolled by wisdom?

But from the day that reasoning became an art, a method, from the day that the virgin Pallas gave birth to the faculty of deduction and calculation, in its pure form, there has existed a regular, uninterrupted and systematic production of human works. The stream flows on, never again to stop—from Solon to Papinian, from Socrates to Descartes, from Archimedes to Newton.[20]

The jurist Papinian, a principal founder of Roman law, with Descartes and Newton, are high points of an evolving historical awareness; according to Michelet their epoch-making discoveries enable humanity to act as its own Prometheus. That is what Greek practical reason means: "Man becomes his own architect and the builder of his own destiny." The autonomy of mind produces democracy, for the equal access to the disciplines of mind should lead to self-liberation.

Michelet's manner of expressing historical generalizations in symbolic form may obscure the sophisticated analyses of mind upon which they are based. In the same passage from *Woman,* he describes in metaphorical terms how ideas can be formulated voluntarily: "To reflect is to turn one's thought back upon itself, to take it for its own object, to look at it as if in a mirror. Thus it will apparently be doubled, so that the thought gazing fixedly upon itself will extend and develop itself, by the analysis of language, or by the inner speech of mute reasoning."

Michelet's analysis, by images, of reflection parallels the theory of intellectual abstraction elaborated by twentieth-century neo-Kantians. Both consider it to be a process by which reason voluntarily transcends perception. Here, for example, is how the historian of philosophy and epistemologist Ernst Cassirer distinguishes between intuition and abstract thought. Cassirer calls the former "mythical thinking" and considers reflection as a voluntary liberation of the mind from sense data:

"Beginning with [scientific conception], we can show that all the intellectual labor whereby the mind forms general concepts out of specific impressions is directed toward breaking the isolation of the datum, wresting it from the 'here and now' of its actual occurrence, relating it to other things and gathering it and them into some inclusive order, into the unity of a 'system.' The logical form of conception, from the standpoint of theoretical knowledge, is nothing but a preparation for the logical form of judgment; all judgment, however, aims at overcoming the illusion of singularity which adheres to every particular content of consciousness." [21] In reflection and productive thought (as opposed to reproductive memory), imagination detaches itself from perception and can thus formulate new thoughts and systems. The processes of abstraction, idealization of complex data, and invention result from a spiritual freedom which both Michelet and Cassirer postulate as the precondition of cultural advance.

History as an Evolutionary Force

Michelet's celebration of the emergence of Western thought summarizes his mission as historian. His concept of history presupposes that humanity is free to act and create itself. The demands of divine Providence, or the necessities of geography, for example, must submit to free will. The very process of an historian's work imitates the goal of civilization. The writer of history first studies the past by examining a mass of unorganized data. Then he or she chooses certain data, and through abstraction and idealization begins to discern a pattern, a meaning. The moral mission of history is derived from this cognitive process. The past must serve the future. Michelet consciously and systematically constructs in his mind an ideal picture of the past in order to define a future society.

This knowledge furthers human evolution because it is practical knowledge. His books on nature and humanity attempt to liberate readers intellectually so that they might consciously master the world itself. Mankind can harness spiritual forces it understands through natural history. The evolutionary view of civilization reminds people of their mental autonomy. That is what Michelet teaches as a naturalist who knows history. History requires disciplined reflection upon the past, which should prepare its adepts to provoke events voluntarily according to a rationally produced plan. His biology completes his history by sketching an ideal image of nature toward which readers might strive.[22]

Civilization should fulfill the phylogeny of spirit started by nature. Michelet's evolutionary vision of society renews the ancient tradition of the microcosm, as he considers humanity as a single organism. The brain of this complex animal is unified by the electric telegraph;* as he writes in *Love*: "The miracle of miracles is not far from being accomplished; and truly, the greatest event that has occurred on this planet is that, by means of electric wires, minute by minute obtaining consciousness of its own thought, the planet achieves a kind of identity and becomes like a person." [23] The historian's image of a worldwide communications network as a self-conscious personality stresses the continuity of nature's evolution and human invention. Technological advances increase the effectiveness of human reflection by expanding its self-awareness. His analysis of thought leads him to hope that the electric telegraph will help both the individual and the collective mind to renovate that second nature, civilization, through a rational synthesis of information.

Michelet further extends his image of telegraphic communication. For his long-range goal is to define the political consequences of his theory of mind. He believes that the insights achieved by the collective mind could renew international relations. His touchstone of spiritual progress is again incarnation. Material (political) and spiritual (moral) unity go hand in hand. Writers and inventors measure the higher progress of civilization and create an intellectual communion which might lead to harmony between nations. This is the message of such didactic books:

"To Providence we owe those other providences, the great souls who bit by bit bind this globe together, who enlighten it, and make it fruitful, who bring it, or soon will bring it, into the harmony and unity of one single human soul." By degrees [such readings tell us] of those material communions (which prepare

---

* The electric telegraph was a recent development in France, causing great excitement in Michelet's day. The *Larousse du XIX⁰ siècle,* a witness to the contemporary scene, states that until Arago's speech to the government in 1845, France had made no progress in establishing "that rapid system for the communication of thought" (s.v. "Télégraphe"). It was only in 1845 that a trial cable was placed on the Paris-Rouen railroad line.

[us] for the moral one), of navigation, commerce, roads, canals, railroads, and the electric telegraph.[24]

Technology can produce a materially unified community which in turn could improve morality. Michelet hopes that the world will become a "person" through communications networks. Today's systems of rapid transportation, mass media, and computerized information-gathering have hardly nurtured the worldwide dialogue which the previous century's thinkers impatiently expected.

Michelet completes his utopian program by revealing the religious basis of his optimism. The author of *Woman* challenges the materialists of his time by interpreting civilization's material ascent as a manifestation of spirit's self-disclosure. He does this when he modifies his statement on material communion by stressing the spiritual origin of inventions:

> *Material?* I conform to the foolish phraseology of our time. They are in no respect material. These things come from the spirit [*esprit*] of which they are the instruments, the forms. In introducing nations to each other, suppressing ignorances and blind antipathies, I maintain that they are as well moral and religious powers, or as I have said, they are communions.

Like many other socialist thinkers of his day, Michelet systematically secularizes the Christian view of a moral society. That is why he insists upon the word "communion" to express his internationalist ideal. Michelet in fact attacks both Positivism and Christianity while preserving what he considers to be their essence.

Yet curiously, Michelet's religious evolutionism reminds us of the Christian evolutionary system of the Jesuit paleontologist and mystic, Pierre Teilhard de Chardin (1882–1955). Teilhard as well considers evolution in collective categories: the "Biosphere" is the agglomerate of living substance which evolves toward greater individuation of organisms, producing capacities of mind; he also views mankind as a single organism which evolves in terms of intellect or reason (in Greek: *nous*): "The Noosphere, final and supreme product, in Man," Teilhard writes, "can take on a full and definitive meaning under one sole condition: that it be considered, in its global totality, as forming a single and boundless corpuscle in which is fulfilled, after more than six hundred million years, the Biosphere's effort of cerebralization."[25] Teilhard's evolutionary teleology, like that of Michelet, traces the emergence of human reason and imagination; and both point beyond the human condition. Despite the profound differences between these kindred spirits (let us not forget too easily Michelet's violent anticlericalism), both were convinced that a process of increasing spiritualization of life was immanent to natural and human history.[26]

Michelet's tremendous faith in technology is thus a consequence of his spiritualistic philosophy. He respected science enough to justify his ideas about human progress by exploring its natural analogues— but only in order to find in both history and nature a divine principle at work. He considered his faith as a non-Christian religion that would serve as an alternative to idols such as Saint-Simonianism, Positivism, and dogmatic Christianity. Michelet's natural religion did not threaten intellectual freedom. Universal moral values were an essential part of his creed and he believed that human freedom could be controlled by love and moral responsibility. A God which was both male and female gave unity to this system. Social progress followed the evolution of male reason and female love, the two principal attributes of God within the world.[27]

Michelet the Artist-Historian

Michelet's organic conception of civilization appears most clearly in his *History of France*. From the *Tableau of France* which introduces volume 2 in 1833 to the 1869 *Preface* to the completed work, he remains faithful to the view of his nation as a living being. "I was the first," he asserts in that preface, "to perceive her as a soul and as a person." The nation that created the Revolution was the most advanced animal in the chain of beings, for in that event the French people realized its identity through an almost transcendent unity of heart and mind.* The author's life reflects his nation's historical evolution, as he states later in the 1869 *Preface*: "My life was in this book, it has been transformed into it." Michelet considered his life consubstantial with his creations.

His mission as an historian thus surpasses his attempt to immortalize his nation in literature. He sought to imbue his contemporaries with the ideals of the past and transform them as he himself had been transformed. Yet this was more than moral propaganda. As an

---

* See beginning of chapter 2, pp. 21–22.

artist-historian (a term Michelet coined early in his career) he would reconstruct, or as he put it, resurrect the past artistically. His verbal world, however, not only preserves the story of civilization but more so it attempts to guide the growth of France and the world. In the last analysis, Michelet viewed himself as an evolutionary force, for he believed that his thought and will would contribute to the metamorphosis of humanity.

In reflecting upon the results of his career, Michelet asserts that his intellectual growth produced a definite increase in the totality of human wisdom. He derives his observation from the common image of humanity as a single organism, a belief which he held from the very start of his career. Michelet most clearly elucidates that view in *The Insect*. There he describes insect metamorphosis as the image of intellectual development. His education mirrors the transformations from larva to cocoon and chrysalis, from which the adult butterfly finally arises. Michelet's life, despite its discontinuity, also preserves one continuous self; thus he writes of himself at the age of fifty-eight:

> Throughout my life I have remarked that each day I would die and be born again; I have undergone many painful moultings and laborious transformations. One more does not surprise me. Many and many times I have passed from the larva into the chrysalis, and into a more complete condition; the which, after a while, incomplete in other respects, has put me on the path of accomplishing a new circle of metamorphoses.
>
> All this from me to me, but not less from me to those who were still me, who loved me, wanted me, or made me; or, whom I loved, whom I made. They, too, have been, or will be, my metamorphoses. Sometimes, a certain intonation or gesture which I detect in myself makes me exclaim: — "Ah! this is a gesture of my father!" I had not foreseen it, and if I had, it would not have occurred; reflection would have changed all; but, not thinking of it, I employed it. A tender emotion, a holy impulse seized me, when I felt my father thus living in myself. Are we two? Were we one? Oh! he was my chrysalis. And I—I play the same part for those who shall follow me, my sons, or the sons of my thought.[28]

The man who taught for over a decade at the Collège de France did not doubt that knowledge increases from generation to generation, as would the body of an individual being. His interpretation of meta-

morphosis from child to adult as an image of intellectual transformations is supported by a very penetrating analysis of the mental process
that Marcel Proust later called "involuntary memory." Michelet interprets memory as proof of organic unity between people. It is true
that memory is a form of continuity of experience. Michelet goes
further in the passage just cited: his involuntary reminiscences of his
father demonstrate to him the *continuity of thought itself*—not just a
simple *contiguity* of experience, as skeptical common sense would have
it. The historian dedicated his life to teaching through speech and
writing because he firmly believed that his knowledge would be absorbed by and help transform humanity as a whole.

Michelet's auto-analysis then affirms the absolute consequence of
his theory of human progress when he imagines a transfiguration
beyond the frontiers of earthly existence. He dreams of an ultimate
metamorphosis which would see the human mind become an immortal
angelic being, or pure bodiless thought:

> I know, I feel, that besides the foundation which I derived from
> my father, my ancestors and masters, besides the inheritance of
> artist-historian which I shall bequeath to others, germs [*germes*]
> existed within me which were not developed. Another man, and
> perhaps better, was within me, who has not arisen. Why were
> not the loftier germs which might have made me great, and the
> powerful wings of which I have sometimes felt myself possessed,
> displayed in life and action?
>
> These germs, though postponed, remain with me. Too late
> perhaps for this life; but in another, who knows?...

Michelet extends his theory of evolution beyond nature into an afterlife. His spiritualistic system proclaims that humanity is ultimately
realized only in that other world. His vision of evolution returns here
to its biographical departure, the agonizing period of Madame Dumesnil's death. He had responded to that loss by extending his idea
of nature's unity to the point of embracing the belief in a life after
death. Michelet bases his conception of himself as a writer on the
doctrine of the transmigration of souls. In this he joins contemporaries
like the historian Henri Martin and their mutual friend Jean Reynaud;
Michelet had indeed found solace in the latter's *Encyclopédie nouvelle*
during Madame Dumesnil's mortal illness. Far from being contrary
to his philosophy of history, Michelet's angelism is a radical conse-

quence of his most fundamental principle: that of mind seeking free-dom from material necessity.

Michelet's conception of his function as a writer thus completes (and perhaps explains) his theory of mental evolution. He exemplifies the physical effects of thought on growing creatures by his nightingale family. Those creatures confirm the principle that imagination (or idea) dominates matter. Nightingale parenthood also symbolizes the creation by an artist's thought of a work of art. In this view, writing appears as an absolute self-liberation from the objective, physical world, because, in creating a verbal universe, the products of imagi-nation or "vision" pass from one's inner, mental cosmos into external reality. This process of artistic expression explains Michelet's his-torical method: he first relives the past within himself by sympathetic imagination and then recreates it in mental images. That is his "in-tegral resurrection" of the past. His mission as "artist-historian" be-comes truly prophetic in this light. He joins the visionary faculties of the artist with the power of literary resurrection of the historian, and foresees the day when his mind will hasten the achievement of hu-manity's apotheosis.

Two: Humanity

5

Nature's Message to a
Declining Humanity

Michelet's great fresco depicts the essential unity of nature and humanity. The ideological thrust of his evolutionism explains why the role of naturalist continues that of the historian committed to save his nation. Like Pierre-Simon Ballanche (1776–1847), the modern prophet, Michelet sought to mediate between past and present in order to transform the future. The nature books effect the characteristically Romantic synthesis of politics and inward inspiration. This mission was symbolized at the time by the myth of Orpheus, the poet-teacher. Maurice Z. Shroder summarizes it as he describes the career of Victor Hugo in terms of Ballanche's *Orphée* (1829):

> "The complete poet," [Hugo] wrote later in his life, "consists of these three visions: Humanity, Nature, and the Supernatural." These correspond exactly to the three functions of Orpheus: to civilize men by establishing political and educational institutions; to reveal nature to them, nature considered in its two aspects—as the material world and as a collection of symbols pointing to a meaning beyond matter; to reveal to them the mysteries by "reading" the symbols of nature, by attending to the supernatural forces of the universe and thus to indicate the routes ordained for man by God, and, finally, to make possible the perception of God Himself.[1]

Michelet the naturalist joins the first two Orphic tasks: he uses nature to civilize and nurture humanity.

Michelet's educational and historical works all challenge the decadence of his century. The historian of the Revolution believed that universal progress had stopped by 1790. The Second Empire was the nadir in a continuum of cultural ups and downs. Sadness and pessimism were not foreign to Michelet. He wrote in his preface to *The People* that the Napoleonic Empire was a period of poverty and gloom for his family. In the *Preface* of 1869 to the completed *History of France* he quotes Jouffroy's famous pronouncement that dogmas had come to an end. Traditional religious faith was no longer possible. "In July 1830," he wrote, "the Church found itself deserted." The Saint-Simonians failed to invent a religion of humanity to replace reactionary Christianity. Michelet deplored the "moral cholera" which flourished during the bourgeois monarchy of Louis-Philippe. The failure of the 1848 Revolution, and the historian's subsequent rejection of Napoleon III, solidified his increasing distance from the Romantic generation's deepest hopes. He dealt with their realistic anxiety in a personal manner. Michelet's production was a protest against despair.

The historian's nature books—*The Bird, The Insect, The Sea,* and *The Mountain*—directly answer the severe moral depression of the Second Empire. It is true, as Pierre Barbéris points out, that this period of expanding capitalist individualism and competition exacerbated the *mal du siècle,* the aimlessness and isolation expressed by alienated writers from the century's beginning. The Restoration made it impossible to believe in the government's moral authority and killed the system of sacred values upon which France traditionally rested. Those dread realities explain Michelet's optimism, but not, as Barbéris explains, because of the historian's escapist bourgeois ideology. Michelet's faith did not deny his era's anxiety; he understood the material realities which excited his compassion and sadness. Michelet was simply compelled to counter fatalism and meaninglessness with hope. His readers craved evidence of humanity's self-affirmation: against the threat of fate and death, against the Second Empire's emptiness and meaninglessness.[2] That is why Michelet, like many contemporaries, combines democratic idealism and the belief in human immortality.

Michelet's nature books present a revitalization program which harmonizes science and faith. He exemplifies the struggle to reconcile idealist Romanticism and Positivism in a transitional age. This struggle is reflected by Michelet's mixture of poetic and rational discourse. He puts the scientific studies upon which the nature books are based into the framework of didactic poems which follow Boileau's injunction to "please while educating." Michelet usually expresses his inspirational and practical messages by a traditionally allegorical method, interpreting the animate world as symbolic of human concerns. However, this conventional pedagogic device did not suffice. He completes these abstract lessons in esthetically seductive passages in which he exercises his gift for poetic lyricism or dramatically evokes personal experiences. Readers of his day were touched by the author's incandescent style while their minds were convinced by his obvious analogies to humanity. The nature books' immense success was due to the fact that they spoke at once to individual needs and to those of European society at large.

The Bird: *Transcendence of the Earthly Life*

Michelet begins his naturalist series with a book whose main theme is religious. The epigraph which graces the cover of *The Bird*— "Wings! wings!" —expresses the metaphysical aspiration at the heart of the author's study of nature. He cites the expression from the German poet, philosopher, and Orientalist Friedrich Rückert (1798–1866) and completes it later in the book:

> Wings above life!
> Wings beyond death!

Michelet's initial presentation of the "divine tribe" of birds is strikingly anthropomorphic. Birds symbolize humanity's wish to dominate the present and the future.

Was Michelet's second wife solely responsible for this extension of the historian's religious ideas? It is true that *The Bird* originated in Athénaïs' research and writing. Its inspirational motto became the trademark of the Michelets and they would often seal their letters with the phrase "Des ailes!" imprinted in the wax. But the historian's diary reveals that the book's theme existed well before his second marriage. That theme emerged from Rückert's poem on wings. Michelet first encountered the poet's work on a trip to Germany which followed the death of Madame Dumesnil. He left France on 19 June 1842 with his son and daughter, Charles and Adèle, and his son-in-law to be, Alfred Dumesnil. His goal was not mere distraction, but the conquest of his despair. His contact with the Rückert poem was colored by this severe emotional stress, in his absorption with thoughts of death and immortality, as he noted in his diary on 2 July:

[Rückert] is so German that it is no longer just German; it is, beyond Germany, the higher region in which Germany joins with the Orient: the dying flower (*"Wings! wings! O sea, o sun, o rose!"*) and the admirable piece about the swallow.... Philosophy, poetry, oriental erudition, all harmonies melded into a powerful melody, a concentrate of the world itself.[3]

Michelet found in Rückert's images a profusion of mystical yearnings he had always associated with mysterious Germany, that Orient of Europe. The historian's secret past becomes alive again fourteen years later as he celebrates, in *The Bird,* his new love and the renewal of his faith in life.

The personal significance of the book, however, does not prevent the author from utilizing a rigorous rhetorical technique. Part 1 of *The Bird* elaborates a single allegory: Michelet first introduces the flight of birds as a symbol of mankind's desire to be released from its bodily limits. He then traces the natural history of wing development while interpreting flight as symbolic of increasing spiritual freedom. Finally he applies to humanity the lesson he learns from animals.

Michelet characterizes the human condition as a play between aspirations for the ultimate and a sense of limits. *The Bird* symbolizes this view through the flight of Icarus, a dominant myth of Romanticism. Mankind, like all nature, yearns for a condition of absolute freedom of will. Only birds dominate the world physically and by sight; they realize what Michelet and many others believed was the goal of historical progress:

> It is in his best age, his first and richest existence, in his youthful dreams, that man has sometimes the good fortune to forget that he is man, a serf of weight and chained to the earth. Behold, yonder, him who takes flight, who hovers, who dominates over the world, who swims in a sunbeam; he enjoys the ineffable felicity of embracing in one glance an infinity of things which yesterday he could only see one by one. Obscure enigma of detail, suddenly made luminous to him who perceives its unity! To see the world beneath oneself, to embrace, to love it! How divine, how sublime a dream!...[4]

A deep conviction rings through the artist-historian's cry for full mental freedom. But only flying birds appear to be released from gravity and from the partiality of normal sight. Birds indeed appear to attain an ideal vision which reflects an almost divine knowledge.

Michelet, a faithful disciple of Vico, interprets the winged gods of mythology as a projection of the human desire to become an angel. He too wishes to become an angel, a person existing as a pure mind entirely freed from its material prison, the body.

Here we encounter the paradox of Michelet's spiritualism. On the one hand, he is the national historian of France, toiling to capture and to recount worldly events of utmost significance, while another side of Michelet desires to escape from earthly reality and enjoy a pure, atemporal existence. He boldly asserts this otherworldly wish in the sentence that closes the chapter under discussion, explicitly stating its lesson: "Something tells us that these dreams are not all dreams, but glimpses of the true world, momentary flashes revealed behind our foggy world below, certain promises to be hereafter fulfilled, while our so-called reality would be but a bad dream." [5] How did Michelet reconcile these contradictory attitudes toward the mundane?

He symbolizes his attempt by the fall of Icarus. Michelet's fleeting glimpse of absolute freedom becomes restricted, as was that of Icarus, by physical necessity. Like other artists of mystical temperament, he must postpone his dreams of ultimate transcendence and embrace the workaday world:

> Do not wake me, I pray you, never wake me!... But what is this? Here again are the day, the uproar and labor; the harsh iron hammer, the ear-piercing bell with its voice of steel, dethrone me and dash me down headlong; my wings have melted. Heavy earth, I fall back to the earth; bruised and bent, I return to the plow.[6]

The negative lesson is that complete spiritual freedom in this life is impossible. Michelet affirms social responsibility: "I return to the plow." His "harsh iron hammer" even expresses a willingness to deal with the industrialism from which he seeks repose. Humanity's contrary desires give a dimension of religious hope to an otherwise flatly materialistic view of existence.

He then translates the allegory of wing evolution to teach a similar combination of activism and resignation. The frigate bird, which is all wing, like Baudelaire's albatross, cannot maneuver while grounded. Michelet's history of the evolution of wings concludes that "no existence is really free here below . . . no wing can suffice. The most powerful one is a bondage. The soul must await, ask and hope for others." [7] Nature's eternal desire reinforces its powerful aspirations although progress remains implacably limited.

Part 2 of *The Bird* describes the evolution of moral and artistic qualities within the animal world. The allegorical technique of subordinating nature to mankind is reversed: qualities usually associated with human beings now serve to illuminate the natural world. Michelet's anthropomorphism expresses literally the spiritual equality of nature and humanity. His argument relates matter to spirit: the smaller the physical size of the bird, the fuller its creative and moral capacities. Michelet's treatment of little birds is democratic in its social ideology; yet he is mainly interested in their artistic genius. For him artistic creativity and love are nature's fullest spiritual attainments.

The book's last two chapters return to the bird as an image of the human soul and creative imagination. Their very title, "The Nightingale, Art and the Infinite," stresses the religious orientation of Michelet's account of birds' mating songs.* The Conclusion of *The Bird* states its underlying theme of wildlife conservation, that civilized people should preserve nature. Michelet's natural history of birds aims to reconcile humanity with these misunderstood creatures. We should respect the avian race as spiritual equals who aspire as we do to conquer physical necessity. The religious yearnings which propel mankind's Icarian quest should enrich daily life with a faith in the transcendent, while if we imitate the artistic imagination of birds, human civilization would be pushed forward.

The Insect: *Immortality and Civic Responsibility*

The coexistence of the earthly and the heavenly in Michelet's vision is elaborated more deeply in *The Insect* (1857). This second naturalist book both defends the doctrine of metempsychosis and expresses the author's absolute commitment to social justice. The book's introduction stresses nature's moral dimension. The insect "loves most truly"; "that maternal genius extends so far, that, surpassing and eclipsing the rare gropings of birds and quadrupeds, it has enabled the insect to create republics and establish cities!" [8] The moralist-historian discovers in insect collectivities his fundamental political and

---

* In chapter 4 I analyzed these mating songs in terms of Michelet's theory of animal creativity. These same texts clarify the author's understanding of religious experience; see chapter 6, section "Is Michelet a Pantheist?"

social values; as he says at the very end of the book: "The noblest work of the world, the most elevated goal to which its inhabitants tend, is without any contradiction the city." [9] Michelet's ideal of natural moral perfection is thus a democratic society. It also conquers time. "How shall we elude death?... Let us create society." The historian's dream of a utopian community reveals the spiritualistic basis of his passionate dedication to social transformation.

Book I, with the loaded title "Metamorphosis," defines *The Insect*'s properly religious view of human possibilities. The author supports his allegorical demonstration with scientific rationalizations of ancient beliefs in personal immortality. His entomology is guided by the Egyptian mythology of insects. Metamorphosis refers to the transformation of an egg into a larva, cocoon (or mummy), and finally an adult insect. Michelet interprets this natural process in such a way as to call into question the usual categories of life and death. Insect metamorphosis represents for him "the identity of three beings. It seems as if there could be no intermediary deaths; one single life is continuously carried on." [10] He then translates this "miracle" of the insect world into human terms. He cites a passage from an unnamed "ingenious philosopher"—directly after the text describing his own "metamorphoses"—in which the author associates the process of foetal development with an adult's aspiration for a life after death:

> If the human embryo, while imprisoned in the maternal womb, might reason, it would say: "I see myself endowed with organs of which here I can make no use, —limbs which do not move, a stomach and teeth which do not eat. Patience! These organs convince me that nature calls me elsewhere; a time will come when I shall have another residence, a life in which all these implements will find employment. . . . They are standing still, they are waiting... I am but a chrysalis of a man." [11]

Michelet's citation of the word *chrysalis* to describe the prenatal stage of human existence is the final link in his equation of the insect with the human life cycle. This passage reasons exclusively by analogy and suggests that beyond this world lies another, more advanced realm of being. Like the insect, earthbound people may be called to fly in the beyond.

Michelet's attempt to defend his belief in personal immortality was so crucial that in *Woman* (1859), in which he proposes, among other things, a non-Christian religious faith, he takes pains to elucidate the inspirational intent of *The Insect*. He quotes the same passage and explains its references: "The eloquent words of today's religious men, the *migrations* of J. Reynaud and the *consolations* of Dumesnil, sustain [the innocent woman], and give her hope. In the book of metamorphoses (*The Insect*) did she not read ... [here he quotes]. A Scotsman (Ferguson) spoke these grave, ingenious words, of striking truth...." [12] The latter example is the philosopher and historian of the Roman Empire, Adam Ferguson (1723–1816), though Michelet does not elaborate.* More familiar is Michelet's friend, the mystical socialist Jean Reynaud, who defended the doctrines of metempsychosis and the afterlife in his articles "Ciel" (1837) and "Terre" (1840) which Michelet had read in the *Encyclopédie nouvelle* by January 1841.[13] Michelet cites Reynaud's complete religious and philosophical statement, *Terre et Ciel* (1854) in *The Witch* (1862), along with the name of a disciple of Reynaud, Michelet's friend and fellow historian, Henri Martin,† and *La Foi nouvelle* (1850) and *L'Immortalité* (1861) by his son-in-law, Alfred Dumesnil.[14] The immortality of the soul was very much a live issue in France well into the 1860s, and our author—in a variety of books—takes a firm, unequivocal stand in its favor.[15]

Michelet completes his discussion of immortality in the four chapters on bees which terminate *The Insect*. In "The Bees of Virgil," he interprets the fable of Aristaeus (*Georgics, 4*) which tells of bees generated spontaneously from the entrails of sacrificed bulls; the Virgilian poem is "a song full of immortality, which, in the mystery of nature's transformations, embodies our highest hope: that death is not a death, but the beginning of a new life." [16] The historian then uses this literary reference to give symbolic meaning to a visit he actually made (dated in the text) to the grave of his son, Yves-Jean-Lazare,

---

* Adam Ferguson's masterwork is his *History of the Progress and Termination of the Roman Empire* (1783). Michelet had read his *Essay on the History of Civil Society* around 1824 (see Paul Viallaneix, *La Voie royale*, 1959 ed., pp. 149–50).

† Henri Martin (1810–1883), the author of a seven-volume *Histoire de France* (1837–1854), was a disciple of Jean Reynaud and defended the Druidic belief in personal immortality.

He should not be confused with the Christian Thomas Henri Martin (1813–1884) who devoted his life to research for a history of the physical and astronomical sciences of antiquity. He was dean of the Faculté des Lettres of Rennes when he published *La Vie future: histoire et apologie de la doctrine sur l'autre vie* (1855).

the only child of his second marriage who had died three months after birth (1850): "I had named him Lazarus in my religious hope of the awakening of the nations... Oh vanity of our hopes!" Michelet considered his life and his works as one and the same; in the present episode, the presence of some "Virgilian bees" on his son's tomb excited promises of his power as an artist-historian to bestow immortality; the insects reminded him of his capacity to resurrect the integral life of the past.[17] Michelet's visit to the tomb of Lazarus suggests that the historian, like Christ, could quicken the dead and that his writing could produce some sort of messianic redemption.

Michelet defines the theoretical bases of his apostolic mission in book 3, "Societies of Insects." His democratic ideology implies a precise political morality. His allegorical lesson now elaborates the traditional image of ant colonies as the ideal republic. The author is particularly concerned with the problem of slavery and with the relation of individual to collective values in society. His entomological inquiry begins and ends with an ethical perspective:

> What! I turn aside from the history of men in search of innocence; I hope at least to discover among beasts the evenhanded justice of nature, the primitive rectitude of the plan of creation. I seek in this people [that is, ants], whom I had previously loved and esteemed for their laboriousness and temperateness, the severe and touching image of republican virtues... and I find this indescribable horror![18]

He goes on to describe (following Pierre Huber), in very dramatic fashion, how an army of red ants abducted the young of a black ant colony: "It was an exact replica of a descent of slave-dealers on the coast of Africa."

The parallels between this natural history and problems of international ethics are obvious. The historian's analysis of this ant colony's social structure is more subtle. The little black ants are enslaved and toil for the victors; though they held no governmental power, they nevertheless retained their creative autonomy, for they controlled the *culture* of the red tyrants: "And who knows but that the pride of governing the strong, and of mastering the masters, may be for those little blacks an inner liberty—an exquisite and sovereign freedom— far superior to any they could have derived from the equality of their native land?"[19] Michelet's ultimate value is mental autonomy. Political freedom is a lesser virtue than intellectual independence in his primarily spiritual system. His interpretation of ant slavery recalls the cultural domination of Greece over her Roman conquerors: "the class of the little ants, who build the city and by education build the people, is truly the city's essential part, its life, its genius, its soul; the one which of itself could, if need be, constitute the motherland." [20] At the end of the chapter Michelet reiterates that political values are ultimately derived from spiritual ones: "Singular triumph of intelligence! Invincible power of the soul!"

His model of a perfect democracy appears in *The Insect*'s penultimate chapter, "Architect Bees. The City." His moral ideal of political union seems to be realized by this apian collectivity:

> If the wasp's nest resembles Sparta, the beehive is the veritable Athens of the insect world. There, all is art. The people—the artist elite of the people—incessantly create two things: on the one hand the City, the motherland, —on the other, the universal Mother whose task it is not only to perpetuate the people, but moreover to become its idol, its fetish, the living god of the City.[21]

The queen bee is a constitutional monarch who is fed and sustained by her people; yet her authority depends upon *their* will, in the way that Rousseau describes the people's "general will" as the removable basis of a social contract. The final sentence of the book's last substantive chapter in fact describes the beehive according to principles which sustained the Revolution of 1789: "[The people] guard her, and wait upon her, but with the pride worthy of a people who adore only their own handiwork, chosen by them, nourished by them, created by them, *able to be undone by them* [my italics]. It is their pride that when necessary they know how to create their God." [22] Michelet considers the personal freedom and creativity of insect citizens in this social system as another vehicle of "the tenderness of the universal Love in the universality of the soul." This last sentence of the book's summary asserts once and for all that natural morality springs from a divine power available to all.

The Sea: *Natural and Human Vitality*

After *The Insect* Michelet wrote two books on marriage and femininity; he completed his *History of the Renaissance* and returned to the natural world in his study of *The Sea*. He develops in that book one basic metaphor: the sea as the earth's womb. His theory of creation was one result of his desire to demonstrate that intuition scientifically.* This organic imagery finds another important application. Michelet uses it to justify his proposal that bathing in the ocean could renew his exhausted nation. His idea that the sea is a single organism adds essential philosophical consequences to this social mission.

The author leads us into his way of thinking with a calculated strategy. He introduces his book by systematically leading us from *comparisons* of the sea to an animal to the *literalization* of those comparisons. Volcanoes, for example, produce the two life-giving currents of warm water "which *might be called* the two aortas of the globe." [23] (All italics in this paragraph are mine.) The Indian and American oceans "*seem* to be the deep womb, the tender and warm cradle, of a world of living organisms." "Such is the sea. She *seems* to be a huge animal arrested in the first stage of organization." Michelet's transition from comparisons based on his speculative animism to their literalization is authorized by the American "poet of the sea," Lieutenant Matthew Fontaine Maury. Michelet gives a penetrating analysis of Maury's masterwork, *Physical Geography of the Sea* (1855) — French selections of which were published in the *Revue Britannique* in 1858—and discovers support for his own cause in the scientist's style: "He endows the sea with a pulse, arteries, even with a heart. Are these mere figures of style, mere poetical comparisons? Not at all. He cherishes (and it is the secret of his genius) an overruling and invincible feeling for the personality of the sea." [24] The sea emerges for Michelet, literally, as a complex organism. He adds to the "soul" or "personality" of birds, insects, and jellyfish the *person-ness* of the earth's womb.[25]

Michelet's "scientific" defense of this organicist thinking produces the rich description of evolution of book 2, "Genesis of the Sea," whose contents we have examined. *The Sea*'s philosophical agenda is equally essential. The prodigious fertility of sea creatures demonstrates Michelet's vitalism. He characterizes animal reproduction as a continuing genesis independent of divine intervention. He views the sea as "the great female of the globe, whose indefatigable desire,

---

* See above chapter 2, "Evolution: The Constant Metamorphosis."

permanent conception, and prolific birth never cease." [26] We know that these doctrines are fundamental to his theory of evolution, for nature's inherent spirituality hinges upon the power of matter to form living organisms. Michelet boldly asserts his panvitalism as he cites Lamarck as his authority (incorrectly, for Lamarck, a product of eighteenth-century materialism, was thoroughly mechanistic): " 'Everything,' he said, 'is alive or has lived. All is life, past or present.' This was a great revolutionary effort against inert matter, which will continue until the inorganic is suppressed." The sea and its self-forming power of life, like the mental liberty of black ant educators, testify to the action of an immanent spiritual process.

Michelet concludes this passage from *The Sea* with an echo of the profession of faith in progress which underlies his historian's manifesto of 1831:

> The word [life] has swollen with a mighty breath the sails of the nineteenth century. . . . We are now launched on the voyage of inquiry, asking of each thing, in history or natural history: "Who are you?" — "I am life." — Death has taken flight before the gaze of the sciences. The spirit [or mind: *l'esprit*], continuing its triumphal advance, ever forces it to retreat.

Michelet's vision of infinite advance unifies his historical and "scientific" works. Had he not affirmed in his *Introduction to Universal History* that the world was the theater of liberation? What more could humanity seek than the conquest of death itself?

Michelet's spiritualistic interpretations of science show him to be a Romantic son of the French Revolution. He adds to the Enlightenment doctrine of progress a religious dimension it did not originally possess. For example, he termed Lamarck's putative vitalism a "great revolutionary effort." His manner of enlisting materialists to preach his gospel of the spirit appears in his presentation of Condorcet's *Tableau des progrès de l'esprit humain* (1794). This epitome of atheistic optimism was written during the Terror while the author was hiding from the Jacobins. Michelet interprets it using his own century's categories in a passage originally published in his *History of the French Revolution*. Condorcet, for him, symbolizes the mission of modern history:

> By the end of March [1794, Condorcet] had relived, saved, and consecrated every century and age; the vitality of the sciences,

their power to bestow eternity, seemed to be manifest in his book and in himself. What is history and science? The struggle against death. The vehement aspirations of a great immortal soul to communicate immortality carried away the sage to the point of expressing his wish in this prophetic form: "Science will have conquered death. And then, no one will die any more." [27]

Michelet descends from eternity to current events in book 3, "Conquest of the Sea." There he is concerned with the protection of certain marine species threatened with extinction. He anticipates the desire of today's ecologists to preserve nature and stresses the importance of humanity's moral balance. Michelet recounts gruesome stories of animal slaughter by thoughtless and sadistic men. He then gives many examples of love in rabbits, bats, even crustaceans while emphasizing the insensitivity of human beings to the moral superiority of aquatic mammals, such as whales and sea cows: "How much more do love, the family, and marriage in its literal sense, exist among the tender amphibians!" [28] The nineteenth century was especially avid for seal pelts. It is brutally ironic, states Michelet, that people butcher those creatures which have perfected qualities not yet realized in human society. His practical suggestion is to establish an international code to regulate exploitation of the marine world.

Michelet then focuses pragmatically on the decline of *human* civilization in the final book 4, "Renaissance through the Sea." This title expresses the author's hope for the physical and intellectual rebirth of his nation. The term *renaissance* refers to reincarnation, physical and spiritual rebirth, as well as to the enormous intellectual energy of the French sixteenth century. The nature books, in effect, complete Michelet's *Renaissance,* published in 1855 one year before *The Bird.*[29] In *The Sea,* Michelet turns to the Second Empire's decadence of spirit and body in the terms of nineteenth-century materialists who explained mental activity in terms of physiology.[30] Our naturalist acts as a physician. He first describes the sea's pervasive vitality and then explains how it can heal mankind. The deteriorating fishing industry of Dieppe and Etretat symbolizes his society's immense fatigue. He then attributes this exhaustion to the prodigious advances of science and technology made available to large masses through a plethora of newspapers and popular books. The century's principal malady is thus a "dispersion of mind" which, according to Michelet, consumes his fellow citizens:

We pour forth from our brains a wonderful flood of sciences, arts, inventions, ideas, products, with which we deluge the globe, the present, even the future. But at what cost is all this achieved! At the cost of frightful expenditure of vital strength, of cerebral force which proportionately enervates the entire generation. Our works are prodigious and our children miserable.[31]

Michelet proposes that the government establish public health spas on the ocean, available at no cost to all social classes. Vacations at the seashore should cure the strains suffered by his rapidly industrialized nation. Overworked parents would no longer weaken their progeny through the inheritance of their acquired degeneration.

The final chapter of *The Sea* expands the Dantesque symbolism of its title, "*Vita nuova* of the Nations," into a vision of the sea as a fountain of human regeneration. Since the ocean is the original and eternal source of earthly life and the cradle of the universal vital mucus (its water!), bathing in the sea could restore the body of humanity, and consequently its mind. Michelet stresses the social utility of his book in a confidence published in its final chapter: "While I was finishing this book, in December 1860, the resuscitated Italy, the glorious mother of us all, sends me some beautiful New-Year's gifts. A brochure, a bit of news, reaches me from Florence... [which] contains a seed of incalculable consequence, and which might change the world." [32] He had received a medical pamphlet telling how the lives of two sick children were saved by sending them to the seashore. He again underlines the pragmatic seriousness of *The Sea* in two notes he added to its second edition (also 1861); there he confirms through a message from his friend Dr. Lortet of Lyon the medical virtues of sea bathing. The author's final note, anticipating success, starts thus: "I learn with great satisfaction that the Parisian Board of Public Welfare is now founding an establishment of this kind [health spas on the sea]. May I be permitted to express some suggestions..." Michelet's didactic poem on *The Sea* combines fantasy, science, and realistic social criticism in a sincere attempt to restore his overworked nation.

The Mountain: *The Regeneration of Mankind*

Michelet had completed his *History of France* by the time his final nature study was published in 1868. After a period of intense introspection he wrote a new preface to his *History of the French Revolution* and drafted an examination of his entire career as an historian. At the age of seventy the author of *The Mountain* could thus trace the inspirational message of his nature series with confidence. He did so in the section of the book in which he describes his physical and emotional renewal through mud bathing at Acqui, Italy. His rebirth revealed the theme his *History* shared with his social and naturalist works: "[Nature] had increased me with life and power. May I be worthy of her (I told myself), may I draw from her sources, and with a more prolific heart enter into her sacred unity! Such was the origin of *The Bird, The Sea, The Insect,* as well as of *The Renaissance,* and of that which created them, and which creates all: *Love.*" [33]

Michelet's naturalist, social, and historical writings all attack the pessimism of early Romanticism which persisted in his day. It was a sacred duty to refute those literary masterpieces which lent authenticity to the discouragement of his contemporaries:

> Cries of despair have been uttered from century to century. Grainville, around 1800, wrote *Le Dernier Homme* [*The Last Man*]. Senancour and Byron, and so many others believed in the end of the world. I believe it to be immortal. By many unforeseeable aspects and still youthful but unsuspected fibers, it always revives.[34]

The obscure Jean-Baptiste Cousin de Grainville (1746–1805), constitutional priest and protégé of Bernardin de Saint-Pierre (1737–1814), drowned himself in the Somme River after the failure of his ambitious epic poem. The poem then became popular with the Romantics. Michelet gives great importance to this forgotten piece, and in an appendix to his *History of the Nineteenth Century* (volume 2, 1873) he summarizes its story of human annihilation while affirming that mankind can be redeemed through love. Etienne Pivert de Senancour (1770–1846) created the memoirs of the disenchanted *Obermann* (1804) which describe a young man adrift in the world who surrenders to reverie and neurotic melancholy. The satanism of Lord Byron (1788–1824) also nourished the Romantic generation, whose rootlessness is typified in Alfred de Musset's quasi-autobiographical *Confession d'un enfant du siècle* (1836). In mid-century, the disgust with life which Michelet resolutely opposed achieved its finest literary expression in *Les Fleurs du Mal* (1857) of Charles Baudelaire and his posthumous prose poems (1869) which express his ennui, or metaphysical boredom, and his ferocious anguish at the poverty and degradation of city-dwellers.

A comparison of how Baudelaire and Michelet handle their gloom could focus a valuable theology of culture. Both writers suffer from acute sensitivity to social affliction and are obsessed with the absence, or injustice, of God. They agree that mankind's yearning for the infinite can strengthen civilization. Yet they grew up in different periods and formed opposing views of human nature. Baudelaire sees humanity as enslaved; his compassion alternates with anger at displays of original sin and God's indifference. Michelet's pity and resentment are excited by mankind's corruption of its essential goodness and he is exalted by human freedom. Michelet was nurtured on the dreams of the Revolution and grew to full intellectual maturity before 1848. While Baudelaire, born in 1821, disgusted by Louis-Philippe and the Empire of Napoleon III, could not sustain such idealism. Baudelaire plunged into his era's anxiety; Michelet revolted against it. The historian's last nature book defines that struggle. *The Mountain* was written within the three years preceding the disastrous Franco-Prussian War. It resists the moral lassitude of the crumbling Second Empire and seeks once and for all to counteract this literature of despair.

Part 1 of *The Mountain* attempts to establish a modern faith on science, while part 2 defines Michelet's prophetic conception of history. The book begins with a trip around and then within the earth. This geological journey is meant to demonstrate scientifically the earth's powers of creation. He then interprets this geology allegorically and presents the mountain as a symbol of human aspirations. Michelet draws his lesson in the chapter, "The Upward Progress of the Earth—Its Aspiration," as he interprets philosophically the rise of liquid rock toward the sun. It becomes another incarnation of nature's Icarian quest:

> With the force of her [earth's] restrained impulse toward him [the sun], her bosom seems, at times, to heave and expand... Regret? Aspiration? ever vain, incomplete, and powerless, like all things in this world. The aspiration falls back to earth as if after reflection it had overcome its yearnings, though not without a sigh.[35]

Physical reality limits the freedom of all creation, humanity included. Yet this vision does not preclude an essential hope. For the "sigh" of aspiration which nourishes desire and progress is as eternal as Mother Earth.

Michelet defines his career as an historian in book 2. The allegory takes the form of a journey on the earth's surface. He studies plants and trees and then translates the meaning of this odyssey in the chapter, "Forests—The Tree of Life—The Golden Bough." Four years before, Michelet had published a sweeping history of world religions, *The Bible of Humanity* (1864). In *The Mountain* he borrows from it various religious interpretations of the tree (Persian, Egyptian, Celtic, Virgilian, and so forth) and relates the tree as a symbol of inspiration to his own mission:

> Vast forest! sea of leaves and dreams... How long have I wandered in its glades! How was my youth spent, if not in gloomy seeking? up to the day when at last I found and seized that golden bough, with which I summoned departed nations from the world of shadows.[36]

Michelet translates these symbols autobiographically. He equates the forest with the underworld of *The Aeneid,* his Orphic power as artist with that of the golden bough, and his *History of France* with a resurrection of the dead. In *The Insect* he described the "Virgilian bees" on his son's tomb which symbolized his ability to resuscitate the Lazarus of nations. Now he uses the Virgilian branch of mountain trees to portray the talisman which allows him to enter the past and return from darkness with lost souls. That "golden bough" is his empathy with the dead and his artistic gift of reliving their events through sympathetic imagination. Michelet's powerful compassion explains his almost magical conception of himself as a writer.[37]

Michelet reappears as the moral judge of his nation in the chapter on "The Pass of the Grisons—The Death of the Mountain." These notations are based on a trip the Michelets made to the Engadine region of Switzerland. The stark landscape provided images of both geological and moral erosion: "How closely does nature resemble man! While writing this, my soul was horror-stricken with the thought of the moral *lapiaz* which I have witnessed in these days." [38] Michelet then explicates his condensed metaphor, "moral *lapiaz*" (*lapiaz* is a technical term referring to cracks made in rock by water) :[39]

> But what will happen if this devastation, from the lower grades
> and the vulgar *lapiaz* of egotism and moral sterility, should extend
> further, and if the process of erosion gain upon the immense
> masses [of the people], indifferent to all things, and deficient
> both in the desire and the capability of good?

The term "vulgar *lapiaz* of egotism" combines natural and social ecology as it describes the self-seeking, morally corrupt and indifferent
middle classes portrayed throughout the century by Balzac, Stendhal,
Flaubert, and Zola, among many others. Egotism is Michelet's term
for amoral individualism, unfeeling self-interest. He fears that the
natural goodness he believes the common people to possess will be
contaminated by the social putrescence of the Second Empire. Michelet
literalizes the geological metaphor he used in *The People* to describe
the simple classes: that the vital heat comes from below. Twenty-three
years later the author of *The Mountain* trusts that a morally committed
science (exemplified by his own approach) will reveal to middle-class
France "the wellsprings of the spirit and the moral flame."

He recapitulates this message in his long final chapter, "Will
Our Era Succeed in Ascending?" There he defines conclusively the
educational purpose of his career. *The Mountain* attempts to establish
the study of nature as the basis of a new moral order. The following
year, in 1869, Michelet particularized his methods in the masterful
treatise on education, *Our Sons*. The final paragraph of *The Mountain*
suggests how the author's experience of writing can change his reader's
life:

> This is the whole secret of this book. If it has again reno-
> vated me, if it has blotted twenty centuries from my memory,
> may you, young traveler, who come with strength and all the day
> before you, may you find herein a starting point! May it be for
> you one of those midway summits where we halt at dawn, to ex-
> amine oneself a brief moment, to mark the goal with a sure eye,
> and then to ascend, to thrust oneself even higher upward.[40]

The historian shares his homeopathic cure by the study of nature. This
book and Michelet's entire corpus should show the path to self-knowledge. Readers would then be liberated by the understanding that nature
is a source of eternal power; they could then, like birds and mountain
climbers, "thrust [themselves] even higher upward." Michelet encourages us to view the world as a reflection of our own creative genius.

6

Michelet's Mysticism

Nature as a Symbol of Spirit

Michelet completes the third and final task of the Orphic poet-teacher, that of bringing readers into the direct presence of God. His passion for the Christian Middle Ages survived his break with the Church and sustains the rich tone of his early historical efforts. Joachim de Flores and Joan of Arc were permanently entrenched in his mythology. His *History* was truly an "eternal gospel." Even Michelet's violent polemics against the Jesuits (in his courses of 1842–1843 and his first educational book, *Priest, Woman, and Family,* 1845) betray a sympathetic, though ambivalent, obsession with prayer and mysticism. History is charged with "sacred moments" in which God is revealed to humanity: the invention of printing during the Renaissance, the intellectual passion of Voltaire, Rousseau, and Diderot (described in Michelet's "Credo of the Eighteenth Century"), and, of course, the Fête of the Federations in 1790, when the French people, in all their diversity, became a nation and reached an almost transcendent harmony of thought and feeling. Michelet's history of religions, *The Bible of Humanity* (1864), remains one of the great inspirational syntheses of the century. The study of religion unlocked cultures and history revealed divine concern.[1]

Michelet surpassed this scholarly mission. He sought to transform not only minds, but souls as well. The diary of this anticlerical articulates his dream, curiously, the day before Christmas 1853. He wanted his contemporaries to pray authentically. Modern prayer, he writes, as opposed to medieval devotion, should be disinterested; "it should be a harmonization of the individual with the universal love which creates the unity of things. Why, during this age of transition, do people no longer pray?" ² Michelet's naturalist works accept the challenge: "Although everyone today should pray for himself, accomplish his harmonization according to his own needs, I wish however a book could be written that could put the soul on the path of an active and voluntary harmonization at the moment of death."

Life is defined by the beyond. Michelet's faith in nature requires faith in an accessible living God. He defends these beliefs by evoking direct experiences of the Deity which complete the proofs of natural science. He was convinced that mystical intuitions were available to anyone with an open mind. His preference for religious experience over dogma reflects his individualism; it advanced the battle against Catholicism which he characterized in his *History of the French Revolution* as a principle of arbitrary grace negating moral and intellectual autonomy.³ As he asserts in *The People,* France herself, defined by the ideals of 1789, must become the religion of Europe. Michelet the naturalist attempts to rival the spiritual masterpieces of Christianity and replace them with a nonclerical Bible of Nature. The lyrical passages of his nature books are his liturgy; they are like psalms that relate a modern man's contacts with the divine.

Their most enduring moments are rhapsodic evocations of the world revealing itself as a form—a symbol—of spiritual forces. Michelet presents himself in scenes of vivid intensity as an example of what his readers might attain. As a naturalist he applies his genius for reliving history to identify with the inner life he imagined the animate world to possess. These passages convey the experiential foundation of his moral fables. His most poetic prose demonstrates that the nature books are didactic poems in which the author realizes his dual role as mystical poet and natural philosopher.

Analysis of Michelet's religious symbolism of nature also clarifies a crucial ideological issue. The author of *The Bird* and *The Mountain* has been generally considered, by friends and foes alike, to be a pantheist. Hostile critics—both Catholic and materialist—have used the volatile term *pantheism* to discredit his natural religion.⁴ Simply stated, Pantheism is a doctrine that considers God and nature as one identical substance. Can the divine force demonstrated by Michelet's theory of evolution become an object of personal experience? Can direct contact with God be achieved through nature? Michelet's answer is yes; but in the final analysis he clearly believes in a God who, in essence, is not identical with creation. In delving into the dynamics of Michelet's imagination of nature as a symbol of spirit, we shall understand why he is *not* a pantheist: his religious experience demonstrates that his deep feeling for God's immanence depends upon a persistent quest for nature's ultimately transcendent source.

Understanding Nature as a Symbolic System

Michelet inaugurates his naturalist series by explaining how to discover the world's spiritual foundation. This method consists of exploring intellectually what his intuition first revealed. He summarizes this procedure in *The Bird* when he imagines the Paris Museum of Natural History to be "the crypt of that great church" which is nature; the museum is the microcosm of all that is organized in creation. The author's vocation is to awaken a desire to pursue its secrets:

> There has never been an unlettered, ignorant man, no insensitive or blasé mind, who can shield himself against a feeling of respect, I might almost say of terror, upon entering the halls of our Museum of Natural History. . . . This sublime harmony is felt instinctively; it imposes and seizes the mind. The inattentive traveler, the chance visitor, is unwittingly affected; he pauses, and he dreams. In the presence of this vast enigma, of this immense hieroglyph which for the first time is displayed before him, he would consider himself fortunate if he could read a character, spell a letter.[5]

Our understanding of the world is colored by religious fear and respect provoked by a naïve confrontation with its grand harmony.[6] Such first impressions endow nature with extraordinary significance. Michelet hopes that we will interpret this vague but sublime unity as a manifestation of divine mysteries.

He gives force to this sense of initiation as he characterizes nature as an "enigma," an esoteric "hieroglyph," a code to be deciphered by a learned priest: "How often have common people, surprised and tormented by such fantastic forms, inquired of us their meaning! A word would set them in the right path, a simple indication would charm them; they would go away contented, promising themselves to return." He stresses the compelling beauty of the zoological display in order to awaken an intellectual passion. That is Michelet the naturalist's mission. This evangelist considers his readers as tourists in the church of nature and himself as their benevolent guide.

Michelet extends the procedure illustrated by the structured museum to his reactions to brute nature. In both instances, intuitions of infinity lead to a spiritualistic vision. He takes the sublime of nature as a sign of God's presence in the world. Nature thus conceived is a vehicle of the divine; its grandeur incites the bold mind to seize its meaning directly. Michelet trains his reader's sensitivity by retracing in remarkable detail the workings of his own symbolic imagination. This model of *participation mystique* (to use Lévy-Bruhl's term) with an immense natural spectacle completes his *theory* of nature. He wants his representations of sublime grandeur to arouse in thinkers a passion to understand the beyond.

Michelet makes his readers participate in the subjective foundation of his naturalist books as he unfolds his insights into natural symbolism. His detailed analysis of imagination demonstrates how to interpret the physically endless as a spiritual revelation:

> Three forms of nature expand and elevate our soul, make it leave itself and soar into the infinite:
>
> The variable ocean of the air, with its festival of light, its vapors and its *chiaroscuro,* its mobile phantasmagoria of capricious creations, which so swiftly vanish.
>
> The fixed ocean of the earth, its undulations which we follow along the crest of lofty mountains, the upheavals which witness to its ancient mobility, the sublimity of their heights with their eternal ice.
>
> Finally, the ocean of the waters, less mobile than the first, and less permanent than the second, obedient in its regular alternation to the celestial movements.[7]

Michelet's first reaction is to project his need to transcend the ego into these impressive appearances. The visual boundlessness of air, earth, and sea excites his fantasy beyond the concrete givens. These masses are all "oceans," that is, they are a material form of infinity. Yet because they differ in mobility these masses create specific movements of imagination.[8] Notice how Michelet bestows upon his impulses the dignity of objective knowledge. Even before he specifies how and what he fantasizes he insists that sublime nature bespeaks God's presence: "These three forms compose the gamut, or musical scale, in which infinity speaks to our soul."

Such intuitions personalize Michelet's allegorical lessons. *The*

Bird, we have seen, depicts the human thirst for transcendence; it traces "the heart's flight toward light." Now Michelet describes how his aerial reveries crystallized into that religious insight:

> The first [thing: air] shifts so constantly, that we can scarcely observe it; it deceives, it decoys, it amuses; it scatters and interrupts our thoughts. It is one moment the boundless hope, a day spent in the infinite; in which we will pierce even to the depth of God... No, everything flees; the grieving heart is disturbed and filled with doubt. Why was I permitted a glimpse of that sublime dream of light? I can never again forget it, and because of it the world remains darkened.

Thought is propelled by a will to know the divine and it flies into the air creating illusions of transcendence. But sadly, this insight is but momentary and only increases a yearning for God who remains hidden, beyond nature. Mankind discovers the essential otherness of the divine when it realizes its physical frailty. *The Bird* translates this religion of hope bound by the limits of finite perception, without abolishing nevertheless "that sublime dream of light." Michelet's symbolism of air attempts to keep alive humanity's desire for spiritual cognition.

The immobile earth leads imagination in the opposite direction: "The fixed ocean of the mountains does not escape thus. On the contrary. It arrests us at every step, and imposes upon us severe but salutary gymnastics. Contemplation [of earth] can only be purchased by the most violent action. Yet the opacity of earth, like the transparency of air, frequently deceives and leads us astray." Opacity and transparency are two irreducible obstacles to intelligence. At least the earth provokes the effort to enter its depths. That very process stimulates the geological reveries Michelet developed in *The Mountain* and to a lesser degree the microscopic examinations he described in *The Insect:* the mystery below the earth's surface animates speculations on its internal processes and entomology demands disciplined concentration in order to penetrate that world of darkness.

Only the sea encourages our struggle to explain the universe. When he interprets his experience of this element, his exposition switches to a more analytical mode. The "Book of Nature" leaves its exalted position as the symbol of a divine process to serve a traditional allegorical technique.[9] Our dreamer "reads" the myriad lives of the deep and formulates a theory of creation:

The Ocean is a voice. It speaks to the distant stars, responds to their motions with its grave and solemn language. It speaks to the earth and to the shore with a pathetic tone, and holds a dialogue with their echoes; alternately plaintive and menacing, it roars or sighs. Above all, it addresses itself to man. Since it is the prolific crucible wherein creation began and wherein it continues in all its potential, it possesses life's living eloquence; it is life speaking to life. Those millions, those billions of organisms which issue from it, are its words.

Thought is no longer stopped by substance. The sea answers Michelet's query, for it is literally a language which can be deciphered and explained: "The Ocean *is* a voice." In other words, the sea itself carries a specific message. Its speech, its sonorous articulation, is its waves, tides and exploding population. He translates it into the terms of science. The code of the sea not only divulges the evolutionary origin of life; it also demonstrates the action of a continuing creation. It points to a life force inherent in matter. The text of the sea resolves a universal enigma. What had begun as an intuition of the infinite now explains the process of life.

Michelet's naturalist books define lessons when the view of the world as a system within itself becomes suggestive of human concerns. The sea's fertility and harmony, in the former perspective, is the source of life. In the latter view, speaking allegorically, it illustrates God's relation to nature and to humanity:

> What does it say? *It speaks life,* eternal metamorphosis....
> What does it say? *Immortality.* At the lowest level of nature lies an indomitable force of life. How much more so at nature's highest point—in the soul!
> What does it say? *Solidarity.* Let us accept the rapid exchange which takes place in the individual between his various elements. Let us accept the higher law which binds together the living members of one and the same body: humanity. And, beyond all, that supreme law which makes us cooperate, create in conjunction with the great Soul, associates (according to our degree) with the loving Harmony of the world, partners in the life of God.

Michelet has come a long way from the overly ambitious attempts of his reverie to find meaning in the unfathomable air and earth. However, the emotional power of those encounters did imbue reflection with a sense of the absolute. Hence the sea, first understood scientifically, and then religiously, links God to nature's vital thrust. The "indomitable force of [physical] life" proclaims its heavenly cause, "the loving Harmony of the world." *Yet it is not identical with it.* It is critical to understand that the *"higher* law" which binds dispersed humanity is subordinate to the *"supreme* law" of God which alone is the ultimate source of nature's unity. A pantheist would identify the natural laws and divine laws without distinction. Michelet is not a pantheist for he depicts a creativity immanent to nature while clearly asserting the existence of a supernatural divinity.

Michelet thus elucidates his theological presuppositions when he translates his allegory. Nature reveals a spiritual process. Creation for him is more than a metaphor of God, however. Were it not for his disdain of the Bible he would exclaim with the psalmist: "The Heavens declare the glory of God and the firmament proclaims His handiwork. . . ." If we apply terminology relevant to literary metaphors to Michelet's understanding of the structure of the world,* we understand that, according to his symbolism, God or the loving Cause of life (the tenor) manifests itself physically by natural evolution (the vehicle). Michelet does not confuse the two distinct realms of nature and spirit with their "meeting place," the world. The common quality that permits the metaphorical equation or comparison is called its "ground." Michelet discovers the "ground" of spirit and matter in nature's and humanity's constant upward development.

His passionate declarations have a pedagogical function related to his implicit theology. The subjective experiences he describes, and his obvious fascination with the workings of imagination aim to educate our poetic sense of nature as an image of spiritual reality. Michelet tries to convince us that intuition reveals a system of analogous functions in the world, that identical forces motivate humanity and nature. Hence, the intellectual complexity of such passages should not mask their essential purpose. Michelet renders his religious symbolism intelligible by analyzing its dynamics while he intends his lyrical style to reinforce those sources of insight anyone may unknowingly possess.

Intuition and Scientific Knowledge

The nature books popularize scientific knowledge as well by appealing to subjective procedures of verification. Their imaginative

---

* See beginning of chapter 3, p. 23.

features complete the author's bald scientific arguments. The method he uses to reconcile the authoritative science of the Second Empire with fantasy follows the pattern of his religious understanding. The Romantic historian's "scientific method" consists of hypothesis, observation, analysis, and then generalization—with this important exception: if one is especially sensitive, one can seize scientific truth directly. This is another mode of knowledge by participation. Even minute observations lead easily to impressive generalizations when magnified by excitement. Michelet's dramatic examples of this process, characteristic of much scientific writing before the experimental era,* are calculated above all to inspire the reader's tacit assent.[10]

Michelet's justification of the idea that sea-water is life's basic element is paradigmatic of his "scientific" procedure. If this hypothesis is correct according to today's science, his explanation harks back to Lamarck and Oken, who supposed that a primordial mucus was the first organic substance. The author of *The Sea* leads us from emotionally tinged observations to his immediate (and experimentally unjustifiable) generalizations. He accomplishes this by reliving the possible genesis of his insight as he describes how he derived his understanding of sea-water from a *touch* experience contaminated with the *idea* of mucus as vital matter:[11]

> Sea-water, even the purest, when procured in the open ocean, free from all admixture, is of slightly whitish color and somewhat viscous. Held between the fingers, it *runs smoothly* [like oil; in French: *filer*] and passes through them slowly. Chemical analyses do not explain this characteristic. It originates in an organic substance, which analyses can attain only by destroying, depriving it of its specificity, and reducing it violently to general elements.
>
> Ocean plants and animals are clothed with this substance, whose mucosity, consolidated around them, has a gelatinous effect, sometimes fixed and sometimes wavering.[12]

Michelet's incredible observation that sea-water is white and viscous can be explained by this notion that the sea is a womb and its water,

---

* The scientific eras of observation and of classification preceded the experimental era. The birth of modern experimental science can perhaps be traced to 1865, the year of publication of the revolutionary *Introduction à l'étude de la médecine expérimentale* by the physiologist Claude Bernard (1813–1878). Cf. Michel Foucault, *Les Mots et les choses* (Gallimard, 1966), especially chaps. 5 et seq.

"the sea of milk," amniotic fluid, thickened by an abundance of fish semen and eggs. Literary psychologists could easily analyze Michelet's obsessions with sexuality and feminine nurturance which dominate his thoughts about sea mucus. In fact, the period during which Michelet composed *The Sea* was one of intense preoccupation with sexuality. With delicious naïveté he exposes in his diary, 15 June 1860, the basis of his associations: "The entire program of *sea-water* has been assimilated with the mucus of the... vagina." [13] His theory of knowledge is more subtle. He proposes an epistemology which opposes analysis; he considers analysis obtuse for it fragments organic substance. He prefers intuition which is by definition immediate, synthetic, and more apt to seize life which is itself integrity.

For Michelet the *manner* of understanding is as important as its subject *matter*. He is at pains to erect his impressionistic observation into a systematic empirical method. He assumes that children possess acute intuitive capacities and attempts to validate his insight by finding its origin in a childhood impression. In the passage which directly follows the one just cited, Michelet unwittingly but perspicaciously analyzes his perceptual distortion. He considers his insight objective because of the very power of this trauma and the durability of his interpretation:

> [The sea mucus] is what most vividly impresses a child when for the first time he sees a fish. I was very young when this event occurred, but I can perfectly recollect the keen impression produced. That shiny, slippery creature, with its silver scales, threw me into an indescribable state of astonishment and rapture. I attempted to seize it, but I found it as difficult to hold as the water which escaped from my little fingers. It appeared to me identical with the element in which it swam. I had the confused idea that it was nothing other than animalized, organicised water.
>
> Long afterwards, when I had reached manhood, I was not less surprised at discovering on a shore some species of radiata— which, I do not remember. ... It seemed to me as it had seemed to the ancients, and even to Réaumur, who simply designated these beings as *gelatinized water*.

Michelet does not remember any rational mediation between experience and conclusion in this event. His tactile impressions were oriented by astonishment and led to an inference as intellectually broad as it is emotionally intense. Michelet gives equal weight to three different

realms of investigation: his reveries on a peculiar sensation, ancient
legends, and modern science. René Réaumur (1683–1757), the physi-
cist and naturalist known as the "Pliny of the eighteenth century," caps
this remarkable concord. Michelet hopes to guarantee his reader's full
participation by evoking the scene with breathless zeal.

Michelet concludes his lesson by placing his inquiry in an indis-
putably solid framework, that of materialistic science. He finalizes his
original intuition with the testimony of a professional master who follows an analogous process of understanding. The scientist's leap from
observation to absolute conclusion is the same; the only difference is
that he qualifies his instantaneous assertion. Here is the last scene of
this epistemological drama:

> Preoccupied with these thoughts, I went to see an illustrious
> chemist, a man of practical and solid mind, an innovator as pru-
> dent as courageous, and, without preface, I abruptly launched
> my question at him: — "Sir," I said, "what in your opinion is
> that viscous, whitish element which we detect in sea-water?"
> — "Nothing other than life."
> Then, by way of explaining an utterance too simple and too
> absolute, he added: "I mean to say, a substance half-organized
> and already capable of complete organization. In certain waters
> it is only a density of infusoria, in others, what is becoming, will
> become life. — Besides, this subject has still to be studied; its
> investigation has not yet been seriously begun." (17 May 1860).

The chemist's response to the abrupt question reproduces young Michelet's thrill at encountering a slimy fish.* The scientist is intellectually
excited by the problem as would be the observer of a sublime landscape. An "exemplary chemist" thus sustains the historian's gigantic
claim. Even though the former recognizes that little experimental proof
for his judgment exists, he does imply that sea-water consists of vital
mucus. Michelet delights in portraying a prudent and practical member
of the scientific establishment who, like himself, literally jumps to con-

---

* Michelet's diary of 16 May indicates that the chemist was Marcelin Berthelot
(1827–1907), then professor at the Ecole supérieure de pharmacie. His special interest was the synthesis of compounds in organic chemistry. His contributions to the
field were so great that he was interred in the Pantheon in Paris. On 4 June 1860
Berthelot wrote a detailed letter to Michelet on the composition of sea-water, citing
the most recent scientific sources (unpublished letter conserved at the Bibliothèque
historique de la Ville de Paris, A. 4844bis).

clusions. The general reader, heartened by the example of a rigorous experimentalist guided by intuition, should accept this "fact" as gospel.[14]

Is Michelet a Pantheist?

Michelet's analyses of nature as a symbol of spirit and his scientific procedure combine precept with example. His presuppositions are less explicit when he evokes his experiences of the Deity. Many commentators have indeed considered his "pantheism" quite obvious.[15] The term *pantheism* is a commonplace of Romantic criticism and is still used loosely to label any literature which poetically evokes a divine presence within nature. Michelet's case is complicated by the nineteenth-century ideological situation. In the polemic vocabulary of his Christian antagonists, pantheism was a theological heresy because it deified matter. A materialistic pantheist, through his disdain of a transcendent God, rejected the authority of any religion sanctioned by a revelation from that essentially transcendent Deity. What, then, could justify the Church's political power? Atheistic materialists, on the other hand, deplored the historian's outbursts of otherworldly yearning which they saw as a reduction of matter to spirit and an evasion from the present. These criticisms are all partially true. However, none recognize how Michelet's natural religion reconciles the present and the future, the here and the beyond.

True, his vitalistic theory of evolution posits the existence of a force or spirit which is immanent to the world. And his often excessive celebrations of that divine presence may suggest that, at least momentarily, he abolishes any distinction between God and nature. Yet, a close analysis of the historian's most ecstatic passages demonstrates that although he asserts that God resides *in* nature, he does not perceive Him as identical *with* it. The historian is not a pantheist; rather he is *panentheistic:* he can say "All is *in* God" but never "God *is* the All." [16] By necessity Michelet insists upon God's ultimate otherness in order to preserve the dialogue between matter and spirit fundamental to his philosophy. More pragmatically, the historian's dedication to freedom requires that God remain essentially separate from human will. At the same time mankind's nostalgia for transcendence nourishes an endless striving.

Biographical information shows that the themes of immanence

and transcendence complement each other in Michelet's imagination. His gradual conversion to a natural religion was completed during his therapeutic mud bathing at Acqui, Italy. He presents to the public in 1868 in *The Mountain* the experience which he had described and analyzed fully in his diary of 7–28 June 1854.[17] In both texts he dwells upon the immanence of the spirit in mineral substance. The year following his mud baths, in 1855, he began to write *The Bird,* in which he emphasizes the desire to transcend the earth. The two poles of earth and air, of immanence and transcendence, express two simultaneous tendencies of his religious quest. We can resolve the enigma of Michelet's sense of God as both essentially other than physical existence and yet manifest within it by scrutinizing his two most celebrated accounts of mystical contact with nature's soul.

Michelet began and ended his naturalist career by writing about his mud baths. In 1854 the ailing historian recuperated at a health spa in the small Italian village of Acqui. He remained attentive to the population's political and economic woes, but his cure had a more lasting influence. He transformed each significant experience into a symbol and understood that his physical rejuvenation was produced by his union with the eternal powers of Mother Earth. Michelet imitated the Antaeus of Greek mythology, the giant wrestler who regained his power when touching the earth, his mother. Michelet began with the preconceived idea of the earth as a vital source so that his immersion in its substance dramatically confirmed that common symbolism.[18] In *The Mountain* he relives that myth in a sophisticated analysis of his own mental processes. He guides the reader's fantasies while convincing his or her mind.

The drama elaborates the theme of his rebirth and that of the human spirit in general. He introduces the bath as a burial: "on the 19th of June [1854], well prepared, I was finally interred, but only up to my waist. In my magnificent coffin of white marble, I underwent the first application of the black mud [*limon*]." [19] Michelet uses the French *limon* in preference to *boue,* common mud, for *limon* denotes the clay from which Adam was formed by God in French translations of the Bible. In this way Michelet suggests that his mud bath was a second creation.

What occurs within his mind is even more significant. His immersion in the hot mud leads to an impressive intuition *by physical participation* of nature's spiritual substratum. He relates in scrupulous detail how reverie lulls his mind and then annuls the barrier between himself and the earth:

> Ideas disappeared in my profound absorption. The only idea which remained was that of *Terra mater.* I felt her plainly, caressing and pitying and warming her wounded child. From without? Internally also. For she interpenetrated my frame with her vivifying spirits, entered into and blended with me, insinuated into my being her very soul. The identification between us grew complete. I no longer distinguished myself from her.

Michelet projects his imagination into the substance that envelops his body. The "idea" which dissolves is the conscious separation of inner thought from the perceptual world. His hypnotic concentration on the symbolic value of his therapy, his absorption in the idea of Mother Earth, intensifies the physical event and lends it extraordinary significance. Michelet thus "knows" the earth's vitality through an absolute form of participation: *"I no longer distinguished myself from her."* He senses the intimate caress of the mud and his own pleasure as identical. Michelet creates an image of the earth which becomes a mirror of his mind.

He then fulfills the potential of his identification by absorbing the earth's energy. He benefits from a concrete form of esthetic reciprocity, a relation in which the spectator awakens within himself the vitality which he "perceives." That experience produces the most strikingly pantheistic moment in Michelet's works:

> From this point up to the last quarter of an hour, that part of my body which she did not cover, which remained free— my face—was restless and importunate. The buried body was happy, and it was I. The head, which remained unburied, lamented, and was no longer I; at least, I thought so. So strong was the marriage, and more than a marriage, between me and the Earth! One might more fitly have called it *an exchange of nature.* I was Earth and she was man. She had taken upon herself my infirmities and my sin. While I, becoming Earth, had assumed her life, warmth, and youth.

The author's marriage with, or return to the womb of Mother Earth actualizes the original identity of that one force which mankind and nature share. The invented term *exchange of nature* (italicized by Michelet) expresses both a physical process of chemical exchange and a spiritual "trading." It presupposes that nature is intrinsically vital and eternal while humanity is essentially fragile and transitory, unless it communes with nature. Michelet's identification with telluric substance realizes concretely the spiritual reality of the symbolic *Terra mater*.

The author's conclusion is clear. The theological dilemma now comes to the fore since he interprets this single experience of renewal as a contact with the occult source of organic matter. This is the subjective insight upon which he based his critical evaluation of various geological theories in *The Mountain*:

> Years, labors, anxieties, all remained at the bottom of my marble coffin. I was renewed. When I emerged, an indescribable unctuous gleam shone upon my body. A certain organic element, wholly distinct from minerals, and whose nature we are ignorant of, gives the effect of a living contact, of having communicated with the invisible soul, and the happy inspiration which that soul communicates in its turn.

Michelet immediately translates his delight at being invigorated by burial in mud into a scientific hypothesis, albeit couched in spiritual terms. He makes a bold synthesis of poetic and objective knowledge, as he affirms the action of an indwelling soul in nature. He reinforces his assertions by the emotional and analytical commentaries which accompany his drama. We might find in this text a model of the pantheistic imagination were it not for his cautious inability precisely to label this "*invisible* soul," to analyze the "*indescribable* unctuous gleam." Michelet's insistence on the quality of mystery, of the unknown— stressed by the words I have italicized—proves that he recognizes a still elusive (that is, transcendent) force at work. Two "natures" had worked as one, although in essence they remained distinct.

Even if a sense of divine presence within matter does prevail in this experience, an examination of Michelet's aerial fantasies proves that he does not identify God with His creation. We can borrow the categories of Gaston Bachelard to describe Michelet's dreams of transcendence provoked by the freedom of flight, as well as reveries of repose and intimacy (immanence) in his terrestrial encounters.[20] The historian firmly differentiates between the physical aspects of marine life and their ultimate source; he understands nature to contain spiritual and physical levels—which allow nevertheless for intuitions of

God. His peak experiences with the bird world, in particular, imply the primacy of spirit over matter while symbolizing humanity's desire to be released from earthly limits. *The Bird*'s most ecstatic evocation of God's immanence takes nature as a point of contact with the mystery which he never ceases to pursue.

Michelet admits that duality but prefers to celebrate certain privileged moments in which the veil falls, when nature rewards him with "a living momentary revelation of the Inscrutable" (to use Goethe's terms).[21] The historian-naturalist's supremely mystical communion takes place as he identifies with the mating song of a nightingale and realizes the religious significance of that artist. His prose poem achieves a masterful synthesis of lyrical evocation and philosophical interpretation.

Michelet begins his experience by becoming passively receptive to the nightingale's song. The contemplation which ensues is reminiscent of his mud bath reverie and of Saint Teresa of Avila's descriptions of spiritual marriage:[22]

> This is the time that you should hear [the nightingale], hear him in his native forest, that you should participate in the emotions of that fecundating power, the most proper perhaps to reveal, to enable us to comprehend here below the great hidden God which eludes us. He recedes before us at every step, and science does no more than put a little further back the veil wherein he conceals himself. "Behold," said Moses, "behold him who passes, I have seen him from behind."
> — "Is it not he who passes?" said Linnaeus, "I have seen him in outline." And as for me, I close my eyes, I feel him with an agitated heart, I feel him flow into me on a night enchanted by the voice of the nightingale.[23]

This rapture combines vision of divine immanence and transcendence. The Hidden God, who Pascal hoped would obsess the reader of the *Pensées,* suddenly becomes experientially manifest to Michelet. Romantics in general considered the Deity as more accessible than had non-Christian writers of more orthodox periods. The author represents the bird's song as inseparable from its *Gestalt,* the forest which symbolizes natural unity. That harmony conveys a sense of the divine presence within nature's "fecundating power." The mating bird reflects the spirit of life which, while immanent in the world, is ultimately transcendent: it is "the great hidden God which eludes us." He insists that a scientific, rational examination of physical laws (here, the classifications of Linnaeus) cannot lead to religious insight; he also rejects biblical revelation in the person of Moses. Personal experience, inward receptive intuition are superior.

The remainder of the passage details the structure of Michelet's religious vision of nature. It clarifies how his ode to the nightingale distinguishes and separates the physical and spiritual levels:

> If you draw near, it is a lover; but if you keep distant, it is a god. The melody, now vibrating with a flaming call to the senses, grows in the distance and becomes amplified by the effects of the wind; it is a sacred canticle which resounds through all the forest. Seen closely, the bird is occupied with the nest, with his beloved, and the son to be born; but seen from afar, another is the beloved, another is the son: it is Nature, mother and daughter, eternal lover, which hymns and glorifies itself; it is the infinite Love which loves in everything and sings in everything; these are the tendernesses, the canticles, the songs of thanksgiving, which go up from earth to heaven.

Michelet's prose poem arises from his attempt to embrace the universe in words. At the same time, he has structured the text according to the logic of his nightingale symbolism. The human perspective is decisive. Viewed at close range as an individual animal, the bird is a lover and family man. In the broader context of the forest, the bird father exemplifies the eternal force of Love; "it is a god." The fertility of these creatures alludes to superior powers as does the fecundity of the sea. The nightingale's love thus illustrates God's immanence, "the infinite Love which loves and sings *in* everything." God is All here—but not *as* nature, rather *within* it.

That Michelet does not, either in theory or in practice, identify God with creation should refine our appreciation of his nature poetry. Hippolyte Taine's otherwise brilliant review of *The Bird* represents the usual misunderstanding of Michelet's immanentism. The materialist philosopher quotes this very passage and damns it by his praise: "This is the profound, passionate and mystical pantheism at which that talent arrives, the point at which that philosophy [of nature] arrives. The artist perceives in all things Love and Vitality. . . . One is tempted as he is to confuse all things in one single being, and it is understandable how an artist, glimpsing the face of the eternal goddess, has stated that her name is Love." [24] Taine develops the commonplace that emotional artists resist subtle distinctions. He erroneously identifies the three terms implicit in Michelet's symbol with one of them: that is, Taine believes that Michelet considers the vehicle (bird reproduction) as identical with its source, the tenor (God), whose common "ground" is a love force. The contrary is true. Michelet refuses to consider natural love (the vehicle) as consubstantial with God (the tenor). Even Michelet's nightingale mysticism reaffirms the one principle at the foundation of his philosophy: that of the ultimate independence of spirit.

Michelet's nature studies strike a balance between God's immanence and transcendence. Inseparable in his personal mythology are an Antaeus who regains strength from touching Mother Earth and a soaring Icarus who dreams of an existence beyond this world. All the naturalist books testify to the author's faith in an essentially hidden God, who is apprehended only at certain privileged moments and in exceptional places. He considers his mystical poetry as part of a modern liturgy designed to help us enter those sanctuaries; it aims to animate within us a dialectic of religious aspiration and esthetic satisfaction. Michelet hoped that mankind's striving would be fortified by such moments of ecstasy, those "flaming melodies" which sing from his pen. His natural religion was meant to enrich daily toil with a savor of the Infinite.

7

The Two Sexes of the Mind

Michelet's Analysis of Creative
and Moral Thought

Michelet's naturalist and social lessons do more than inspire people with the author's optimistic faith. They aim to stimulate a radical
renewal of humanity. They contain a program to transform people's
minds which should in turn effect a social and political revolution.
With this goal in sight, Michelet sought to understand humanity, first
through historical research and then through the study of nature. The
final chapter of *The Mountain* explains that he combines the two
realms to illuminate the inner life: "Europe is powerfully lucid. Its
singularly inventive genius, which pierces to the depth of things, cannot fail to turn back upon itself, and to see within man. Among the
numerous arts which it has created, another, and the loftiest, will yet
arrive—that which makes and remakes the soul." [1] The historian first
takes the outer world as his primary object; he then returns home to
the human spirit. His history and science must reveal the powers of
the inner person.

Michelet extracts his philosophical anthropology equally from human and natural history.* To his mind, these two bodies of knowledge
are adapted to male and female audiences respectively: he thought that
women were sensitive to nature, while men could more readily find
meaning in the turmoil of social conflict. He represents his own historical ("male") and naturalist ("female") insights in a description of
the bisexual androgyne. This image of the complete human being was

---

* Michelet did not himself use the term "philosophical anthropology," but
ever since *The People* (1846) he committed himself to the task of defining the essential nature of the person. His historical studies are thus completed by his exploration of thought, imagination, and the emotions.

very common in the nineteenth century; it occurs, among others, in the works of the gentle mystic of Lyon, Pierre-Simon Ballanche, Honoré de Balzac (most particularly in *Séraphîta*), the religious socialist Pierre Leroux (1797–1871), and August Comte (1798–1857), the founder of Positivism.[2] The historian's analysis of the "two sexes of the mind" (a phrase he first uses in *The People*) defines the ideal person who would guide a just social revolution.

He describes this intellectual synthesis, characteristically, by focusing upon the *manner* in which we know. A full apprehension of the world involves a bisexual form of understanding which in *Woman* he calls "the modern religion." Nonclerical of course, this religion joins man's perception of life's physical forms with his mate's intuition of their ultimate cause:

> The two legitimate and reasonable sides of religion are displayed in the tendencies of man and woman, represented by each of them. Man perceives the infinite in the invariable Laws of the world which are like the forms of God. Woman [senses it] in the loving Cause and the Father of Nature who is creating it from good to better. She feels God by that which is its life, its soul and the eternal act: love and reproduction.
>
> Are these points of view contradictory? not at all. The two harmonize in this: that the God of woman, *Love, would not be Love if he were not Love for all,* incapable of caprice or arbitrary preference, *if he did not Love according to Law, to Reason and Justice,* that is to say, according to the idea that man has of God.[3]

Like virtually all his contemporaries Michelet is a "male chauvinist," he subordinates woman to man. But we discover beneath this prejudice a solid analysis of cognition. The author's description of male and female perception is both literal and symbolic. The two religious perspectives—subjective and objective—are *"represented* by each of the two sexes." Woman instinctively perceives the spiritual substratum of life, its "loving Cause," while man rationally apprehends its physical laws, "the forms of God" accessible to science. The two sexes thus point to two distinct (but interdependent) domains of reality and together they determine a universal system of ethics.

When intellect and intuition cooperate the lessons of nature and history can be executed. Theory can create practice. Michelet assumes that his readers' insights will necessarily lead them into social involvement, that their understanding of his theory of mind, if morally committed, will transform reality. His mythology of man and woman also represents society. The emotional woman epitomizes the sage instincts of the common people, while the man exemplifies the rationality of the educated elite. Michelet applies this traditional primitivism to the ailing Second Empire. He attempts to defend woman's role as social guide so that all classes would become as harmonious as the ideal family.

The Man of Genius as Ideal Humanity

Why did the historian model society after thinking processes? Because his spiritualistic philosophy considers mind as the source of civilization. Culture and institutions embody the free action of intelligence (or spirit) upon matter. His interpretation of civilization can also be traced to the political ideology elaborated in his seminal manual of human transformation, *The People*. Paul Viallaneix, in his encyclopedic study of Michelet's historical and social thought, *La Voie royale* (1959), demonstrates authoritatively that categories elucidated in *The People* explain the historian's entire career. This same book describes the androgynous mind of genius which foreshadows the author's later preoccupation with the intellectual faculties. In fact, the androgynous man of genius symbolizes society and represents creation itself:

> Genius, the inventive and productive power, supposes . . . that the same man is endowed with two powers, that he combines in himself what may be called the two sexes of the mind—the instinct of the simple and the reflection of the wise. He is in a way man and woman, infant and mature, savage and civilized, people and aristocracy.
>
> That astounding duality, which the vulgar often regard as a strange phenomenon, a monstrosity, is the very thing which makes him, to the highest degree, the normal and legitimate character of man. To say the truth, he alone is man, and there are no others. . . . He alone is complete, and is also the only one who can truly produce; and he is charged with continuing the divine creation.[4]

The androgynous man, "who alone is complete," contains the sum of human potentialities. His creative process mirrors that of all nature: both produce by means of a marriage of ("female") matter and ("male") spirit, and both illustrate the action of a divine life force. It follows, in the logic of Michelet's imagination, that society could imitate his example. The key to social harmony is the agreement of "the instinct of the simple and [of] the reflection of the wise."

Michelet insists that the political city can be understood only in terms of the "interior city" of the mind. His program for social revolution depends upon an understanding of spiritual forces. The problem is how to discover God's scheme. It can be found in the creative method of genius, a technique available to all:

> Ah! were you to reveal that, you would illuminate not only art, but moral art as well, the art of education and politics. If we knew how genius cultivates the darling of its own thought, how they live together, by what skill and gentleness, without impairing its originality, it animates thought to produce according to its own nature, we would have attained at one time the rule of art and the model of education, and of initiation into civic duty.

The secret of systematic and inventive thinking unlocks the gates of human progress; it unfetters the Promethean impulse to control history. Civilization steps beyond nature because the human intellect is more conscious and freer than animal instinct. Michelet's discussion of the mind of genius ends with a plea to master the psyche. A science of the human mind could rebuild civilization.[5]

Toward a Phenomenology of Mind

Michelet did not cease to ponder this science of the "inward city." He describes how it could be exploited twenty-two years later in *The Mountain,* when he details the process by which ideas and concepts are formed. Despite his ardent defense of the instinctual faculties, he considers reflective thought superior to "feminine" intuition. Intuition is tied to matter because it tends to be automatic, unconscious, and instinctual; intuition is the child of necessity, not of freedom. In *The Bird* had he not immortalized his dream of dominating the world, his desire to release thought from finite perception? Michelet's analysis of the thinking process extends his view of evolution as a progressive liberation of mind from matter. His theory of thought establishes reason as the ultimate director of human progress.

The Mountain develops a phenomenology of mind which relates in astonishing detail the intricate process of insight. The author guides those with no philosophical background with images which render his description concrete. He uses bird flight to picture the process by which thought abstracts itself from the immediate data of sight: birds soar far above the earth and conquer space with a single glance. Human beings possess a sort of interior vision by which they synthesize the fragmented givens of perception; the person who can reconstruct various ideas mentally feels like he or she possesses the world. Thus the flying bird achieves a synthetic vision very much like that of abstract thought.

The human mind, according to Michelet, proceeds no differently. Pure thought and reflection—like the flying bird's sight—presuppose an interior vision which voluntarily transcends perception and gains its autonomy. Michelet continues a philosophical tradition started by the ancient Greeks when he explains that thought arises when sensual data are idealized by the mind.[6] He dramatizes this process of abstraction as a meditation at the summit of a mountain. Secure aloft this traditional place for contemplation the intellect achieves complete objectivity.[7]

The procedure begins with pure sight unimpeded by the details of physical space; the mind then creates for itself an image truer than that of the outside world. Michelet intends his analysis of thought to enable mankind voluntarily to govern itself and the world:

> I wish I could bestow upon the men who could renew us a few of the meditative days I spent at Pontresina! A peculiar silence extinguished, subdued all the foolish noises that mingle with our thoughts. There the senses seized upon every object with more certainty. The transparency of the air which clears away the mirages of mist and fog, also diminishes distance, and enables us not only to see things remote, but also to see a multiplicity of things at one time. We embrace here in one great whole that which elsewhere we see in detail. A grand harmony in which everything is included, is yet subject to a certain control, so as to exclude the illusive, and to protect the truth.
>
> This harmony enriches and extends our prospect, even beyond the limits of what we see. Thus in the wonderfully harmonious landscape of the Roseg, I divined, guiding myself by striking analogies, certain aspects, and, with the mind, *I saw what I did not see* [my italics]. This is the secret of vision spoken of by the ancients, and not without reason, but without their being able to afford a proper explanation. Hence they could say that the seer could pierce through bodies with his glance.[8]

Before anything can be accomplished within the mind, one must perceive the world's essential harmony.* One must be convinced intellectually of the unity of thought and truth. Only then can Michelet, like the yogi, still his senses in order to liberate thought from passive perception. He is convinced that mental discipline and self-knowledge can enable humanity to reach a thoroughly objective understanding of the world. He insists that such "vision" masters such physical impediments as "the mirages of mist, fog, and distance." Michelet's bird's-eye glance at the totality of nature produces a synthetic vision which is far superior to normally fragmented perception.

A mental (or spiritual) process then transforms perception into an idealization of reality. The result is a sort of divination, or intuition by analogy: *"I saw what I did not see."* This "insight" confirms Michelet's theory of reflection: ideas are images of empirical reality recreated in an idealized form. If we define imagination provisionally as the faculty of reproducing images independently of perception,[9] we understand that Michelet's ideal (mental) vision of the world extends his interpretation of bird vision. The bird perceives an external totality which symbolizes (to use Kantian terms) the *inner manifold* produced by the synthesizing imagination.[10] In simpler words, the "mind's eye" joins previous knowledge with perception and grasps more of reality than can just plain sight.

But Michelet pushes beyond. He links self-consciousness and epistemological judgment. A detached observation of nature sharpens one's reflection upon mind. The basic task of Michelet's analysis is to educate mankind's intuitive and learned sources of self-knowledge. His theory of rational reflection is thus essential to his ideal of mind. The goal of his meditation is nothing less than an attempt to define humanity:

> It is much more difficult to penetrate into oneself: that is the great effort of meditation, the object of the ancient sage in his sojourn upon the mountain. It is there that he can obtain mastery over his own nature, disengage his own essence [*son génie propre*] both from the well-worn furrows of routine and from the entanglement of the crowd, —and even from his inner self; briefly, he must by his own effort fly above himself [*planer de soi sur soi*].

* For an excellent group of studies of Romantic conceptions of harmony in esthetics, religion, science, literature, see *Romantisme* 5 (1973).

The soul feels itself as infinite, and its initiative increases. Humanity itself weighs little in the balance. Who does not remember that the world was on one side, Copernicus, Galileo on the other?

In the presence of the Alps, all false greatness perishes. There no worldly authority can preserve its false prestige. Only one voice subsists there: reason, truth, conscience.

Michelet's interior scrutiny anticipates the type of psychoanalysis based on intellectual self-understanding, for it supposes that a conscious will can prevail over forces which inhibit freedom: habit, social pressures— in sum, the artificial identity imposed by the outside world upon even the "inner self." He distinguishes between what today's phenomenologists call "being-for-oneself" and "being-for-others." In Freudian terms, the conscious ego removes itself, thanks to a moment of lucidity, from the socially conditioned super-ego. The bird analogy again expresses the mind's "own effort to fly above itself"; that is, it describes the systematic separation of thought from itself in a voluntary act of objectification. Conscious reflection is the heart of Michelet's rationalism and it epitomizes nature's evolutionary goal. He believes self-conscious humanity able to dominate reality if it remains faithful to the principles of "reason, truth, and conscience."

Michelet's theory of practical reason is based on a theory of pure reason, according to another episode in *The Mountain*. Even the synthetic imagination that enables one to master the world is subordinate to free imagination or absolute abstraction. Michelet announces his philosophical idealism in a description of thought seeking an entire independence from matter. He illustrates his theory of pure mind by a reverie which takes its departure from a total vision of the earth. His extraordinary perception takes place in a georama, a large spherical room whose walls picture the globe's surface:

> The spectator, placed in the center, would see the earth from all sides [at once], from inside to outside. . . . But no representation can do justice to reality. . . . Our senses betray us: it is too large, and everything escapes us. From a balloon, at a moderate elevation, we see scarcely more than a vast geographical map. It is rather through thought, solitary imagination, far from any distracting object, that we can embrace this beautiful and prodigious being, infinitely more complex than any creature which has issued from its womb.[11]

Michelet's style becomes increasingly lyrical as it frees itself from realistic description and his georama changes into a "beautiful and prodigious creature." This reverie defends an implicit philosophical position which revolves around the ambiguous word *representation*. It denotes both an artificial rendering of an object and an image formed in the "mind's eye" through perception.[12] The historian deplores any dependence upon physical sight and equates the two terms *thought* and *solitary imagination* in order to differentiate abstract thinking from perception. Intellect must separate itself from the sensorial apparatus which reproduces the world passively. Reflection can flourish only when it remains "far from any distracting object." For Michelet, the autonomous imagination which finally comes into play does not negate or distort "reality"; it produces the purest awareness of truth.

The Sexuality of Creative Thought

If thought is more complete when it transcends the world, what function is left for nature? Is Michelet's ideal person an abstract thinker, a theoretician? Was this lover of angelic purity the same historian fully committed to preparing social revolution with his pen? Michelet was fascinated with absolute abstraction and defined an idealist theory of knowledge. But he was more deeply attentive to the utility of such thought. Man, that "abstractor of quintessences" as he called him, must be led to active involvement in social problems. That was woman's crucial role. Michelet counted on the "feminine" faculties of intuition, love, and pity to help males apply their abstract principles.

Michelet in fact initiated his career as moral educator by arguing that women were necessary to humanize men. His mythology of female intuition and male analysis appears in the first educational book, *Priest, Woman, and Family* (1845): "She, who remains in the sphere of common sense and sentiment, she understands nothing of your [male] formulas; and rarely, very rarely, do you [the man] know how to translate them into human language." [13]

This characterization of male and female minds is sexist in its literal sense: Michelet seems to believe that women and men belong to separate races. His view of women's marital role is more bizarre and reveals many psychological problems.[14] In *Love* and its sequel *Woman* he portrays women as suffering a loss of will and self-sufficiency because of their monthly "wounds" or "sicknesses." He establishes a program in which the young wife should be formed by her older, more worldly mate. This blatantly contradicts the book's feminist theme which insists that husbands respect their wives as individuals. Michelet idolizes females but demands that women worship their husbands in return. At the same time he vindicates women's social rights sincerely and persistently. He extols their intellectual prowess and political heroism in *Women of the French Revolution* (1854), and elsewhere. What is the basis of Michelet's ambiguous feminism?

The historian's creative process elucidates that question. He considered the genesis of the sea cow mother's hand to be an *incarnation* of her *idea* of love. That episode from *The Sea* concretizes the author's abstract principle of maternal evolution. His understanding of the human mind follows a similar process of literalizing his symbolism of male and female minds. Although Michelet was unaware that his theory of the two sexes of the mind was figurative in the way I describe, his "medical" explanation of creative thinking in females can be interpreted as a metaphor of the ideal mind.

What is necessary for an idea to become an act, for an abstraction to be expressed? The "incubation" of an idea (to use Michelet's word) demands an emotional commitment, a feeling of love that seeks to preserve the thought. Michelet describes an intellectual gestation by elaborating the image of childbirth, for it epitomizes the joining of spirit to matter:

> It is doubtless difficult to observe this gentle power of germination, of incubation, which is in woman.
>
> Man's power is in abstracting, in dividing; but woman's power is in not knowing how to abstract; it is in preserving everything, every idea entire and living, so to be able to render it alive and to fructify it. . . .
>
> Your [the man's] brain, an arsenal of the finest steel blades, contains scalpels which will cut through everything. Anatomy, war, critical philosophy: behold the head of man. But the organ of woman is another thing. That sweet organ, which is a second brain to her, dreams only dreams of love. The peace of heaven, God's peace, the peace of union, unity itself: those are the treasures of her bosom [*sein*].
>
> By what means would you have her employ your divisions, how seize the rough instrument of analysis? If one of your subtle thoughts should come to her, it is that she, by her maternal process

of incubation, has brooded on it for your sake, has put it into her-self, *conceived* it [Michelet's emphasis], and out of the idea makes her child.[15]

This way of characterizing women would be intolerable if only taken literally. Michelet's interchange of physiological and intellectual terms translates his description of female emotive responses into a metaphor of thinking: "by a *maternal* process she has *conceived* your *idea.*" Woman's power of intellectual synthesis, her dreams of harmony with the divine, flow from her identity with nature. Her womb, like the sea, is a fitting symbol of natural creation. The French *sein* can denote both heart and womb: Michelet's ambiguity is intentional: the *sein* is woman's second brain (unfortunately her first one does not enter into his analysis). The author implies that her role is to complement man's more flexible mind.*

Michelet's theory of the "two sexes of the mind" concretizes his interpretation of the relation of matter to spirit. Female is subordinate to male in this system, as physical nature is subordinate to the will of God. Yet women are presumably capable of inventive thought, even though Michelet does not stress this consequence of his theory. All that is necessary for life to emerge, in both the natural and the mental realms, is for matter and spirit to "marry." Michelet's ideal mind pro-duces in the following manner: the "feminine" intuition of life's wholeness creates a synthesis of concept and sentiment; what results is —in its physiological and intellectual senses—the *conception* of a new being *in the world.*

Michelet's doctrine of feminine thinking is more than a theoreti-cal insight. He verifies his physiology of thought historically. He leans upon a medical theory of the genesis of heroes, superior men who cre-ate civilization. According to Michelet, the conception of a child also incarnates the ideas present in the mother's mind during sexual inter-course. (Such was his interpretation of the "sacred moments" of plant and animal reproduction.)† The human child's quality is proportional to the woman's quest for a superior ideal: "It is that exaltation of our mothers, their effort to conceive an infant God, that has made us the

---

* Michelet reflects Jean-Jacques Rousseau's view of woman in *Emile* (1762). It was continued by the French Revolution, legalized by the Napoleonic code, and persists, in France as elsewhere, to this very day.

† See chapter 3, section "Evolutionary Emergence of Love," pp. 54–56.

little that we are; through this dream she has put within us the best of ourselves. And whoever is strong upon the earth, it is because woman has conceived him in heaven." She literally incarnates an aspiration, a "dream" (like that of plants and animals) through an act of will. This eccentric view of history attests to Michelet's fidelity to a vision in which physical life conforms exactly to a spiritualistic system.

Michelet's discovery of the French Revolution's inception is the most striking verification of his theory. Imagine its importance to the historian who considered the events of 1789 as a culmination of universal history. This odd supposition introduces *Women of the French Revolution,* a collection of biographies based on his seven-volume history. There he explains with utmost seriousness that woman's mental apprehension of the ideal during coitus was the origin of the world's greatest self-liberation. The heroic generations of revolutionaries in politics and science were conceived during an orgasm as spiritual as it was physical:

> The natural and very simple cause of the phenomenon was the overflowing vital sap of the moment.
>
> The first epoch (about 1760) was the dawn of Rousseau, who owed the beginning of his influence to the first and powerful effect of *Emile;* to the passionate emotions of the mothers who wanted to nurse and stay close to the cradle of their child.
>
> The second epoch was the triumph of the ideas of the century, not only by the universal knowledge of Rousseau, but by the long-foreseen victory of his ideas on law, by the great actions of Voltaire, his sublime defenses of Sirven, Calas and La Barre. The wives became still, meditated under the influence of these powerful emotions, they brooded the salvation to come. All the children of that moment bear on their foreheads a sign.
>
> Powerful generations sprang from these noble thoughts of an augmented love, conceived in the heavenly flame, born of the sacred moment, too short alas, when the woman, beyond her physical passion, glimpsed, adored the Idea.[16]

From Theory to Practice

All this is not so mad if you believe that acquired traits are hereditary. Yet Michelet's approach to historical causation, his analysis of the "sacred moments" of revolutionary mothers, must be understood on more than one level. The physiological theories of *Love* and *Woman* simply extend (and literalize) the figurative description of the mind of genius he developed over a decade before in *The People*. His analysis of "female" thought not only completes that picture of the androgynous mind. It explains for the author how knowledge leads to action. Michelet's cult of the female is due in large part to his belief that women possess the secret of ethical sensitivity and activism. Only women, he thought, could fulfill the ideals to which he devoted his life. Only women could make his books effective.

His theory of "active thought" explains how ideas are acted upon. His analysis extends the metaphor of feminine thought as did his analysis of creative mind. In both, a concrete sense of life leads insights to expression; in his terms, "female" emotions actualize "male" ideas. Michelet again rationalizes his mythology by describing physiological functions:

> What to man is only light is to woman first of all warmth. An idea takes the form of sentiment. If the feeling is lively, it vibrates and becomes nervous emotion. A thought, an invention, some useful novelty, affects your brain pleasantly, and makes you smile, as with an agreeable surprise. But she, she feels at once the good which will result from it, a new happiness for humanity. This touches her heart [*sein*]; she trembles, —at the spine, she shivers with agitation, is well-nigh weeping.[17]

Woman's heart or womb (both *sein* in French) is a perceptual organ. The male light of reason becomes animated upon contact with the feminine warmth of emotion (and vice versa). These metaphors recall Michelet's description of the earth's liquid heat seeking the sun. When spirit and nature meet they create a new reality; "the idea becomes a feeling" and then an action. Michelet speaks to men about their mates as he summarizes this principle: "Whatever you give to her as abstract, as generality, as collectivity, she makes of it an individual. You speak to her of the motherland, of the free community: and she has already dreamed the hero." [18]

Michelet's theory of feminine thought also explains his apparently excessive lyricism. How could he not assume a "feminine" warmth in order to animate his ideas and to touch readers he imagines dessicated by Positivist objectivity? Unsympathetic critics have scorned the sentimental gush of the educational works written after his second marriage.[19] But considered dispassionately their style is appropriate to their inspiration. The author was appealing to the "feminine" sensitivities of his readers, male or female, as he defended women's social status. He hoped to awaken a delicate moral sense capable of launching a veritable "cultural revolution." His brand of feminism combats the ethical drought and egotism of the French Empire, while, at the same time, demonstrating to men that their female companions exemplified a morality of action.

The author of *Love* and *Woman* believed that the female sex could realize his country's cultural potential. In other words, "feminine" emotions were required to apply the abstract moral values upon which France was founded:

> Few, very few ideas are new. Almost all those which burst forth in this century, and seek to sweep it along, have appeared many times before, and always uselessly. The arrival of an idea is not so much the first appearance of its formulation as its definitive incubation, when, having been received in the powerful heat of love, it blossoms fecundated by the force of the heart.
>
> Then, then, it is not a word, but a living thing. . . .
>
> The great, the difficult thing is for the useful idea, at the decisive moment, to meet prepared a hearth of good moral willingness, of heroic warmth, of devotion and sacrifice... Where will I find the primitive spark in the universal coldness? This is what I say to myself.
>
> I have addressed myself to the indestructible spark, to the hearth which still burns on the ruins of the world, to the immortal warmth of the maternal soul.[20]

Michelet's books on women responded to a practical problem. Families were disintegrating at an alarming rate largely, he thought, because his culture gave men freedom while requiring proper women to stay at home. The historian promotes the social independence of women because he felt that a renewal of the institution of marriage would help rebuild French society. But the feminist apostle's more general goal is revealed by his metaphorical language: the "incubation" of an idea requires the same personal interest as compassion. His theory of androgynous ethical insight explains how transformation of the mind produces historical change. Moral sympathy or "the powerful warmth of love" can help society realize the principles described by theory ("an idea

... its formulation"). Michelet intended the warmth and passion of his style to call forth, in the hearts and lives of the French people, heroic acts worthy of national tradition.

Michelet's view of cooperation between the sexes is severely limited by the culture which it seeks to transform. He seems unable to do more than oversimplify the actors' parts. But what could his theory of androgyny say to an age in which social roles are more flexible? Today such roles are being modified: more and more women enter occupations that were formerly the domain of males, and husbands are starting to take more responsibility at home. Still most marriages reflect Michelet's view of the mother as the cook charged also with the complex of tasks demanded by the family. On the other hand, Michelet did deplore, in 1845, the system in which a man risks becoming deformed by his speciality, by his technical or time-consuming and competitive profession.[21]

If we apply his ideal of the androgynous mind to today's men and women, we might see how to modify rigid social stereotypes of both by criticizing the psychological stereotypes by which they are justified. We might then arrive at more balanced mental health models by educating in each sex the intellectual and emotional gifts represented metaphorically by the other. What might result? Men who are less exclusively socially aggressive yet still professionally effective; fathers who are sensitive to feelings and to the subtle needs of family and friends; mothers who might also consider themselves active participants in the larger concerns of the country. A new understanding of unmarried people could also evolve. An updated version of Michelet's fable of the two sexes of the mind defines a fuller image of humanity.[22]

Michelet's Ethics: The Harmony of Law and Compassion

Active thought produces Michelet's cultural revolution and an ethical theory based on androgynous thought guides it. The two sexes of the mind account for physical and mental creativity and they harmonize the lessons of natural and human history. Doctors and jurists should establish their ideals according to those studies. Together they compose what Michelet calls "the modern mind":

> The modern mind has but two component parts:
> The *sciences of life,* which are those of love. They teach us of

life's identity, our common parentage, and the fraternity of all beings.

The *sciences of justice,* which are superior charity, and impartial love. This is fraternity also.

. . . The more does law ennoble and humanize itself, the more also does the natural and medical brotherhood, the sciences of life, of love and of pity. . . .

This is the modern science, the only one, identical, of two sexes. You comprehend it through justice and truth, order and harmony. While *she,* your young pupil, feels it through pity and gentleness. Both of you though love.[23]

Michelet translates his theory of knowledge into a "school for wives": objective moral judgment and intuitive sympathy produce the same loving insight. His expressions *"superior* charity and *impartial* love" represent an androgynous union of moral faculties. The italicized adjectives refer to the rational (male) domain; these special word combinations (almost oxymorons) represent stylistically such a marriage. His term "the *sciences* of justice," on the other hand, points to the organic (or material) basis of law which is, in principle, derived solely from abstract universals. Michelet's analysis of moral perception describes a complete system of ethics, "the modern science, the only one, identical, of two sexes"—of which conjugal love is the social vehicle.[24]

However, Michelet reflects the bourgeois mores of his time when he sustains the superiority of "masculine" reason. Man is more effective than his partner because he can formulate universal obligations, while she remains dominated by emotionality. Michelet turns his mythology of the sexes into this social observation:

Nevertheless, law and justice are the sovereign principles of modern life. Superior and complete principles too, for impartial and kind justice (as justice ought to be, to be justice at all) has the effect of love—that loftier love which embraces the City.

If woman, in ancient times, ever rose to an appreciation of this, it was by an extraordinary effort. As her great mission here below is to bring forth children, to incarnate individual lives, she takes everything individually, and nothing collectively by masses. Woman's charity consists in bestowing alms upon whoever asks—in giving bread to the hungry. And man's charity consists in those laws which assure to all the action of all their powers; which make all men free and strong, capable of providing for themselves, and living with dignity.

Michelet claims, as does Kant, that a fully realized moral stance derives from an objective code of ethics. Egalitarian laws form the foundation of the City, the nation or nation-state. This democratic ideal is, for the historian of France, the apex of mankind's evolution. And this ideal can be *practiced* only within nature. Women, love, and pity are necessary.

Michelet's complete program of moral education and his model of a perfect society integrate woman's immediate sympathy and man's universal law. He never forgets that ideas must be embodied. Although the laws upon which society rests are dead without emotion and a concrete sense of life, Michelet insists that intellect, because of its spiritual freedom, rules moral and creative action. His theory of mind remains valid if it recognizes the fact that women and men are equally capable of rational and intuitive thinking. Michelet's social view of the female sex shares the limits of his epoch's stereotypes, but his commitment to rationality does not. This Romantic reminds us that a nation's laws must be both intellectually sound and compassionate.

8

Michelet the Poet of History

Conclusion

Michelet's mission to transform France and Western Europe thus enjoys a solid theoretical base. His reconciliation of law and compassion, of reason and intuition, realizes the single goal of his historical and naturalist works. Together they appeal to the complete person, to the "male" and "female" faculties of the mind. In his final book on education Michelet outlines the curriculum meant to form the ideal individual. *Our Sons* begins by refuting systematically the Christian view of human nature defended by the influential liberal Catholic, Monseigneur Dupanloup, in his book *L'Education.** Our Sons* continues the principles Michelet announced in *Priest, Woman and Family* by elaborating a philosophy of education which presupposes that human nature is essentially good and the individual free from Original Sin. People become morally responsible and creative by recognizing within themselves natural forces. Both *Our Sons* and *Priest, Woman and Family* argue that women are necessary for true education to be realized.

Michelet wrote *Our Sons* toward the end of his life, and it is almost a guidebook to the completed *History of France*. He stresses the unity of his varied career as he reiterates that women reveal the secrets of nature and men penetrate the order of human history. All children can exercise the powers of Prometheus if guided by their parents.

---

* Félix Dupanloup (1802–1878), Archbishop of Orléans, became a member of the Académie française in 1854. The first volume of *De l'éducation* appeared in 1850; the three-volume sixth edition was published in 1861–1862. For a judgment of Dupanloup which would have pleased Michelet see Ernest Renan, *Souvenirs d'enfance et de jeunesse.*

Michelet leans upon the theories of Rousseau and Pestalozzi as he formulates his program of liberating a child's essential nature. He wants older children prepared to receive the lessons of history and the life sciences. Michelet summarizes in *Woman* the manner in which his career defines the complete education: "The judge of truth is *the conscience*. But controls are necessary. These are *history,* the conscience of the human race, and *natural history,* the instinctive conscience of nature. . . . When the three agree, you may believe." [1] Michelet sees his works as sources of the modern faith; they replace Christianity as the foundation of Western civilization.

Young Michelet had considered the Enlightenment doctrine of progress as the answer to Christianity. The mind challenged the material realities of nature and forged its way forward endlessly. Then the historian began to assimilate the recently developed life sciences into his system and discovered in nature the eternal forces which he had believed to be the exclusive domain of humanity. Each object of his universal curiosity furnished proof of the progressive triumph of freedom. The animal kingdom produced organisms which refined their individuality to the point of creating families. Animal "societies" based on love and cooperation flourished without mankind. History demonstrated that the French people struggled for centuries toward the unity realized during the Revolution. Nineteenth-century technology appeared to continue this promise by restoring the personhood of the nation and by extending it into a worldwide communications network. Michelet's natural history buttressed his hopes for social renewal, while his mysticism of nature convinced him of life's eternal ground.

Evolution is universal, in this view, extending from the lowest mineral to the human precursor of an angelic being. All nature aspires toward a condition of greater spiritual freedom, in which the "person," the self-conscious personality, remains responsible for its actions, its creations. This process is peaceful and demonstrates that the divine order upon which it is grounded is benevolent. According to Michelet nature challenges mankind to realize its creative potential, while providing models of moral harmony. The artistic creativity of birds, for example, can impel human beings to master their inventive faculties; the realization of a constitutional democracy by bees reminds people to exploit their superior freedom and establish just and congenial nations. Animal families show how shamefully egotistical human society has become. Michelet buttresses these arguments with a vivid style in which the author's forceful presence compels readers to identify with his passion.

From the very beginning of our inquiry, the interpenetration of the writer and his work has become increasingly obvious. I suggested in chapter 1 that Schelling's conception of the world as the metaphor, the outward form, of God's mind anticipates Michelet's system. The historian's philosophical idealism—his belief that pure abstract thought reveals facts about the outside world—supports this view. The chronological development of his works suggests that his *a priori* ideas about history guided, and even produced his naturalist philosophy. Michelet's autobiographical preface to *The People* of 1846 as well as the retrospective self-analysis of 1869 which introduces the *History of France* stress the identity of the author with his creations. How does the artist-historian's universe mirror his mind?

Michelet's Self-Portrait

These theories reveal their creator. Michelet's synthesis of natural and human history is a projection of the androgynous mind which produced it. His idealization of women illustrates the emotionality and intuition he obviously enjoyed. That explains why he absorbed his wife's naturalist research with such ease and sought to mold her personality in accordance with his. From the beginning of their relationship, in fact, Michelet expected Athénaïs to serve his vision.* In his preface to *The Bird* he stated with pride that the book was created by a "woman's heart," both his and his mate's. The basis of his philosophical anthropology is, however, the image of a perfect *man*. Michelet's clearest self-portrait is his description of that ideal.

Writing the *History of France* involved a drama in which the author relived his nation's painful growth. Michelet defines his personality when he reflects upon the historical art. He had glimpsed his method as a child at the Museum of Historical Monuments, where he filled the silent tombs with his fantasies. As a mature writer, however,

---

* Michelet made this note on his wife's diary of 1850, the year after their marriage: "She wants to be transformed into me so that we can be together in the life to come" (unpublished manuscript conserved at the Bibliothèque de l'Institut, 4855). Madame Michelet analyzed this aspect of their relationship in a comment she added to her husband's diary on 19 October 1868. Finally she wanted to be herself.

he became acutely aware of the dilemma posed by his subjective approach. We recall the astute criticism Michelet received from Gasparin in 1842: "You are still an excellent narrator... But at the same time you are a man of imagination who excessively tries to put facts into a mythical system, one which not everyone can accept." Michelet always claimed to be the first French historian to exploit the National Archives systematically and he was quick to defend the scholarly solidity of his *History of France* against critics who, like Taine, considered him a mere poet. He answers many criticisms in the 1855 introduction to *The Renaissance*. All his life Michelet struggled to reconcile his inner vision with intellectual detachment. In his *Preface* of 1869 he stoutly rejected the possibility that his national chronicle derived from his imagination: "Without arguing with those trustful souls [that is, with the actors of the past] who beg for resurrection, art, while welcoming them, in restoring their vital breath, art, nevertheless, retains within itself its full lucidity." [2]

Michelet was fully aware of the problems involved in historical knowing. He illustrates the view held much later by the philosopher and historian of ideas R. G. Collingwood: that the historian understands the past by reenacting it in his mind. Michelet's language is dramatic and metaphorical, but his thinking is sharp. The historical art requires both love of the objects of inquiry and a reflective awareness of the perceiving subject. Michelet relives the feelings and ideals of historical figures while attempting to do so with a self-consciousness approaching objectivity. He insists time and again that his original contribution was to have exploited unpublished documents previously buried in archives. He counterbalances his admitted partiality for certain historical figures by his respect for evidence. Michelet's dilemma is far from being idiosyncratic; it typifies that of all modern historians as defined by Ernst Cassirer: "It is a keen sense for the empirical reality of things combined with the free gift of imagination upon which the true historical synthesis or synopsis depends." [3]

Modern historiography has left its mark on Michelet's reputation as an exact historian, and he is respected today primarily for his brilliant visionary poetry. In spite of his exaggerations, however, this poet of the archives still provides historians with a useful model when he describes how to avoid excessive emotional involvement with historical events. Moral insight is crucial. The art of observing society teaches us to utilize our minds. The living, like the dead, call forth two types of empathy or "pity," which correspond to male and female minds. In his words, "female" pity is a purely sentimental empathy while "male" pity involves a self-aware though compassionate identification with human distress:

> There are two types of pity—that of the womanly, and that of the strong—that of overly sensitive souls which weep for their own woes, and that of disinterested hearts which contentedly accept their lot and pour out continual benedictions upon nature; while, not ignorant of the world's ills, they draw from their very sorrow fresh strength to act or create.[4]

The historian eschews the passive, immobilizing, "feminine" pity which surrenders to emotion. He erects into a method the virile art of empathy. "Male" compassion is no less deep and sincere than its "female" counterpart, but it profits from intellectual lucidity. The observer's self-control increases his confidence in the world; as a result of that self-confidence, when touched with moral concern, he will act.

Michelet's distinction between "male" and "female" pity explains the decisive role played by nature study in his life. Why was he always at pains to demonstrate that nature was essentially peaceful and harmonious, even against Darwin's evidence of a "struggle for life"? Perhaps because Michelet saw himself as a woman. He described his temperament as feminine because of his acute sensitivity to human agony. Michelet's natural history project was meant to cure the depression caused by Louis-Napoléon's *coup d'état* and the anguish of writing the history of the Terror. His sojourns in Nantes and Italy, and his young wife's nature research began to soothe that pain. That is why in his autobiographical preface to *The Bird* he conceives of love and nature as the counterpoint of history: "The sweetness [of nature] contrasted strongly with the thoughts of the present, and with the gloomy past which then occupied my pen. I was writing of '93. Its heroic and dismal history enveloped, possessed, shall I say, consumed me. . . . It was a daily battle of affection and nature against the somber thoughts of the human world." [5]

Michelet draws a valuable lesson from the equilibrium he finally achieved. After he completed both his nature series and the *History of France* he reflects upon how he reconciled these apparently contradictory realms. He considers that his method as "artist-historian" answers the pessimism and moral neutrality of his time:

By a successful alternation between History and Nature, I was able to preserve my height. If I had followed man alone, and his savage story, melancholy would have enfeebled me. If I had wholly devoted myself to nature, I would have fallen (as many today have done) into an indifference toward the right. But I frequently exchanged the two worlds. When I found my breath failing in my human studies, I would touch *Terra mater* and would recover my flight.[6]

Michelet bases his understanding of the world on two types of "pity," compassion provoked by human disasters and identification with an evolving, eternal nature. He symbolizes its optimistic aspect with the myth of Antaeus, the giant wrestler who gained strength by touching his Mother Earth. Natural science demonstrates that human vitality is eternal. But the naturalist's optimism must not lead to moral indifference. Its function is to save the historically sensitive person from a voluntary insensitivity to human suffering as a defense against excessive involvement. The artist-historian's secret of "objective empathy," his esthetic sublimation of an instinctual love for the living and the dead, is moral realism itself.

Historical Imagination and Active Thought

Michelet's analysis of his own historical insights gives rise to an analysis of moral commitment. Historical re-creation is not frigidly dispassionate, although it requires an objective, conscious act of rational evaluation. Michelet's optimistic view of the world stems from an intellectual synthesis of nature and humanity. That mental process is the path to an active faith. He symbolizes that insight as another contemplation from a mountain peak:

From up there, the earth seems a very little thing. The grandeur of its physical expanse is as nothing, and even the long duration of time and the differences of epochs diminish. Our ignorance causes us to exaggerate diversities. From this elevated point, under the different costumes, I see the eternal man.

This does not deter me from descending to the plain beneath, and from reaping my harvest on the fields of history and natural history. But I do like the Swiss: in winter I work below; when my work is done, I ascend again to those solitary summits which

pacify my mind, by permitting me to embrace, in one great simplicity, all the apparent contradictions of things, and to recognize
the profound concord in all that seems discordant.[7]

Michelet describes in metaphorical terms the process of abstraction and
reflection and recalls the bird's-eye view which combines telescopic and
microscopic vision. The historian's separation from details enables him
to "embrace, *in one great simplicity,* all the apparent contradictions of
things." Reflection harmonizes the system of nature with an analogous
human nature, "eternal man." This demonstrates the common foundation of the two realms.

Michelet's description of historical knowing just cited from *Love*
extends the analysis of the mind of genius he developed in *The People,*
twelve years before. In his writer's solitude he was conscious above all
of his own imagination. He analyzed it and sketched the theory of
mind which structured his subsequent educational projects. In that
early book he presented the mind of genius as a combination of male
and female cognition. That consciousness was of course Michelet's own
"two sexes of the mind." He was convinced that a description of his
mental processes could teach others how to transform society.

Michelet's preoccupation with genius seems to contradict his worship of the plebeian class. We associate him with the celebration of the
downtrodden and not with the promotion of superior beings. Indeed,
his *History of France* immortalized the self-creation and liberation of
the masses whose national identity was realized during the French
Revolution. The paradox dissolves (at least theoretically) when we
understand that Michelet believes the man of genius to enjoy, in all
their potential, certain qualities of mind and feeling found in the
lower classes. He identifies the man of genius with children and
working men and women whom he considers gifted with an inherent
finesse. Their instinct and emotional sensitivity reveal a closeness to
nature which the upper classes rarely possess. Michelet thus bases his
portrait of the man of genius on an idealization of the common people.
Michelet's genius combines and perfects the creativity of the lower
levels of society: that of children, women, and the poor.[8]

The historian's personal dilemma in being both genius and common has a pragmatic solution. Mind was universal, social class relative.
That is why Michelet's concept of genius challenges the traditional
notion of the ideal man. Most Romantics considered genius as an ex-

ception, as an abnormal, God-given talent which alienates the gifted individual from the crowd.[9] Alfred de Vigny's "Moïse" was a friend of God but a stranger to his people, while the poet Chatterton was an aristocratic but destitute victim of social indifference. Victor Hugo celebrates the quasi-divine qualities of genius in *William Shakespeare* and in "Les Mages," although his lonely and humble visionary, the shepherd of "Magnitudo parvi," is closer to the historian's democratic approach. Michelet's "superior" individual combines proletarian and feminine sensitivity with the freedom of an educated intellect. He is "a man *par excellence*" because he harmonizes creativity with a moral sense.

Michelet justifies his sociological observations with an analysis of thought. The process by which women and common people formulate and express ideas explains their superiority over highly educated thinkers. It behooves the man of genius to identify with the humble. The mind of the lower classes is especially valuable because it reveals the secret of "active, instinctive thought":

> We may observe that the instinct which dominates [the common people], also gives them an immense advantage in action. Reflective thought arrives at action only through all the intermediate stages of deliberation and discussion; it arrives at it through so many things that it often does not arrive at all. Instinctive thought, on the contrary, *touches the act,* is almost act; it is almost at the same time idea and action.[10]

This description of activist thought was written in 1846 when its revolutionary consequences were more obvious than now. After the failure of the 1848 Revolution the author of *Woman* and *Love* updated this analysis of creative and moral thought in order to redefine the image of humanity degraded by Louis-Napoléon's Empire. He believed even more strongly that the family could educate the male and female aspects of people's minds. The historian's distinction between male and female was also a practical consequence of his philosophy: intuition and reflection represent the physical and spiritual levels of the mind respectively, for instinct reacts to necessity while abstract thought requires a volitional act. His theory of mind completes his social mission. The thinking of common people, in this analysis, combines feeling with idea, so that their insights will be acted upon.

"The Man of Genius is *par excellence* the Simple Person, the

Child and the Common People." So states the title of the chapter of *The People* in which Michelet draws this analysis. Without the instinctive simplicity of the masses the mind of genius would be sterile. Understanding cannot be separated from moral sensitivity. Truth for Michelet involves ethical commitment as well as objective reason. That is why he expends such energy exploring the inner life. He wants to teach intellectuals how to act. He wants to bring abstract reason and analysis down to earth. His solution is to harness intuition:

> They [children and simple people] are fond of comparing and connecting, but seldom distinguish or analyze. Not only does distinguishing, dividing, overtax their minds, but it pains them, — they consider it a dismemberment. They shrink from dissecting life, and everything seems to them to have life. Things, whatever they may be, are to them like so many organic beings, which they would have qualms about altering to the slightest degree. They draw back the moment it becomes necessary to upset by analysis whatever presents the least appearance of vital harmony. A disposition of that kind generally presupposes a natural gentleness and goodness: we call them *good people.*
>
> And not only do they not divide, but as soon as they find something divided, partial, they either pass it by, or they rejoin it in their mind to the totality from which it has been separated; and they recompose this whole with a rapidity of imagination that could not be expected from their natural slowness. They are powerful to compose in proportion as they are impotent to divide. Or rather, it seems, on looking at so easy an operation, that it betokens neither a power nor its want, but is a necessary fact, inherent in their existence. In fact, it is by virtue of this that they exist as *simple.*

Michelet's promotion of a nonanalytical apprehension of life reminds us of his scientific imagination of sea-water. In *The People* he describes in detail how moral and cognitive understanding are interdependent. Simple folk (not to be confused with simpletons) perceive beings in their integrity; their synthetic imagination identifies esthetic wholeness with ethical affirmation. Men of genius are endowed with the synthesizing instinct of the people. In the presence of a divided thing simple people rejoin it "*in their mind* to the totality from which it has been separated" and they "recompose this whole with a rapidity of *imagination*" which astonishes the uninitiated.

Michelet believes that anyone can learn to combine reason and intuition systematically, especially men with an androgynous mind. What is mainly uncontrollable feeling in women, children, and the common people becomes for them a free intellectual act. We can interpret Michelet's man of genius as a symbol of the ideal person who masters an inherent intuition with a learned method of reflective thought. That combination enables him or her to act intelligently, compassionately, and effectively in the world.

Michelet's Poetic Vision

Michelet sees no contradiction between his life of writing and other forms of social activism. His theory produces events because it explains to thinkers how to act upon their principles. Leaning upon his century's sex-role stereotypes, he believes that women and common people, who are born activists, need only to be inspired, and they in turn will inspire the male leaders of the nation. His androgynous man of genius is the perfect activist since he contains the types of thinking characteristic of all classes of society. Michelet defines this ideal person in terms of what he knew best: his own mind. We are therefore not surprised to find that his model of moral action is poetic creation.

Michelet symbolizes the birth of his vocation as artist-historian by describing the origin of poetry in India. The historian's sensitivity to life and death is represented by India's highly developed affinity with the animal world.[11] The author of *The People* describes his own imagination when, in a beautiful insight, he shows how the Indian poet's initial sympathy with nature engenders poetry:

> India was well recompensed for her gentleness toward nature; in her, genius was a gift of pity. The first Indian poet sees doves fluttering about, and while he is admiring their grace and their amorous play, one of them falls struck by an arrow... He weeps; his measured sighs, without his thinking of it, in unison with the beatings of his heart, take on a rhythmical movement, and poetry is born... From that moment on, two by two, the melodious doves, reborn in the song of man, love and fly over all the earth. (Ramayana).[12]

We are witnessing the genesis of the great epic poem of India, the *Ramayana,* born of a desire to preserve the living doves. The poet resurrects their loving in the eternity of an artistic work. The source of this creative act is the poet's ethical sensitivity, his "gift of pity." These emotions transform silent compassion into expressive action. From a total participation of the individual, from the union of a "feminine" sensibility and a "male" productive mind, comes forth a national monument. The author of the *Ramayana* represents the author of the *History of France*.

The ancient poet Virgil is Michelet's most perfect incarnation of the man of genius as *écrivain engagé,* as committed writer. The original poet of the golden bough exemplifies Michelet's dual mission as historian of the common people and poet of nature. Virgil's literary achievements fulfill the two sexes of the mind required by historical writing:

> Tender and profound Virgil!... I who was nursed by him, and brought up on his knees as it were, am happy that this unique glory is his, the glory of pity, and of excellence of heart... This peasant of Mantua, with his virgin-like timidity, and long hair falling down in country fashion, is, however, without his having known it, the true pontiff and augur between two worlds, between two ages, on the half-way road of history. Indian by his tenderness for nature, Christian by his love of man, this simple man reconstructs in his immense heart that lovely universal city, from which nothing that has life is excluded, although each wishes to introduce only his own kind.

Virgil, like Michelet himself, is a poet of both mankind and nature who masters intuition and productive thought. Female or Indian in its bucolic aspect, Virgil's love does not degenerate into "moral indifference": rather, his pre-Christian sensitivity affirms the value of humanity. Endowed thus with these "two sexes of the mind," the Roman poet is able to imagine, to *conceive* the ideal: "he reconstructs *in his immense heart* that lovely universal city." He pictures the world as a vast democracy in which the equality of all citizens, be they animal or human, is that of life itself. No clearer statement of the moral ideal which guided Michelet's historical and naturalist careers can be found.

Michelet's lifelong exploration of the general principles first sketched in *The People* enabled him to amplify, in breadth and in detail, a philosophical anthropology. His nature books interpret the world in a way which confirms his highest hopes for mankind. In spite of the shaky nineteenth-century science upon which it is built,

Michelet's philosophy of nature remains an impressive monument to the Romantic religion of humanity. Indeed, his models of perception, cognition, abstract and productive thought, and his phenomenology of ethical judgment could serve even now to reconstruct the new person. His interpretations of nature and history demonstrate that men should unite with women for thought to be creative, ethics active, and society to be stable and just. Michelet's books all describe their creator, a man of genius possessing the two sexes of the mind, who dedicated his life to a vision of the perfect society.

Appendix

Michelet's Preface *of 1869*
to the History of France

Introduction

Michelet's celebrated *Preface* to the 1869 reedition of the *History of France* was written near the end of the author's life. This Romantic statement of faith, shadowed by the crumbling Second Empire, and barely preceding the disasters of Sedan and the Commune, testifies to the ardent conviction which sustained the historian during his "labor of almost forty years." The final volume of his *History* had gone to press in October 1867. Moved by his persistent need for self-evaluation, Michelet turned to his diary and cartons of notes intending to summarize his life's work. During January of 1868 he began to write *Our Sons* which, with *The People,* is the summa of his educational program. Two other projects were conceived, though never realized, during this period: *The Child* and *The Book of Books.* Michelet immortalized his legacy, rather, in the panoramic and intense *Preface* of 1869 that portrays his vast ambitions while attempting to demonstrate how they reached fulfillment.

The *Preface* establishes firmly the place in history Michelet believed his work deserved. To that end, he takes pains to distinguish himself from his most illustrious French predecessor, Augustin Thierry (1795–1856), whose *Histoire de la Conquête de l'Angleterre par les Normands* was published in 1825. Michelet's preoccupation with Thierry is perhaps due to the fact that their conceptions of historical writing—revolutionary at the time—were strikingly similar. The narratives of both were admired for their brilliance and vividness of style. Both attempted to reconcile art and science; they were among the first to use original authorities—for example, manuscripts, etc.—to correct the contemporary chronicles upon which most historical writing was then based. Michelet rightly argues that he improved upon his elder, for the latter had exaggerated the element of race in his interpretations; Thierry was respected for artistic talent and not for analytical rigor. It remains to be seen, however, if Michelet himself merits a similar reproach.

Michelet directs his criticism of predecessors primarily against their incompleteness of documentary evidence, to his mind both the cause and the effect of their limited vision. He begins with the Swiss economist and historian Sismondi (1773–1842), passing quickly to the outstanding historical Pleiad of the Restoration: Barante (1782–1866), Guizot (1787–1874), Mignet (1796–1884), Thiers (1797–1877), and Augustin Thierry. These men, according to him, as innovative and productive as they were, did not elevate themselves to a higher understanding of France. The ideal method should vitalize enormous efforts of research with intellectual synthesis and penetrating intuition. Michelet claimed to master this remarkable combination of qualities. He proudly displayed himself as the first to perceive France "as a person and as a soul." As he wrote a quarter of a century before in *The People:* "Thierry called history *narration,* and Guizot called it *analysis.* I have named it *resurrection,* and this name will last." *

Michelet glorifies the decisive influence exercised by the Neapolitan philosopher Giambattista Vico (1668–1744) upon his historical vocation. He remained Vico's fervent disciple from the beginning to the end of his life. Michelet was the first to introduce Vico's thought to the French public by his translation and presentation of the *Scienza nuova,* published in 1827. Michelet's theory of history and culture is indeed grounded upon his interpretation of Vico. However, Michelet fails to mention in the *Preface* another decisive model (also influenced by Vico), the German philosopher of history, Johann Gottfried von Herder (1744–1803). It is no coincidence that Herder's *Ideen* were translated and published the same year by Michelet's closest friend, Edgar Quinet. For Michelet, Herder is Vico's invisible partner. Eminent historians of ideas such as Ernst Cassirer, R. G. Collingwood, and Emery Neff clearly establish Herder as the father of modern historiography, stressing his conception of historical writing as artistic resurrection. Those familiar with historiography will also recognize that Michelet's theory of historical imagination resembles that of his British contemporary, Thomas Carlyle (1795–1881). †

Michelet's 1869 *Preface* defines his *History*'s unity for posterity, but

---

* *The People,* translated by John P. McKay (Urbana: University of Illinois Press, 1973), p. 19. The next quotation from *The People* is found on page 152 of that edition, which is available in paperback.

† See Ernst Cassirer, *An Essay on Man* (New Haven: Yale University Press, 1944); R. G. Collingwood, *The Idea of History* (London, New York: Oxford University Press, 1956); Emery Neff, *The Poetry of History* (New York: Columbia University Press, 1947); and Charles Rearick, *Beyond the Enlightenment* (Bloomington: Indiana University Press, 1974).

its true subject is the author himself. Two themes dominate his professional and spiritual autobiography: the artistic problem of historical re-creation and Michelet's changing relationship with Catholicism. Ideology and esthetics are intertwined. The historian makes a last-ditch effort to sort them out.

Michelet repeatedly expresses his ambition to resurrect the integral life of the past throughout his writings. He conceptualizes through images and myths. His task appears as Aeneas's descent into the underworld. The Roman carried a golden bough which allowed him to enter and return unharmed from the land of the dead. Michelet lived constantly in their company. The historian's golden bough is his awareness that he is alive; its power revives the soul of the documents he studies. Michelet is armed with imaginative empathy. As artist-historian he rescues lost souls from oblivion by dramatizing their actions on the printed page.

Michelet was a prophet for whom writing as a resurrection of the past implies a vision of universal justice. The dead receive their reward of eternity by living in the consciousness of the present. The historian's sacred duty was to restore the glories of the past to inspire readers to construct the image of an ideal future. History was Michelet's instrument of social retribution. He symbolizes this grandiose moral and political aspiration as "Caesar's dream"; the historian recounts this imperial image of himself in *The People:*

> It is said that when Caesar was coasting along the shores of Africa, he fell asleep and had a dream; he saw a vast army, weeping and stretching their hands toward him. On awakening, he wrote down upon his tablets Corinth and Carthage, and he rebuilt those cities.
>
> I am not Caesar, but how often I have dreamed Caesar's dream! I saw them weeping, I understood their tears. "Urbem orant." They want their city! And I, a poor solitary dreamer, what could I give to that great silent nation? All that I had—my voice. May it be their first admission into the City of Right, from which they have been excluded until now!

The historian is a Promethean titan who initiates a rebirth of civilizations. The *History of France* immortalizes the past. It also seeks to transform the present. Michelet's greatest competitor was the Catholic Church. Their common goal to define humanity and to decipher the universe explains why, in the mid-nineteenth century, the republican historian of the French Revolution and the Church could not coexist. Michelet's religious evolution reflects that of his era. His love for God and the human spirit could not endure the reactionary politics of the Church. He rejected this mother while remaining fitfully ambivalent toward her.

In his early years, as part of the generation which reached maturity during the Restoration, Michelet was nourished by his powerful sympathy for the Catholic Church. The six volumes of his *History of the Middle Ages* pulse with admiration for the artistic and intellectual triumphs of the Christian spirit. Because of the fervor expressed in these volumes, and because of the original and exhaustive documentation upon which they are based, most historians agree that they are Michelet's lasting historical masterpiece. Does their solidity suffice to explain why the author of the 1869 *Preface*, despite his long-standing hostility toward the Church, persisted in defending them? Political and personal circumstances had turned the historian into a rabid anticlerical, and by 1843, the year of his public lessons attacking the Jesuits, his break with the Church was definitive. Yet, curiously, the 1869 *Preface* defends excessively his youthful appreciation of Christianity. What is the basis of Michelet's obsessive ambivalence toward that religion?

His relative fidelity to his volumes of medieval history can be explained somewhat by his fundamental attraction to all sorts of spirituality, be they natural, human, or even supernatural. There is perhaps an even more basic reason for the compulsion to recall his former love of Christianity: his absolute commitment to an organic conception of history. For the author, the *History*'s esthetic integrity became more compelling than the rectification of its incomplete details. His goal was to depict the living legend of the French people, starting with its first appearance as Jacques, through Joan of Arc, and culminating in the French Revolution. The lesson that *"humanity is its own Prometheus"* (which he derived from Vico) far outweighs any discontinuity which the author's avowed changes of political opinion might betray. Michelet's mission remained constant from the quasi-mystical illumination brought about by the July Revolution to his death in 1874: liberate human energy, celebrate the inherent powers of nature and mankind.

The *Preface*'s most intimate portrait derives from Michelet's contention that artistic production lives by the creator's love for his subject. His comparison of historical writing with a woman's conception and gestation of a child suggests the historian's "two sexes of the mind," his unique combination of "male" analysis and "female" compassion and empathy. If anything of permanent value will survive in Michelet's *Preface*, it is certainly his self-portrait as a man of emotion. He had crossed ten centuries of human struggle, "swallowed too many plagues, too many vipers, and too many kings." He loved or detested his actors with deep passion. Jules Michelet the person lives again in these pages. His work summarizes an entire era. The author exemplifies the sublimity, and the frailty, of a great and tender heart.

The following translation—the first to be published in English—is my own, prepared with the valuable assistance of Perry McIntosh. The sub-titles are mine, although they are based on the original analytical table of contents that Michelet published with the *Preface*. The edition used was that of Charles Morazé (Armand Colin, 1962), and checked against the text of the *Oeuvres complètes,* volume IV, ed. Paul Viallaneix (Flam-marion, 1974). I have added phrases in brackets. We have endeavored to translate this text in a way which would suggest how Michelet might have written it in twentieth-century English. However, we have supplied many connectives in an attempt to render his highly elliptical style more accessible to those unfamiliar with it. We hope that Michelet's final testament has not lost too much of its original vigor.

Edward K. Kaplan

The 1869 Preface

This arduous labor of about forty years was conceived in an instant, in the lightening flash of the July Revolution. During those memorable days a great light appeared, and I perceived France.

She possessed annals, but no history at all. Eminent men had studied her, especially from the political point of view. None had penetrated into the infinite detail of the diverse results of her activity (religious, economic, artistic, etc.). None had yet embraced the living unity of the innate and geographic elements which formed her. I was the first to perceive her as a soul and as a person.

The First History to Embrace All Human Activity

The renowned Sismondi, a persevering worker, honest and discerning, rarely raises himself to comprehensive views in his political annals. And, moreover, he scarcely undertakes scholarly research. He himself admits straightforwardly that, writing in Geneva, he had neither the records nor the manuscripts at hand.

Besides, until 1830 (even until 1836), none of the remarkable his-torians of that epoch had yet felt the need to seek facts outside of printed books, in the original sources—for the most part unpublished at that time—, and in the manuscripts of our libraries, in the documents of our archives.

That noble historical constellation which, from 1820 to 1830, caused so great a stir, MM. de Barante, Guizot, Mignet, Thiers, Augustin Thierry, considered history from specialized and differing points of view. One was preoccupied with the racial element, another with institutions, etc., without understanding adequately perhaps how difficult it is to isolate these things, how each of them works upon the others. Do races, for example, remain the same without being influenced by changing customs? Can institutions be sufficiently studied without taking into account the history of ideas and the multitude of social conditions from which they arise? There is always something artificial about these specializations, which claim to illuminate, but which nonetheless can give faulty profiles, deceiving us about the whole while concealing the greater harmony.

Life has one supreme and very exacting condition. It is genuinely life only when complete. Its organs are completely interdependent and only work as a whole. Our vital functions are linked, presuppose one another. Let one be missing, and nothing will live any longer. In the past it was believed possible to isolate by the scalpel, to follow separately each of our systems; this cannot be, for everything affects everything.

Thus, all or nothing. In order to rediscover historical life, one must follow it patiently along its courses, all its forms, all its components. But one must also, with a still greater passion, reconstruct and restore all its workings, the reciprocal action of these diverse forces in the powerful motion which could again produce life itself.

Géricault, a master with whom I doubtlessly shared, not genius, but a violent will, upon entering the Louvre (the Louvre of that time, where all the art of Europe was collected), did not seem troubled. He said: "Fine! I'll do it all over again." In rapid sketches which he never signed, he went about seizing and appropriating everything. And, were it not for 1815, he would have kept his word. Such are the passions, the madness of youth.

A Living Harmony

Still more complicated, more frightening, was my historical problem, set forth as a *resurrection of the integral life,* not superficially, but in its interior and organic depth. No prudent man would have dreamed of it. Fortunately, that I was not.

In the blazing morning of the July Revolution, in its vast promise, its powerful electricity, this superhuman undertaking did not frighten a young heart. There are no obstacles at certain times. All is simplified by the flame of passion. A thousand tangled things are resolved in it, rediscover in it their true connections, and (harmonizing themselves) are illuminated. Many coil-springs, inert and heavy if they lie apart, roll of their own accord if they are replaced in the system.

Such was my faith at least, and that act of faith, whatever my weaknesses, took effect. History's immense movement shook before my eyes. Those various forces, both of nature and of art, sought each other, arranged themselves, at first awkwardly. The limbs of the great body, peoples, races, regions, grouped from the sea to the Rhine, to the Rhône, to the Alps, and the centuries marched from Gaul to France.

Everyone, friends and enemies, said "that it was alive." But what are the true, unquestionable signs of life? With a certain dexterity, one can obtain animation, a kind of warmth. Sometimes electric charges make it appear to surpass the actions of life itself with its lurches, its efforts, its jarring contrasts, its surprises, its small miracles. The sign of true life is completely different: its continuity. Born in one gush, it lasts, and grows placidly, slowly, *uno tenore.* The unity of life is not that of a little five-act play, but (in an often limitless development) the harmonious identity of soul.

The most severe critics, if they consider the totality of my book, will not fail to recognize in it these lofty conditions of life. It has not at all been hurried, abrupt; it had, at the very least, the quality of slowness. From the first to the last volume, the method is the same; as it is, in short, in my *Geography,* so it is in my *Louis XV,* and in my *Revolution.* No less rare in a labor of so many years, the form and the color are sustained. The same qualities, the same flaws. If the latter had disappeared, the work would be heterogeneous, motley, it would have lost its personality. Such as it is, it is better for it to remain harmonious and a living whole.

France Has Created Herself

When I began, a book of genius existed, Thierry's. Shrewd and penetrating, he was a discerning interpreter, a great chiseler, an admirable worker, but too enslaved to one master. This master, this tyrant, is the exclusive, systematic assumption of the permanence of races. All things considered, what makes this great book beautiful is that, in spite of this system, which could be seen as deterministic, one feels breathing beneath everything a heart animated against fatalistic forces, the invasion; one senses a heart brim-full of the national soul and of the right to liberty.

I greatly loved and admired him. However, shall I say it? neither the physical nor the spiritual approaches were adequate for me in his book.

The physical, the element of race, the common people who carry it on, seemed to me to need under them a good solid base, the earth, to support and nourish them. Without a geographic foundation, the people, the historic actor, seem to walk on air as in those Chinese paintings in which there is no ground. And note that this ground is not only the theater of action. By means of food, climate, etc., it influences in a hundred ways. As the nest, so the bird. As the country, so the man.

Race, a strong and dominant factor in barbarian times, before the great childbirth of nations, becomes less tangible, weaker, and almost obliterated, in proportion as each nation fashions itself and becomes a person. The famous Mr. Mill says quite well: "It would be too easy a means of avoiding the study of moral and social influences to attribute differences of character, and of conduct, to innate, indestructible differences." [1]

Contrary to those who pursue this racial element and exaggerate its influence in modern times, I drew from history itself an enormous, and too little noticed, moral fact. It is the powerful *labor of oneself on oneself,* whereby France, by her own progress, transforms all her rough elements. From the Roman municipal element, from the Germanic tribes, from the Celtic clan—which are annuled, have disappeared—we have produced in the course of time completely different results, even contrary, to a great extent, to everything which preceded them.

Life exerts upon itself an action of self-gestation, which, from pre-existing materials, creates absolutely new things. From the bread, the fruits which I have eaten, I make red and salty blood which does not at all remind me of the foods from which it is derived. —So goes the historical life process, so goes each people fabricating, generating itself, grinding and amalgamating elements, which doubtless remain there as an obscure mixture, but which are relatively insignificant compared to the long, slow travail of the great soul.

France itself has formed France, and the deterministic element of race seems to me secondary. France is the daughter of her freedom. Essential in human progress is the life force, which is called mankind. *Humanity is its own Prometheus.*

To sum up, history, as I saw it represented by those eminent (and several of them admirable) men, still seemed unsubstantial in its two methods:

Not material enough, taking races into account, but not the soil, the climate, foods, and so many physical and physiological conditions.

Not spiritual enough, speaking about laws, about political acts, but not about ideas, about customs, and not about the great progressive interior movement of the national soul.

1. This is the principal point on which I differ from my learned friend, M. Henri Martin. Moreover, this disagreement does not at all diminish my sympathetic esteem for his great and very beautiful *History of France,* which is so instructive, so rich in research and ideas. It would have been infinitely useful, in reviving the all too unrecorded national tradition, for these two histories, which help and compensate for one another, to have appeared simultaneously.

[That form of history], especially, was not very interested in minute scholarly details, where the best, perhaps, remained buried in unpublished sources.

My History and Its Author

My life was in this book, it has been transformed into it. This book has been my only consequence. But this identity of the book with its author, is it not dangerous? Is not the work colored with the feelings, the times, of he who produced it?

That is what always happens. No portrait is so exact, so conforms to the model, that the artist has not added to it a little of himself. Our masters in history have not escaped from this law. Tacitus, in his *Tiberius,* also paints himself with the suffocation of his times, "the fifteen long years" of silence. Thierry, in recounting for us Klodowig, William and his conquest, reveals the interior breath, the emotion of the recently invaded France and his opposition to the regime which seemed that of a foreigner.

If this be a weakness, we must admit that it is very useful to us. The historian who is deprived of it, who attempts to disappear while writing, to not exist, to follow contemporary reports from behind (as Barante did for Froissart) is not an historian at all. The old chronicler, although quite charming, is absolutely incapable of defining for his poor valet who follows at his heels, what is the great, the somber, the frightful fourteenth century. In order to know what it is, all our forces of analysis and erudition are necessary, a great device is needed. What device, what means are needed to pierce the mysteries which are inaccessible to this storyteller? It is the modern personality, so powerful and so elevated.

In penetrating an object more and more, one comes to love it, and from then on one examines it with growing interest. A heart touched with emotion has second sight; it sees a multitude of things which are invisible to those who are unconcerned. History, the historian, merge in this penetrating glance. Is this good? Is this bad? Here something operates which has not been described and which we should reveal:

It is the fact that history, in the progress of time, makes the historian much more than it is made by him. My book has created me. It is I who am its handiwork. This son has produced its father. If it first issued from me, from my storm of youth (which still rages), it has rendered me much stronger, more enlightened, even given me more fertile warmth, more actual power to resurrect the past. If my work resembles me, that is good. The traits which it shares with me are in a large part those which I owe to it, which I took from it.

An Intellectual Autobiography

My destiny has favored me well. I possessed two things which are rather rare, and which have produced this work.

First, freedom, which has been its soul.

Then, some useful obligations which, by slowing down, delaying its completion, made it more thoughtful, stronger, gave it solidity, the sturdy foundations of time.

I was free because of solitude, poverty and simplicity of life, free through my teaching. Under the ministry of Martignac (a short moment of liberality) it was decided to reconstitute the Ecole Normale, and M. Letronne, who was consulted, had the chair of philosophy and history given to me. My *Précis of Modern History,* my *Vico,* published in 1827, seemed to him sufficient qualifications. This dual teaching, which I exercised still later at the Collège de France, opened me to an infinite freedom. My boundless domain included every fact, every idea.

I had no master other than Vico. The principle of the living force, of *humanity which creates itself,* made both my book and my teaching.

I stayed at a good distance from the majestic, sterile doctrinaires, and from the great Romantic flood of "art for art's sake." I had my world within myself. I held my life within myself, as well as my renewals and my fecundity; but also my dangers. Which? My heart, my youth, my method itself, and the new obligation demanded of history: no longer just to recount or judge, but to *summon, remake, revive* the ages. To have enough passionate flame to reheat the ashes so long cooled off—that was the first point, and a dangerous one. But the second, more perilous perhaps, was to relate intimately with the revived dead, who knows? to become finally one of them.

My first pages after the July Revolution, written on the burning paving stones, were a view of the world, of Universal History, as a struggle of freedom, its incessant victory over the world of necessity, brief as an eternal July.

That little book [*Introduction to Universal History*], with an unbelievable impetus and rapid flight, moved forward (as I have always done) with two wings at once, Nature and Spirit, two interpretations of the vast general movement. My method was already there. I said there in 1830 what I said (in *The Witch* [1862]) about Satan, bizarre name for a still youthful freedom, militant and negative at first, but later creative, more and more fruitful.

Jouffroy had just uttered in 1829 the key word of the Restoration: "How dogmas come to an end." In July, the Church found itself deserted.

No free thinker then would have doubted that the prophecy of Montesquieu about the death of Catholicism should not soon be fulfilled.

I was in this respect perhaps the freest man in the world, having had the rare advantage of not have suffered from the deadly education which catches young souls unawares, and immediately chloroforms them. The Church was for me a foreign world of pure curiosity, like the moon. What I knew best about that pale star was that its days were numbered, that it did not have long to live. But who would replace it? That was the question. The Church was entangled in the moral cholera which followed the July Revolution so closely, the disillusionment, the loss of high hopes. Lower down, the masses rumbled. The novel, the theater burst forth with daring ugliness. Talent was plentiful, but the brutality was gross; this was not the fecund orgy of the old cults of nature which have seen their grandeur, but a deliberate intoxication with sterile materialism. Much bombast, and little beneath.

The original text which preceded July had been *Honor to Industry,* new queen of the world, who dominates, subjugates matter. —After July, this was reversed: matter, in its turn, subjugated human energy.

This last fact is not rare in history. Nothing is older than this idea of the right of matter which wants to have its turn. But what made it shocking in the case of the Saint-Simonians was the ugliness of a Janus,[1] who conserved in that ritual the servile imitation of the Catholic institution.

At a solemn meeting to which we were invited, Quinet and I, we saw with astonishment, in this religion of the bank, a remarkable return of what was supposed to be abolished. We saw a clergy and a pope; we saw the preacher receive the transmission of Grace from this pope by the laying on of hands. He said: "Down with the cross!" But it was present in the sacerdotal authoritarian forms reminiscent of the Middle Ages. The old religion, which they claimed to combat, was being renewed at its worst; confession, spiritual direction, nothing was missing. The Capucines were restored: bankers, industrialists. The bland softness of a new Molinos had the odor of sweet Jesus.

Suppress the Middle Ages, fine. But they were plundering it. This was quite apparent to me. When I went home, with a blind and generous impulse, I wrote forceful words in favor of that dying age which was pillaged during its death agony. Those juvenile lines, foolish if you will, but doubtless excusable as a heartfelt emotion, hardly belonged in my little

1. This has nothing to do with the honesty of the individuals. There were some admirable men, people like Bazart, Barrault, Carnot, Charton, D'Eichthal, Lemonnier, etc.

book inspired by the July Revolution and Freedom, inspired by its victory over the clergy. They clashed strongly with Satan, whom this book introduces as a myth of liberty. No matter. Those lines are there, and they still make me laugh. Such apparent contradictions hardly bother a young artist of solid faith, though innocent, uncalculating, sensing little the danger of being soft-hearted toward the enemy.

My First Two Volumes Were Too Favorable toward the Church

I was an artist and writer then, much more than an historian. This is evident in the first two volumes (*France in the Middle Ages*). The documents which have thrown light upon these shadows, upon the abyss of these long woes had not yet been published. The great synthetic effect which emerged from these documents was for me that of a dismal harmony, a colossal symphony, few of whose countless dissonances reached my ear. This is a very serious deficiency. The cry of Reason by Abelard, the immense movement of 1200, so cruelly stamped out, are too little felt there, sacrificed excessively to the artistic effect of the greater unity.

And yet, today, having passed through so many years, ages, different worlds, as I reread this book and see its failings quite clearly, I say:

"It cannot be meddled with."

It was written in a solitude, a freedom, a purity, a high tension of mind, which were truly uncommon. Its candor, its passion, the enormous quantity of life which animates it intercede for it with me, support it against my scrutiny. The rectitude of youth is felt in its very mistakes. Its broad general effect, on the whole is a result of that rectitude. For the first time the soul of France appears in its living personality, while the impotence of the Church is not less exposed.

An impotence which is radical and twice established.

In the first volume one sees the Church, queen under Dagobert and under the Carlovingians, able to do nothing for the world, nothing for the social order.

In the second volume one observes how the Church, having produced a king-priest, a king-abbott, a canon of her eldest son, the king of France, crushes her enemies (1200), smothers the free Spirit, bringing about no moral reform. Finally, eclipsed, overtaken by Saint Louis, the Church is (before 1300) subordinated, dominated by the State.

This is the unquestionably true portion of those two volumes. But in their share of mirage, of poetic illusion, can it be said that all is false? No.

The latter aspect expresses the idea that such an age had of itself, it voices what it dreamed and wanted. It represents the age truthfully in its aspirations, in its deep sadness, the reverie which held it down before the

Church, crying in its stone refuge, sighing, waiting for what never comes.

Nothing was more necessary than to rediscover the idea that the Middle Ages had of itself, to reproduce its impulse, its desire, its soul, before judging it. Who was destined to rediscover its soul? Apparently our great writers who all had a Catholic education. How then can it be that these geniuses, so well prepared for this, walked around the Church without entering it, so to speak, without penetrating its interior? Some seek in the echoes of church entrances or cloisters the themes of their melodies. Others, with great exertion and a powerful chisel, excavate the ornaments, arm the towers, the roofs, with formidable masks, with gnomes and grimacing devils. But all that is not the Church herself. Let us first remake her.

What is remarkable is this: that the only one who possessed enough love to recreate, to restore the inner world of the Church, is he whom she did not raise at all, *he who never communed with her,* who had no faith other than one in humanity itself, no imposed creed, nothing but a free mind.

This mind approached the dead thing with a human sensitivity, having the great advantage of not having had to undergo the priests, the ponderous formulas which have buried the Middle Ages. The incantation of a finite ritual would have accomplished nothing. Everything would have remained as cold as ashes. And moreover, if history had arrived in all its critical severity, with absolute justice, I do not know if those dead would have dared to live. They would, rather, have remained hidden in their tombs.

Love of Death and the Gift of Tears

I had a noble disease which clouded my youth, yet which well suited an historian. I loved death. I had lived nine years at the doors of the Père-Lachaise cemetery, at that time my only place for walking. Then I lived near the Bièvre part of Paris, amidst large convent gardens, another kind of sepulcher. I led a life which the world would have called buried, having no company except that of the past, and for friends, entombed peoples. By recovering their legendary story, I awakened in them a multitude of vanished things. Certain nursery songs whose secret I shared had a sure effect. By my tone of voice they believed me to be one of them. The gift which Saint Louis requests and does not obtain, was mine: "The gift of tears."

A powerful, very fruitful gift. All those for whom I wept, peoples and gods, lived again. This naïve magic had an almost infallible power of conjuring. Egypt, for example, had been spelled out, decoded, all its tombs excavated, but its soul had not been rediscovered. For some the climate, for others certain symbols of empty subtlety was the explanation. I myself found it in the heart of Isis, in the sufferings of the common people, the eternal mourning and the eternal wound of the fellah's family, in his insecure life, in the captivities, the razzias of Africa, the great trade in men, of Nubia and Syria. Man carried far away, bound to hard labor, *man made into a tree* or attached to trees, nailed, mutilated, dismembered, it is the universal Passion of so many gods (Osiris, Adonis, Iacchus, Athis, etc.). How many Christs, and how many Calvaries! How many funereal laments! How many sobs all along the way! (See my little *Bible* [*of Humanity*], 1864).

I had no other skill in 1833. A tear, one only, dropped onto the foundation of the gothic Church, sufficed to summon it forth. Something human surged from it, the blood of legend, and, through that powerful thrust, everything rose toward the sky. From inside to outside, everything sprang out in flowers, —of stone? No, flowers of life. —Sculpt them? Approach them with iron and chisel? That would have horrified me, and I would have thought they would bleed!

History as a Resurrection

Would you like to know why I was so fond of these gods? it is because they die. They all depart in their turn. Each one, just like us, having received a little holy water and tears, descends into the pyramids, the hypogeum, the catacombs. Alas! What ever returns from there? I will not deny that *after three days* (each one three thousand years long), a light breath can reappear from there. The Indian soul has not vanished from the earth; it returns through the love it had for all life. Egypt has always echoed in this world through its love of death and its hope for immortality. The refined Christian soul, in its blandness, can doubtless never expire without returning. Its legend has perished, but that is not enough. It must cast off the horrible injustice (Grace, Arbitrary Judgment) which is its vital center, its heart, the true base of its dogma. It is harsh to say it, but Christianity must die in its very principles, openly accept its penitence, its purification, and expiation by death.

Wise men told me: "It is not safe to live to this extent in such intimacy with the other world. The dead are all so nice! All these faces which have calmed and become so gentle have strange powers of extravagant illusion. Among them you acquire strange dreams, and who knows? attachments. He who lives there too long turns livid from it. You risk coming upon the white Fiancée, so pallid and so charming, who drinks the blood of your heart! At least do what Aeneas did, who did not venture among the dead without a sword in his hand to drive away these images, so as not to be engaged too closely (*Ferro diverberat umbras*)."

The sword! Dismal advice. What! I would have harshly, when those beloved images approached me seeking to live, I would have thrust them aside! What doleful wisdom!... Oh! How unaware the philosophers are of the true essence of the artist, of the secret talisman which constitutes the power of history, allows the historian to pass time and again among the dead!

I would have you know, then, you ignorant people, that without a sword, unarmed, without arguing with those trustful souls who beg for resurrection, art, while welcoming them, while restoring their breath, art, nevertheless, retains within itself its full lucidity. I do not mean *irony*, in which many have placed the essence of art. I am speaking rather of the mighty duality which permits one, while loving them, to see nonetheless what they really are, "that they are the dead."

Creation through Love

The greatest artists of the world, the geniuses who examine nature so tenderly, will allow me to make here a humble comparison. Have you seen at times the touching seriousness of a young girl, innocent, and yet deeply affected by her future motherhood, who cradles the work of her hands, animates it with her kiss, says to it from her heart: My daughter!... If you touch her work roughly, she becomes upset and screams. But this does not prevent her from knowing deep down what this being is that she animates, that she makes talk, reason, that she brings to life with her soul.

This is a little image of a great thing. It represents exactly art at its moment of conception. Such is the essential condition of artistic fecundity. It is love, but also a smile. It is the loving smile which creates.

If the smile is outmoded, if irony begins, and with it harsh criticism and logic, then life becomes chilly, withdraws, shrinks, and nothing is produced at all. Weak and sterile people who, while wanting to bear fruit, blend *although* and *nisi* with their wretched child, these grave imbeciles do not know that no life springs forth in a frigid environment; from their glacial nothingness will issue... nothingness.

Death can appear at the moment of love, in the creative surge. But in that case it should appear with infinite tenderness, with tears and pity (which still express love). In the intensely emotional moments when I incubated and reproduced the life of the Christian Church, and stated plainly the sentence of its impending death, I was also filled with pity for it. Recreating it through art, I told the invalid what Hezekiah asked of God. Nothing more. Conclude that I am Catholic! What could be more inane! The believer does not say an office for the dead for a dying person whom he believes to be eternal.

I Became More Human

These two volumes were successful and accepted by the public. I was the first to have established France as a person. Less exclusive than Thierry, and subordinating the element of race, I strongly underlined the geographic principle of local influences, and moreover, the general labor of the nation which creates itself, fabricates itself. In my blind outburst for the Gothic I had caused the stone to give forth blood, and the church to flower, to ascend like the flower of legends. This was pleasing to the public. Less to me. There was in that work a great flame. I found in it too much subtlety, too much wit, too much method.

Four whole years went by before the third volume (which begins around 1300). In preparing it I tried to extend myself, to become deeper, to be more *human,* more simple. I sat for some time in Luther's house, collecting his table conversations, such virile and strong words, so touching, which slipped from this heroic fellow (1834). But nothing was more useful to me than Grimm's colossal book, his *Antiquities of German Law.* A very difficult book which sets forth the symbols and the formulas—found in all the dialects, all the periods of that language—with which the so diverse Germanies have sanctified the great events of human life (birth, marriage and death, testaments, sales, tributes, etc.). I will tell you some day about the incredible passion with which I ventured to understand and translate this book. I did not shut myself up in it. From nation to nation, I went about collecting from everywhere, I went from the Indus to Ireland, from the Vedas and Zoroaster up to the present, piling up these primitive formulas in which humanity so naïvely reveals so many intimate and profound things (1837).

This made another man of me. A strange inner transformation took place; it seemed to me that until then, I was harsh and subtle, I was old, and that little by little, under the influence of young humanity, I too became young. Refreshed by those living springs, my heart became a flower garden, as if touched by the morning dew. Oh! the dawn! Oh! tender childhood! Oh! good and natural nature! What well-being this created in me, after the witherings of my mystic subtlety. How meager that Byzantine poetry now appeared to me, how sickly and barren, how emaciated. Yet I spared it still. But how shabby it appeared in the presence of humanity! This I possessed, I held it, I embraced humanity, both in the very rich detail of its boundless variety (leafy as the forests of India, where each tree is a forest) and, in looking upwards, I saw its sweet, mild harmony which smothers nothing; I grasped the divine element in its unity worthy of adoration.

So richly watered and nourished by nature, my substance increasing,

I experienced an immense growth of solidity in my art, and (shall I say it? but it is true) a growth of kindness, and a heedlessness, an absolute ignorance about rivalries, —consequently I developed a vast sympathy for mankind (whom I scarcely saw), for society, the world (which I never frequented).

I had the security of a body which had become firm and strong, in which good food had changed and replaced—to the very atoms and molecules—all which had at first been weak. I was not even touched by the maliciousness of the doctrinaires. I was no less indifferent to the ambushes of the Catholics. Everything which I had accumulated (without thinking, without trying), those unquestionable, countless facts, those mountains of truths which, in my persistent work, rose, pushed higher each day, —all that was against them. None of them could have discovered the solid and deep foundation that I found there, to the extent that I had neither the need nor the idea of polemics. My strength made my peacefulness. It would have taken them ten thousand years to understand that what to them seemed weakness, the gentle and peaceful *human sense,* which was steadily growing in me, was precisely my strength and that which separated me from them.[1]

The mongrel half-Catholic salons, in the insipid atmosphere of the friends of Chateaubriand, would have been a more dangerous trap for me. The benevolent and pleasant Ballanche, then M. de Lamartine, wanted to escort me several times to L'Abbaye-aux-Bois. I was perfectly aware that such a milieu, where everything was circumspect and decorous, would have civilized me too much. I had but one single strength, my savage virginity of opinion, and the free manner of an art which was all my own and new. I would have had to adapt myself, become milder, better mannered than was suited for me. The salons were from that period on very hostile toward me. In them, doctrinaires and Catholics have steadfastly waged war on me, attacking me little in particulars, praising me in order to destroy me and to deprive me of any authority: "He is a writer, a poet, a man of imagination."

1. As they sniff out death very well, the moments when the wounded soul might soften, at the time when I had had a painful loss in the family, one of them, seductive and shrewd, came to see me and sounded me out. I was surprised, confused at the idea that he could have believed to have some hold on me, that he could say that we might reach an understanding, having between us but slight differences, etc. I spoke to him in these very words: "Monseigneur, have you ever been on the sea of ice?" — "Yes," he answered. "Have you ever seen a certain crack, over which, from one side to the other, one can speak, converse?" — "Yes." — "But you have not seen that this crack is an abyss...", I continued, "and so much so, Monseigneur, so deep, that through the ice and the earth, it descends without ever reaching bottom. It goes as far the center of the globe, continues across the globe, becoming lost in the infinite."

This began at the time when I was the first to remove history from the vagueness which satisfied them; I established history from the records, the manuscripts, the enormous investigation of thousands of various documents.

History Now Based on Unpublished Documents

No historian that I know of, before the publication of my third volume (a simple thing to verify) had used unpublished pieces. This began with the use I made in my history of the mysterious register of the *Interrogatory of the Temple,* which had been locked up for four hundred years, hidden, walled up, prohibited under the most severe penalties, in the treasury of the cathedral. The Harleys took it from there, it then came to Saint-Germain-des-Prés, then to the National Library. The Chronicles of Duguesclin, then unpublished, also helped me. The enormous repository of the Archives provided me with a multitude of records which supported these manuscripts, and for many other subjects. This was the first time history had so serious a foundation.

What would I have become, in studying the fourteenth century, if clinging to the methods of my most illustrious predecessors, I had made myself the docile interpreter, the servile translator of the contemporary narrative? Entering centuries rich in records and in genuine texts, history came of age, mastered and ruled the reports which it purified and judged. Armed with unassailable documents of which these records were unaware, history, as it were, held them on its knee like a little child to whose prattle it listens willingly, but whom it must often admonish and contradict.

An example, the one which I suggested above, will suffice to make myself well understood. In the pleasant history in which M. de Barante follows our narrators, Foissart, etc., so faithfully, step by step, it seems that he cannot make too many mistakes in clinging to these contemporaries. Afterwards in examining the records, the various documents, then so dispersed though collected today, one recognizes that the recorder failed to appreciate, was unmindful of the broad features of the times. It is already a financial and juridical century, in feudal form. It is often Pathelin masked as Arthur. The advent of gold, of the Jew, the weaving industry of Flanders, the dominating wool trade in England and Flanders—this is what allowed the English to prevail with regular troops, some of which were mercenaries, paid. The *economic* revolution alone made possible the *military* revolution, which, through the rude defeat of feudal knighthood, prepared, brought about the *political* revolution. The tournaments of Foissart, Monstrelet and the Golden Fleece have little influence in all this. It is the incidental aspect.

From this time on (1837), from volume to volume, I would make reference to and often quote manuscripts, whose importance I would underline and which would later be published.

With such supports, superior to all simple records, history continues, serious and strong, with authority. But independent of these natural instruments, it is given immeasurable assistance from everywhere. —From literature and art, commerce, thousands of indirect revelations come to it, and from the side illuminate the central narrative. —History becomes a reality insured by the various controls which all the various forms of our activity furnish.

Here again I am compelled to say: I was alone. —Hardly anything other than political history, governmental records existed, studies of institutions to a slight extent. No one took into account that which accompanies, explains, establishes in part that political history: the social, economic, industrial conditions, those of literature and of ideas.

The third volume (1300–1400) embraces all the aspects of a century. It is not without weaknesses. It does not explain how 1300 was the atonement for 1200, how Boniface VIII paid for Innocent III. It is too harsh toward the legists, toward the intrepid men who slapped the face of the idol with the Albigensian hand of the valiant Nogaret. However, this volume is new and strong in deriving history principally from *the economic Revolution,* from the advent of gold, of the Jew and of Satan (the king of hidden treasures). It vigorously presents the marked *mercantile* character of the times.

How England and Flanders were married by wool and cloth, how England drank Flanders, became saturated with her, enticing at any price the weavers driven out by the brutalities of the house of Bourbon: this is the great fact. An enriched England defeats us at Crécy, Poitiers and Agincourt, with well-regulated troops which bury chivalry. A great social revolution.

The Black Plague, the dance of Saint-Gui, the flagellants and the witches' sabbath, these carnivals of despair impel the abandoned leaderless people to act for themselves. The genius of France in her Danton of the time, Etienne Marcel, in her Paris, her States General, bursts forth unexpectedly in her constitution, admirable in its precosity, —postponed, rubbed out by the petty negative prudence of Charles V. Nothing has been cured. Aggravated, on the contrary, evil arrives at its culminating frenzy, the raging madness of Charles VI.

Resurrection of the Spirit of France

I have defined history as *Resurrection.* If this was ever realized, it happened in the fourth volume (Charles VI). Perhaps, truthfully, that is saying too much. This volume was created in a spurt of agony, in an ecstasy of that soul of yore, savage, sensual and violent, cruel and tender, raging. As in *The Witch,* several places are diabolical, the dead dance there, —not to provoke laughter as in Holbein's ironies, —but in a painful frenzy which can be shared, which almost overtakes the spectator. It whirls with astonishing speed, a horrible rout. And one is breathless. No stopping, no distraction. Everywhere there is an emotional and deep bass continuum; mysterious rolling sounds beneath, a muted thunder of the heart.

In the midst of so many gloomy things, one falls upon a great light, — the death enthroned at the Louvre, —in a wilderness Paris, the real death of France in the form of the Englishman from Lancaster. The king of priests, Henry, the damned Pharisee, tells us "that we have perished only for our sins."

I do not answer him; let the English answer him themselves.

They say that before the battle of Agincourt, each Englishman looked to his salvation, confessed himself; the French embraced each other, forgave each other and forgot their hatreds.

They say that in Spain where the French and English were waging war, the latter dying of hunger, the French fed them. —I will not go beyond that: it is God's choice.

The greatest legend of our time is soon to come. It is seen in a frightening seed sprouting around 1360, and which becomes radiating sublime, charming and touching, in 1430 (third and fifth volumes).

France had glimpsed the city and its towns. But what about the country? Who knows about it before the fourteenth century? That vast world of shadows, those countless, ignored masses, break through one morning. In the third volume (principally erudition), I was not on guard, was expecting nothing, when the form of *Jacques,* standing up on a furrow, blocked my path; a monstrous and frightful form. I felt a convulsive contraction in my heart... Great God! Is this my father? The man of the Middle Ages?... "Yes," he answered, "Look how I am made! Behold a thousand years of sorrows!..." Those sorrows, I felt them immediately as they flowed up into me from the depths of time... It was he, it was I (same soul and same person) who had endured all this... From these thousand years, a tear came to me, burning, as heavy as a world, which soaked through the page. None (friend, enemy) went by there without weeping.

The appearance was dreadful, but the voice was tender. My pain increased with this. Beneath this frightening mask was a human soul. Deep, cruel mystery. It cannot be understood without going back a little.

Saint Francis, a child who does not know what he says, and who speaks the better for it, tells those who ask who wrote *The Imitation*: "The author is the Holy Spirit."

"The Holy Spirit," says Joachim de Flore, "is he *whose reign arrives after the reign of Jesus.*"

It is the spirit of union, of love, finally emerging from the suffocation of legend. The free associations of brotherhoods, free towns, were for the most part under this benediction. Such was, in 1200, in the Albigensian period, the cult of both the free towns, and the knights of southern France, the worship of a new spirit which the Church drowned in torrents of blood.

The Spirit, frail dove, seems to perish there, to disappear. It becomes from that moment airborne, and will be breathed everywhere.

Even in that little book, *The Imitation,* so monastic and devout, are found some passages of absolute solitude in which the Spirit manifestly replaces everything, in which nothing is seen anymore, neither priest nor Church. If one hears its interior voices in the convents, how much more so in the forests, in the free boundless Church! —It was the Spirit speaking, from the depths of the oaks, when Joan of Arc heard it and shuddered; she said tenderly: "My voices!"

Holy voices, voices of the conscience, which Joan of Arc carries with her into battles, into prisons, against the English, against the Church. There the world is changed. The passive resignation of Christians (so useful to tyrants) is superseded by the heroic tenderness which takes our griefs to heart, which wants to set God's justice here below, a justice which will act, which will combat, save and heal.

Who worked this miracle, so contrary to the Gospel? a superior love, *love in action,* love until death, "the pity which was in the kingdom of France."

What a divine spectacle when on the scaffold, the girl, abandoned and alone against the priest-king, the murderous Church, upholds in the midst of the flames her interior Church, and takes flight saying: "My voices!"

My Historical Method Reveals the Genius of France

I should mention at this point how much my history, so glibly accused of "poetry," of "passion," has on the contrary retained its solidity and lucidity, even in touching subjects where it might be excusable to shut one's eyes. Everyone has hesitated at the Joan of Arc story, observing through their tears the flames of the stake. While I was doubtlessly moved, I saw clearly however, and I noticed two things:

1. The innocent heroine, without suspecting it, did much more than rescue France, she rescued the future by establishing the new standard, the opposite of Christian passivity. The modern hero *is the hero of action.* The deadly doctrine, which our friend Renan still praises excessively, of passive, interior freedom, preoccupied with its own salvation, which hands the world over to evil, abandons it to tyrants, that doctrine expires on the pyre at Rouen, and in a mystic form foretells the French Revolution.

2. I have in this grand narration practiced and demonstrated something new, from which the young might benefit: it is the fact that the *historical method* is often the opposite of *strictly literary art*. —The writer occupied with trying to increase his effects, to make things stand out, almost always likes to surprise, to seize the reader, to make him exclaim: "Ah!" The writer is happy if the natural event appears miraculous. —On the contrary, the historian has as his special mission to explain whatever appears miraculous, to lavish it with precedents, the circumstances which lead up to it, —to bring it back to nature. Here, I should say, I deserve credit. In admiring, loving this sublime personality, I have shown to what degree it was natural.

The sublime is not at all outside nature; it is on the contrary the moment at which nature is most itself, in its natural height and depth. In the fourteenth and fifteenth centuries, in their excessive miseries, in their horrible extremities, the heart grows larger. The crowd is a hero. There were in those times many Joans of Arc, at least as regards courage. I meet many of them along my route: example, this fourteenth-century peasant, le Grand Ferré; example, in the fifteenth century, Jeanne Hachette who defends and saves Beauvais. Profiles of these naïve heroes appear often to me in the histories of our free towns.

I have told the facts quite plainly. From the moment when the English lost their mainstay, the Duke of Burgundy, they became very weak. On the contrary, the French, rallying their armed forces of the South, became extremely strong. But this produced no harmony. The charming personality of this young country girl, with her tender, emotional and joyous heart (heroic gaiety burst forth in all her responses), became a center and united everything. She was effective precisely because she had no art, no thaumaturgy, no enchantments, no miracles. All her charm is humanity. She has no wings, this poor angel; she is the common people, she is weak, she is us, she is everyone.

Treading the Path toward the Revolution

In the lonely galleries of the Archives where I wandered for twenty years, in that deep silence, murmurs nevertheless would reach my ears. The distant sufferings of so many souls, stifled in ancient times, would moan softly. Stern reality protested against art, and occasionally had bitter words for it: "What are you fooling around with? Are you another Walter Scott, recounting at great length picturesque details, the sumptuous meals of Philip the Good, the empty Pheasant's vow? Do you know that our martyrs have been expecting you for four hundred years? Do you know that the valliant men of Courtray, of Rosebecque, do not have the monument which history owed them? The salaried chroniclers, Froissart the chaplain, Monstrelet the chatterbox, do not suffice. It was with firm faith, with the hope of justice that they gave their lives. They have the right to say, "History! Settle with us! Your creditors are summoning you. We accepted death for one line from you!"

What did I owe them? To recount their battles, to place myself in their ranks, to go halves with them in victory or defeat? That was not enough. During the ten years of strenuous perseverance when I reproduced the struggle of the northern towns, I undertook much more. I redid everything from top to bottom so as to restore to them their life, their arts, especially their rights.

First, the right which these cities had over the regions; that was the most sacred of rights, for they had created the land itself, reclaimed it from the waters, constructed life-producing canals, the protection, the circulatory system of the region. These cities had produced and created. Their masters have destroyed. Oh how that world, so lively then, is today so pallid! What is the whole of Belgium compared with Ghent or Bruges, compared with that Liège of former days, from which each launched armies?

I dived into the populace. While Olivier de la Marche and Chastellain were lolling around at the meals of the Golden Fleece, I probed the wine cellars where Flanders was fermenting, with her masses of valiant workers and mystics. I piously restored all their powerful *Friendships* (the name of their towns), their *Candid Truths* (the name of their gatherings), not forgetting their bells, and their brotherly chimes. I put back my great bronze friend, the dreaded Roelandt, into his tower, whose solemn voice, which, ringing for ten leagues, made John the Fearless and Charles the Bold quake.

One very essential point which the contemporaries and our moderns neglected is to distinguish sharply, to characterize the particular personality of each city. That is its true reality, the charm of this diversified country. I clung to that task; it was a religion for me to reconstruct the soul of each of those ancient and cherished cities, and that could be done only by showing clearly how each trade and each way of life created a race of workers. I put Ghent aside, deep hive of battles, with its devout people and valiant weavers. Aside as well, the friendly and great Bruges, the seventeen nations of its merchants, the three hundred painters who made of one city an Italy. And Ypres, the Pompeii of Flanders, today deserted, which preserves its true monument, the prodigious market place where all trades met, this cathedral of labor where every good worker should remove his hat.

The conflagration of Dinant, the cruel end of Liège, close this history of the free towns with a heartbreaking tragedy. Myself a child of the Meuse on my mother's side, I had a family involvement with it. Those poor French nations, lost in the Ardennes, between hostile peoples and competing languages, moved me greatly. I gave back to the people of Liège the great renovator, Van Eyck, who transformed painting. I discovered, unearthed from the ashes of Dinant, its lost arts, so dear to the Middle Ages, humble arts, so touching, which were the kind servants, the family friends of all Europe.

How can I thank my friends, my avengers, the good Swiss chroniclers who luckily arrive with their hunting horns and lances at the great hunt of Morat, and who bring to bay the wild boar, that cruel beast, Charles the Bold? Their narratives are heroically gay songs. It is a pleasure to see this frightful swelling bombast punctured, all of a sudden flattened. One undeniably favors Louis XI in his tricky struggle against barbaric pride, feudal brutality. He is a fox who nets the fake lion. Wit at least triumphs. The refined and firm prose of Comines overcomes gross rhetoric, counterfeit knighthood. An irony, still petty and malicious, worthy of the medieval fables, is present in history. Tomorrow, strong and powerful, history will become fruitful in the great days of the Renaissance.

This good king, Louis XI, stopped me for a very long time. My entire fifteenth century came forth from records, manuscript fragments. The extremely vast work of Legrand nonetheless requires verification of his often very inexact transcriptions against the originals (Gaignières, etc.), a work requiring great patience.

I entered through Louis XI into the centuries of monarchy. I was about to undertake this study when an accident made me reflect deeply. One day, passing through Reims, I examined in great detail the magnificent cathedral, the splendid church of the Coronation.

The interior cornice from which you can walk around the church at a height of eighty feet makes it appear enchanting, of flowery richness, a permanent hallelujah. In the hollow vastness, you always think you hear the great official hubbub, spoken by the voice of the populace. You think you see at the windows the birds which were released when the clergy, anointing the king, made the pact between the Throne and the Church. Going back outside over the arches in the immense panorama which embraces all Champagne, I came to the last little steeple, exactly above the chancel. There a strange scene amazed me. The round tower was wreathed with tortured criminals. One has a rope around his neck. Another has lost an ear. The mutilated are more wretched there than the dead. How right they are! What a frightful contrast! What! The Church of festivals, this bride, has taken this lugubrious ornament as a wedding necklace! This pillory of the people is set above the altar. But could not their tears, through the arches, have fallen upon the heads of kings! Fearful anointing of the Revolution, of the anger of God! "I will not understand the centuries of monarchy if first, above all, I do not establish within myself the soul and the faith of the people." I spoke these words to myself, and, after Louis XI, I wrote the *Revolution* (1845–1853).

I Bid Farewell to Modern France

Readers were taken aback, but nothing was more prudent. After many ordeals which I have recounted elsewhere and through which I glimpsed closely the other shore, dead and repudiated, I created the *Renaissance* with centupled strength. When I returned, faced backwards and reexamined my Middle Ages, that superb sea of folly, I was seized with a violent hilarity, and in the sixteenth and seventeenth centuries I made dreadful festivities. Rabelais and Voltaire laughed in their graves. The splintered gods, the rotten kings appeared unveiled. The insipid history of conventionality, that shameful prude with which people were content, disappeared. From the Medicis to Louis XIV a harsh autopsy set forth the character of this government of corpses (1855–1868).

Such a history was sure to succeed, to offend every friend of falsehood. But this means many people, particularly people of approved authority. Priests and royalists howled. The doctrinaires did their best to smile.

These reactions made very little difference to that patient history. It is strong, solid, well established, and it will wait.

In my successive prefaces and in my explanatory notes, one can see from volume to volume the foundations which are underneath, the enormous base of records and manuscripts, or rare publications, etc., on which it rests.[1]

1. I do not want to anticipate here. In only one or two words I can say: It is this book, "this book of a poet and a man of imagination," which, by its successive parts, has told everybody whatever was important to them:

To the Protestants, the very essential fact of the Saint-Bartholemew's Day Massacre toils fifteen days early in Brussels (Granvelle papers, August 10). Then, so many facts about the Revocation of the Edict of Nantes, which they had illuminated very little.

To the Royalists, a whole world of curious anecdotal facts; for example, the legend of the *Iron Mask* and the wisdom of their queen. The letters of Franklin (1863) have revealed the secret, on the authority of Richelieu, and have proven that I alone was right.

To the financiers, Law's system (unexplained by M. Thiers in 1826) is finally elucidated, both by the manuscripts and by the histories of the Paris and London Stock Exchanges.

As for the Revolution, what can I say? Mine emerged entirely from the three great bodies of archives of our times which are in Paris. Could Louis Blanc (despite his talent, his merit which I respect) have guessed the nature of the Revolution? Could he have recreated it in London with a few brochures? I cannot believe it. —Read moreover and compare.

This is how forty years were spent. I hardly suspected it when I began. I believed I was going to write an abridged history of a few volumes in perhaps four years, in six years. But one can abridge only what is well known. And neither myself, nor anyone, knew that history.

After my first two volumes only, I caught a glimpse of this *terra incognita*. I said: "Ten years are necessary... No, twenty more, thirty more... And the road grew longer before me. I did not complain. On exploratory voyages one's heart is extended, grows, sees nothing other than the goal. One forgets oneself entirely. So it happened with me. I lost sight of myself, I stayed away from myself. I lived parallel to the world, and I took history for life.

Behold my history has flowed away. I regret nothing. Well, what would I ask for, cherished France, with whom I have lived, whom I leave with such deep regret! With what companionship I have spent forty years (ten centuries) with you! So many passionate, noble, severe hours we have had together, often winter itself, before the dawn! So many days of labor and studies in the depths of the Archives! I worked for you, I went, came, searched, wrote. Each day I would give of myself entirely, perhaps still more. The next morning, finding you at my table, I believed myself identical with you, strong with your powerful life and your eternal youth.

But how, having enjoyed the remarkable fortune of such companionship, having lived long years through your great soul, how have I not profited more within myself? Oh! The answer is, in order to restore all this for you I have had to tread again that long course of misery, strewn with cruel chance, with hundreds of diseased and deadly things. I have drunk too much bitterness. I have swallowed too many plagues, too many vipers, and too many kings.

Very well! My great France, if in order to retrieve your life, a man had to give himself, to cross and recross so many times the river of death, he will get over it, he thanks you still. And his greatest sorrow is that he must leave you here.

Paris, 1870.

Notes

Unless otherwise noted, all French books cited in the endnotes were published in Paris and all English books cited were published in New York.

Introduction

1. Ernst Cassirer, *An Essay on Man* (New Haven: Yale University Press, 1944), p. 185.

2. For accounts of Michelet's place as a philosopher of history see Oscar A. Haac, *Les Principes inspirateurs de Michelet* (New Haven: Yale University Press; Presses Universitaires de France, 1950) and Paul Viallaneix's masterwork—indispensable to all Michelet scholars—*La Voie royale: Essai sur l'idée de Peuple dans l'oeuvre de Michelet* (Delagrave, 1959; Flammarion, 1971). See also Emery Neff, *The Poetry of History* (Columbia University Press, 1947); John Atherton, "Michelet: Three Conceptions of Historical Becoming," *Studies in Romanticism* IV, 1 (1964), 220–39, and Charles Rearick, *Beyond the Enlightenment: Historians and Folklore in Nineteenth-Century France* (Bloomington: Indiana University Press, 1974).

The reviews *L'Arc, Europe,* and the *Revue d'histoire littéraire de la France* have devoted special issues to Michelet, in response to the centenary of his death; see also the collective volume *Michelet cent ans après* (Presses Universitaires de Grenoble, 1975); *Clio* was the first American journal devoted to Michelet (Winter, 1977).

3. According to the stipulations of Madame Michelet's will, these journals were inaccessible to the public until 1950. See the excellent editions of: *Ecrits de Jeunesse. Journal (1820–1823). Mémorial. Journal des Idées,* ed. Paul Viallaneix (Gallimard, 1959); *Journal,* vol. 1 (1828–1848), ed. Paul Viallaneix (Gallimard, 1959); *Journal,* vol. 2 (1848–1860), ed. Paul Viallaneix (Gallimard, 1962); *Journal,* vols. 3 and 4 (1861–1874), ed. Claude Digeon (Gallimard, in press).

4. Quoted by Paul Viallaneix in his introduction to *l'Histoire de France,* vol. 4 of the *Oeuvres complètes* (Flammarion, 1974), p. 99. This is the definitive edition, published under the direction of M. Viallaneix with the aid of the Centre de recherches révolutionnaires et romantiques of the University of Clermont-Ferrand.

5. Reprinted in Taine, *Essais de critique et d'histoire,* 6th edition (Hachette, 1892), p. 101; originally published in the *Revue de l'instruction publique,* February 1855.

6. *The People,* trans. G. H. Smith (D. Appleton and Co., 1845) p. 22; *Le Peuple,* ed. Refort (Marcel Didier, 1946), p. 26; McKay translation, p. 16.

7. Ernst Cassirer, *An Essay on Man,* p. 187. See R. G. Collingwood, *The Idea of History* (Oxford University Press, 1946), especially part v, sect. 4; cf. Leon Goldstein, "Collingwood's Theory of Historical Knowing," *History and Theory* IX

(1970), 3–36. The next quotation is from Emery Neff, *The Poetry of History* (Columbia University Press, 1947), p. 217.

8. Cited by Paul Viallaneix, *La Voie royale* (Flammarion, 1971), p. 362.

9. See Roland Barthes, *Michelet par lui-même* (Le Seuil, 1954; 1962), especially pp. 177–80 on how to read Michelet. I have been inspired by Barthes (and Bachelard), but have preferred to take Michelet's ideas more seriously.

10. Gustave Flaubert, *Correspondance: Supplement,* vol. II, edited by R. Dumesnil, J. Prommier and Cl. Digeon (Louis Conard, 1954), p. 20; to Madame Roger de Genettes, November 1864.

11. From his preface to Michelet, *Oeuvres complètes,* vol. I (Flammarion, 1971), p. 10.

12. René Wellek, "The Concept of Romanticism in Literary History," in *Romanticism: Points of View,* 2nd edition, edited by Robert F. Gleckner and Gerald E. Enscoe (New Jersey: Prentice-Hall, Inc., 1970), p. 193; cf. Morse Peckham, "Toward a Theory of Romanticism," as well as the other outstanding essays in the same collection.

The most recent and far-reaching explorations of the various forms of Romanticism are: Henri Peyre, *Qu'est-ce que le romantisme?* (Presses Universitaires de France, 1971), and Hans Eichner, editor, *'Romantic' and its Cognates: The European History of a Word* (Toronto: University of Toronto Press, 1972), especially Maurice Z. Shroder's contribution on France, pp. 263–92. These two books will provide all the bibliographical information necessary for an extensive examination of theories of Romanticism. See also Arthur O. Lovejoy's now classic essay, "On the Discrimination of Romanticisms," *Essays in the History of Ideas* (Baltimore: The Johns Hopkins Press, 1948), reprinted in the Gleckner and Enscoe anthology.

13. See *The People,* final chapter of part three, entitled "God in the Nation."

14. For the context of Michelet's social Romanticism see Maxime Leroy, *Histoire des idées sociales en France,* vol. 3, *D'Auguste Comte à P. J. Proudhon* (Gallimard, 1954), and D. O. Evans, *Le Socialisme romantique: Pierre Leroux et ses contemporains* (Marcel Rivière, 1948).

For lively introductions to the question see Albert L. Guérard, *French Prophets of Yesterday: A Study of Religious Thought Under the Second Empire* (D. Appleton and Co., 1913) and Frank E. Manuel, *The Prophets of Paris:* Turgot, Condorcet, Saint-Simon, Fourier, Comte (Harper Torchbooks, 1962). The most recent and detailed study of the poet-teacher in literature is the superb book of Paul Bénichou, *Le Sacre de l'écrivain, 1750–1830* (José Corti, 1973).

Michelet commits himself to the Romantic socialists in the following letter he wrote to the Minister of Public Education, in February 1848:

Monsieur le ministre:

L'Académie des sciences morales et politiques, la fille de la Révolution, le laboratoire futur des réformes sociales, n'a que trente membres. Les autres académies plus anciennes, en ont quarante.

J'ai l'honneur de vous demander qu'elle soit complétée par la nomination des citoyens, dont suivent les noms; ils ont, à titres divers, bien mérité de la patrie.

Béranger. Il acceptera sans doute maintenant qu'il s'agira d'une coopération sérieuse.

Arago

Lamennais

Lamartine

Quinet

Louis Blanc

Mickiewicz (Tout polonais est français)

Pierre Leroux (l'illustre ouvrier)

J. Reynaud (le premier métaphysicien du temps, jusqu'ici écarté de l'Institut par l'éclectisme.)

Ajouter à ces noms celui de George Sand, le premier écrivain socialiste, qui vient dans ses deux derniers ouvrages de créer une littérature nouvelle, espoir immense d'avenir.

Je vous prie, Monsieur le ministre, d'agréer mon hommage fraternel.

(Unsigned draft of an unpublished letter conserved at the Bibliothèque historique de la Ville de Paris, Ms. *cote* A. 4822*bis*, f. 225.)

15. A. L. Chassin, *Edgar Quinet* (1859), p. 64; cited by Gabriel Monod, "Michelet dans l'histoire de son temps," *Bibliothèque universelle et Revue suisse,* ser. 4, vol. 60 (June 1911), 465, n. 1. The next quotation is from Jules Vallès, *Le Bachelier* (Garnier-Flammarion, 1964), chap. 6, p. 89; cited by Paul Viallaneix, "A l'école buissonnière," *L'Arc,* no. 52 (1973), p. 60.

16. Marcel Proust writes of Michelet's great preface of 1869 to *The History of France* and his preface to *The History of the French Revolution* in a way which also defines the essential role of the historian's educational works: ". . . les plus grands écrivains ont manqué leurs livres, mais, se regardant travailler comme s'ils étaient à la fois l'ouvrier et le juge, ont tiré de cette auto-contemplation une beauté nouvelle extérieure et supérieure à l'œuvre, lui imposant rétroactivement une unité, une grandeur qu'elle n'a pas. . . . ne peut-on dire . . . de ce dernier [Michelet] qu'il incarne si bien le XIXe siècle que, les plus grandes beautés de Michelet, il ne faut pas tant les chercher dans son œuvre même que dans les attitudes qu'il prend en face de son œuvre, non pas dans son *Histoire de France* ou dans son *Histoire de la Révolution,* mais dans ses préfaces à ces deux livres? Préfaces, c'est-à-dire pages écrites après eux, où il les considère, et auxquelles il faut joindre ça et là quelques phrases commençant d'habitude par un 'Le dirai-je?' qui n'est pas une précaution de savant, mais une cadence de musicien" (*A la recherche du temps perdu,* vol. III, "Bibliothèque de la Pléiade" [Gallimard, 1954], p. 160). This reference is due to the attentive friendship of Professor Albert J. Salvan, Brown University.

17. The only published study of Michelet's natural histories, until the present work, was Robert Van der Elst, *Michelet naturaliste: Esquisse de son système de philosophie* (Delagrave, 1914). Van der Elst's use of quotations out of context leads him to a complete misunderstanding of Michelet's philosophy: reacting against the historian's anticlericalism, the author mistakenly demonstrates that he is a pantheist. See chapter 6, especially note 4.

Add to this work the sensitive and subtle Yale University doctoral dissertation of Linda Orr, *Michelet the Naturalist: The Dialectics and Stylistics of Metamorphosis* (September 1971) which is much more psychologically oriented than my own dissertation (Columbia University, May 1970) which was the starting point for the present book. Professor Orr has extended her thesis in *Jules Michelet: Nature, History, and Language* (Ithaca, New York: Cornell University Press, 1976) which I could not consult before *Michelet's Poetic Vision* went to press.

18. *La Montagne,* 1st edition (Librairie internationale, 1868), p. iv; *The Mountain,* translated by W. H. Davenport Adams (London: T. Nelson and Sons, 1872), p. vii.

1 Jules Michelet: Historian, Philosopher, Naturalist

1. *The People*, trans. G. H. Smith (D. Appleton and Co., 1846), p. 19; *Le Peuple*, ed. Lucien Refort (Didier, 1946), p. 17. The following passage is from pp. 19 and 18 of the English and French versions respectively. There is a good updated translation of *The People* by John P. McKay (Urbana: University of Illinois Press, 1973). In my text I quote from the Smith translation (with my corrections), but shall also give page references to the McKay version. The above pages are to be found in McKay, pp. 13–14.

2. *The People*, p. 23; *Le Peuple*, p. 24; McKay, p. 18.

3. *Journal*, vol. II (1849–1860), edited by Paul Viallaneix (Gallimard, 1962), p. 191. See the entire entry (pp. 191–94) for one of Michelet's most significant moments of self-examination.

4. The drama of Michelet's attitudes toward different regimes is succinctly described by Gabriel Monod, "La Place de Michelet dans l'histoire de son temps," *Bibliothèque universelle et Revue suisse*, ser. 4, vol. 60 (June 1911), 449–70. The historian's exchange with Carnot cited below is from Monod, p. 466. See also Jacques Seebacher, "L'attitude politique de Michelet," *Revue des travaux de l'Académie des science morales* (1967), pp. 107–22.

5. *The Bird*, translated by A. E. [W. H. Davenport Adams] (London: T. Nelson and Sons, 1869), p. 52; *Oiseau*, 6th edition (Hachette, 1859), p. xlix.

6. Taine, *Essais de critique et d'histoire*, 6th edition (Hachette, 1892), p. 134. First published in the *Revue de l'instruction publique*, 24 March 1856.

7. *Ma Jeunesse* (1798–1820) (Marpon et Flammarion, 1884); *Mon Journal* (1820–1823) (Marpon et Flammarion, 1888); *Rome* (Marpon et Flammarion, 1891); *Sur les chemins de l'Europe* (Marpon et Flammarion, 1893). Madame Michelet's corruptions of her husband's manuscripts have been studied: see Roland Barthes, *Michelet par lui-même* (Le Seuil, 1954), pp. 180–81; Paul Viallaneix in his introduction to *Ecrits de Jeunesse*, pp. 23–36; introduction to *Journal* I, pp. 11–28.

8. *Journal* II, p. 290.

9. Disputes as to the nature books' value as a true expression of Michelet's concerns and imagination originate in Mme. Michelet's legal litigation, after her husband's death, to support her role as "collaborator," so that she could collect fifty percent of the author's rights. Michelet's last will and testament indeed states: "Ce fut seulement en 1856 que ma situation commença à se relever par le succès de *L'Oiseau*. Ainsi toute notre fortune a été acquise pendent la durée de mon second mariage. Ma femme y contribua non-seulement par sa vie économique, mais très-activement par une *collaboration* continuelle. Elle revoyait mes épreuves et préparait mes livres d'Histoire naturelle (*Oiseau, Insecte, Mer, Montagne*) par des lectures, extraits, etc. Et même elle a écrit des parties considérables de ces livres" (from "Dépôt du testament olographe de Mr. J. Michelet, 16 février 1874," conserved at the Bibliothèque historique de la Ville de Paris).

10. The manuscripts are at the Bibliothèque historique de la Ville de Paris (*cotes* A. 3842–3853).

11. From Papiers Dumesnil. Correspondence 1855: provisional *cote* 5740 at the Bibliothèque historique.

12. *Journal*, vol. I (1828–1848), edited by Paul Viallaneix (Gallimard, 1959), pp. 405–6. Hereafter cited as *Journal* I.

13. *Introduction à l'Histoire Universelle* (with *Tableau de la France, 1869 Préface à l'Histoire de France*), ed. Charles Morazé (Armand Colin, 1962), p. 35;

also published in Michelet, *Oeuvres complètes,* vol. II, edited by Paul Viallaneix (Flammarion, 1972), p. 229.

14. *1869 Préface à l'Histoire de France,* ed. Morazé, p. 183.

15. *Nos Fils* (Calmann-Lévy, 1903), p. 115.

16. *Histoire de la Révolution française,* vol. I, ed. Gérald Walter (Gallimard, 1952), pp. 58–59; cf. ibid., pp. 415–16 on Kant. Michelet's affinity with Kant can be explained somewhat by Kant's own affection for Rousseau. One can explore the remarkable conjunction of possible influences suggested in the present chapter in Ernst Cassirer, *Rousseau, Kant and Goethe* (Harper Torchbooks, 1963). Cf. also Vallois, *La Formation de l'influence kantienne en France* (Félix Alcan, 1924), and especially Oscar A. Haac, *Michelet et l'histoire allemande* (Unpublished dissertation, Yale University, 1948).

17. *Nos Fils,* pp. vi–vii.

18. "[L'homme] est le puissant ouvrier, il est le créateur fort d'un prodigieux monde de science, d'industrie, de richesse.... A côté de la nature, il en a bâti une autre de son génie et de sa force" (*L'Amour* [Calmann-Lévy, 1894]), p. 426. See also *Nos Fils,* p. 245, and *Histoire de la Révolution française,* vol. II, p. 821.

19. At the level of a general history of ideas, Michelet should be added to J. B. Bury, *The Idea of Progress* (London: Macmillan and Co., 1920) which does not mention him. For contemporary witnesses see Eugène Pelletan, *Profession de foi du XIXᵉ siècle* (Pagnerre, 1852), and Jean-Félix Nourrisson, *Tableau des progrès de la pensée humaine, depuis Thalès jusqu'à Leibniz* (Didier, 1858; 3rd edition, 1867: ... *jusqu'à Hegel*). Cf. *Larousse du XIXᵉ siècle,* s.v. "Progrès," for the perspective most characteristic of the time.

20. *Nos Fils,* pp. 258–59.

21. Perhaps the most interesting of the books which both reflects and studies Michelet's period is A. de Quatrefages, *Charles Darwin et ses précurseurs français; Etude sur le transformisme* (Germer Baillière, 1870). Also Edmond Perrier, *La Philosophie zoologique avant Darwin,* 3rd ed. (Félix Alcan, 1896).

On Lamarck, see M. Landrieu, *Lamarck, le fondateur du transformisme* (Soc. Zool., 1909), which is still the best introduction. For the most recent state of affairs see Ernest Mayer, "Lamarck Revisited," *Journal of the History of Biology,* 5, 1 (Spring 1972), 55–94.

For a broader sense of the period see Bentley Glass, O. Temkin, and W. L. Straus, Jr., eds., *Forerunners of Darwin* (Baltimore: Johns Hopkins Press, 1959), and, of course, Loren Eiseley, *Darwin's Century: Evolution and the Men Who Discovered It* (Doubleday and Co., 1958). There remains to be written for the nineteenth century what Jacques Roger did for the eighteenth in *Les Sciences de la vie dans la pensée française du XVIIIᵉ siècle* (Armand Colin, 1963); a beginning has been made by Judith Schlanger in her excellent *Les Métaphores de l'organisme* (Vrin, 1971), which does not include Michelet.

22. Words of Geoffroy Saint-Hilaire cited without reference by F. Godefroy, *Histoire de la littérature française, XIXᵉ siècle,* vol. 2, 2nd edition. Paris, 1881 (Liechtenstein: Kraus Reprint Ltd., 1967), p. 612.

23. I follow in general the account of the debate by Théophile Cahn, *La Vie et l'œuvre d'Etienne Geoffroy Saint-Hilaire* (Presses Universitaires de France, 1962), chaps. 20, 21. Also useful was Edmond Perrier, *La Philosophie Zoologique avant Darwin,* and "[Etienne] Geoffroy Saint-Hilaire: Sa vie et sa doctrine," *Revue Britannique,* ser. 8, 11 (October 1857), 257–95. The primary texts are published in the

Annales des sciences naturelles: for a summary of the debates (March–April 1830), vol. XIX, "Revue bibliographique," 18–47; for Cuvier's first attack against Geoffroy, "Considérations sur les Mollusques, et en particulier sur les Céphalopods," ibid., vol. XIX (March 1830), 241–59; and "Réflexions de Goethe sur les débats scientifiques de mars 1830 dans le sein de l'Académie des Sciences," ibid., vol. XXII (1831), 179–88, followed by a defense of Goethe by Geoffroy Saint-Hilaire, pp. 188–93.

24. Cited by Cahn, *La Vie et l'œuvre*, pp. 197–98.

25. *Annales des sciences naturelles*, vol. 19 (1830), p. 45; and cited by Goethe, ibid., vol. XXII (1831), pp. 186–87.

26. See C.-A. Sainte-Beuve, "M. Ampère," in *Portraits littéraires* (Garnier, 1862); article originally published, with one by Emile Littré, in the *Revue des deux mondes* (15 February 1837). Cf. the anonymous article of Ampère (cited by Michelet, *L'Insecte*, p. 380) in *Annales des sciences naturelles*, vol. II (1824), pp. 295 ff. See Cahn, pp. 203–4 for the next quotation.

27. *Conversations of Goethe with Eckermann and Soret*, trans. John Oxenford (London: George Bell and Sons, 1882), pp. 479–80. For Michelet's accounts: *L'Oiseau*, pp. 38–39, *L'Insecte*, p. 380. Cf. Stephen F. Mason, *A History of the Sciences* (Collier Books, 1962), pp. 385–86.

28. See Gabriel Monod, "Isidore Geoffroy Saint-Hilaire et Michelet," *Revue politique et littéraire. Revue Bleue* (14 October 1911), pp. 481–84. I have gathered and transcribed for publication Isidore's letters to Michelet which will appear with my critical edition of *L'Oiseau* and *L'Insecte* in the *Oeuvres complètes*, Flammarion.

29. Isidore Geoffroy Saint-Hilaire, *Histoire naturelle des règnes organiques, principalement étudiée chez l'homme et les animaux*, vol. I (Victor Masson, 1854), composed of papers first presented to the Academy of Sciences in 1851. Isidore Geoffroy, pp. 332–33.

30. See Schelling, *Ideen zur einer Naturphilosophie*, 1797; *Weltseele*, 1798; *Entwurf eines Systems*, 1799. The best works on Schelling are Emile Bréhier, *Schelling* (Félix Alcan, 1912), and the classic, Heinrich Knittermeyer, *Schelling und die Romantische Schule* (München: E. Reinhardt, 1929).

A basic work to be read in conjunction with the present study is Alexander Gode-von Aesch, *Natural Science in German Romanticism* (AMA Press, 1966; 1st ed. 1941).

31. Wilhelm Windelband, *A History of Philosophy*, vol. II (Harper Torchbooks, 1958), pp. 598–99.

32. It would be valuable to trace Schelling's influence in France, starting with Mme. de Stael *De l'Allemagne* (1810). To that end I cite references included by Isidore Geoffroy (pp. 295–97): Willm, *Histoire de la philosophie allemande depuis Kant jusqu'à Hegel*, vol. III, 1847, pp. 72 et seq.; pp. 204–37, pp. 366 et seq.; vol. IV, 1849, p. 605. Ch. de Rémusat, *Rapport: Mémoires de l'Académie des sciences morales et politiques*, vol. V, 1847, pp. 223–37. Matter, *Schelling, ou la Philosophie de la nature et la révélation*, Paris, 1845. Barchou de Penhoen, *Histoire de la philosophie allemande depuis Leibnitz jusqu'à nos jours*, Paris, 1836. See also, Louis Wihl, "Des phases diverses de la philosophie allemande depuis Kant," *La Revue contemporaine* (September 1858), pp. 308–25; ibid. (October 1858), pp. 470–95. See also Judith Schlanger, *Les Métaphores de l'organisme*, op. cit.

33. This and the following quotations are from Isidore Geoffroy, pp. 304–7.

34. This and the following from Isidore Geoffroy, pp. 116–17. These epistemological matters, concerning Michelet's thought, have been treated in our chapter 7, "The Two Sexes of the Mind."

35. Henri Milne-Edwards, *Rapport sur les progrès récents des sciences zoologiques en France.* "Publication faite sous les auspices du Ministère de l'instruction publique" (L'Imprimerie impériale, Hachette, 1867), p. 15.

2 Evolution: The Constant Metamorphosis

1. The quotations in this and the next paragraph are from the *Oeuvres complètes,* vol. IV (Flammarion, 1974), pp. 383–84; also *Tableau de la France,* ed. Morazé (Armand Colin, 1962), pp. 158–59.

2. This and the next quotation are taken from *The Sea,* trans. W. H. Davenport Adams (London: T. Nelson and Sons, 1875), pp. 118–20; *La Mer,* 1st ed. (Hachette, 1861), pp. 149–52.

3. This terminology relating to the structure of the metaphor is borrowed from I. A. Richards, *The Philosophy of Rhetoric* (1936), chaps. 5–6; it is examined by Max Black, *Models and Metaphors* (Ithaca, N. Y.: Cornell University Press, 1962), p. 47, note 23.

4. *Dictionnaire universel d'histoire naturelle* (1839–1849), ed. Charles d'Orbigny (1860–1876), s.v. "Transformation." Cf. *Larousse du XIXe siècle,* s.v. "Métamorphose" (published in 1874) which quotes Michelet on insects. The only appropriate use of "metamorphosis" to imply modern evolution theory is a geological usage: "The concept of metamorphism, i.e., the transformation of preexisting rocks into new types by the action of heat, pressure, stress and chemically active fluids, was later defined by Sir Charles Lyell" (René Taton, ed. *Science in the Nineteenth Century,* trans. A. J. Pomerans [London: Thames and Hudson, 1965], p. 322).

5. See Loren Eiseley, *Darwin's Century,* p. 118, note. For a beginning for what should prove to be a fruitful study of the influence of natural history on French literature see S. de Sacy, "Balzac, Geoffroy Saint-Hilaire et l'unité de composition," *Mercure de France* (1 June 1948), pp. 292–305, and (1 July 1948), pp. 469–80; Théophile Cahn, *La Vie et l'œuvre de Geoffroy Saint-Hilaire,* chap. 23, "Balzac et l'œuvre de Geoffroy Saint-Hilaire," Pierre Albouy, *La Création mythologique chez Victor Hugo* (Corti, 1963); Hélène Tuzet, *Le Cosmos et l'imagination* (Corti, 1965); Judith Schlanger, *Les Métaphores de l'organisme,* op. cit.

6. [Jean-Louis] A. [Armand] de Quatrefages [de Bréau], *Charles Darwin et ses précurseurs français* (Germer Baillière, 1870), pp. 11–12.

7. See Gertrude Himmelfarb, *Darwin and the Darwinian Revolution* (Doubleday Anchor Books, 1959), chap. 7, p. 443, note 1; cited by Etienne Gilson, *D'Aristote à Darwin et retour* (Vrin, 1970), p. 88, note 9, a book which contains an excellent summary of this historical problem. For a summary at a glance of the state of the word evolution in Michelet's day see *Larousse du XIXe siècle,* s.v. "Evolution" (pub. 1870).

8. *Sea,* p. 318; *Mer,* p. 423; cf. *Mer,* pp. 166–67.

9. The history of this idea has received its definitive treatment in the classic work of Arthur Lovejoy, *The Great Chain of Being* (Harper Torchbooks, 1960; 1st ed. 1936).

10. See Joseph A. Mazzeo, *The Design of Life: Major Themes in the Development of Biological Thought* (Pantheon Books, 1967), pp. 41–42 et seq. for a short history of the vitalism/mechanism controversy—a lucid and far-ranging introduction to the history of biology.

11. *The Mountain,* trans. W. H. Davenport Adams (London: T. Nelson and Sons, 1872), p. 113; *La Montagne,* 1st ed. (Librairie internationale, 1868), p. 119.

The following two quotations are found on pp. 113–15 and 119–20 of the English and French versions respectively.

12. *Montagne*, pp. 372–73; cf. ibid., pp. 127–28; and *Oiseau*, pp. 292–93, 300.

13. This and the following passage are taken from *Sea*, pp. 98–100; *Mer*, pp. 115–24. Compare to Michel Serres, "Michelet, la soupe," *Revue d'histoire littéraire de la France* 74 (September–October 1974), 787–802. M. Serres uses the model of thermodynamics as the interpretive grid in his analysis of *La Mer*.

14. Stephen Mason, *A History of the Sciences*, p. 345.

15. *Sea*, p. 100; *Mer*, pp. 123–24.

16. For a more psychological analysis of this text by the man who first revealed Michelet as an imaginative writer, see Gaston Bachelard, *L'Eau et les rêves* (Corti, 1942), pp. 160–61; and Gilbert Durand, *Les Structures anthropologiques de l'imaginaire* (Presses Universitaires de France, 1963): "Le culte de la nature chez Hugo et les romantiques ne serait pas autre chose qu'une projection d'un complexe d'un retour à la mère" (p. 246); ibid., pp. 243–46. The most subtle analysis of Michelet's psychological attitudes toward women is Linda Orr, *Jules Michelet: Nature, History, and Language* (Ithaca, New York: Cornell University Press, 1976). Professor Orr uses Freud and Lacan to great advantage.

17. In *L'Insecte* (Hachette, 1859), pp. 32–35, Michelet cites the evidence of a "calcium cycle" in the sea to support his vitalistic hypothesis: "Ces myriades de morts, ayant alimenté de leur calcaire ce qui fait notre nourriture, ont passé dans notre substance. D'autres aussi réclameraient. Le caillou même, le dur silex, il eut vie et nourrit la vie" (p. 33). "Récemment les marins anglais [Nelson, Darwin] ont découvert au fond des mers cette manufacture de craie, qui la fait passer sans cesse de l'état vivant à l'état inorganique" (ibid., p. 35). In note 3 to *L'Insecte* he gives his authorities: "Quant aux fossiles microscopiques, infusoires, etc., leur grand coup de théâtre a été la découverte d'Ehrenberg. Voy. ses mémoires dans les *Annales des sciences naturelles*, 2e série, vol. I, II, VI, VII, VIII. Au vol. I, p. 134, année 1834, il spécifie le point où Cuvier laissa la science, et ce que sa découverte y a ajouté" (ibid., p. 376). The seriousness of Michelet's note underlines the importance of the vitalistic theory of evolution which it supports. Cf. also *Montagne*, note, pp. 374–78.

18. This and the next three quotations are from *Sea*, pp. 95–96, 110; *Mer*, pp. 116–17, 137–38.

19. "L'homme, depuis le moment où il est conçu jusqu'à celui où il atteint sa maturité, remonte donc tous les échelons de la vie animale, et son âme passe par des états analogues à ceux que traverserait celle du dormeur amené graduellement d'un sommeil complet à l'état complet de veille" (L.-F.-Alfred Maury, "Du sommeil dans ses rapports avec le développement de l'instinct et de l'intelligence," in *Le Sommeil et les rêves*, 3rd ed. [Didier, 1865], p. 354; see whole essay, pp. 351–408).

20. This and the next two passages are from *Sea*, pp. 126, 130–32; *Mer*, pp. 160, 166–68.

21. *Sea*, p. 140; *Mer*, p. 179.

22. *Oeuvres complètes*, vol. IV, ed. Viallaneix (Flammarion, 1974), p. 383. Compare to text cited in note 1 of this chapter.

23. This and the next quotation are from *Sea*, p. 145; *Mer*, p. 186; *Sea*, p. 168; *Mer*, p. 219.

24. This and the next quotation are from *Sea*, pp. 176–78; *Mer*, pp. 230–34.

25. This and the next quotation are from *Sea*, p. 185; *Mer*, p. 243; *Sea*, p. 189; *Mer*, p. 248.

26. *Sea*, pp. 193–94; *Mer*, p. 254.

27. *"The frequent use of any organ, when confirmed by habit, increases the function of that organ, leads to its development and endows it with a size and power that it does not possess in animals which exercise it less,"* Lamarck, *Zoological Philosophy,* trans. by Hugh Elliot (Hafner Publishing Co., 1963), I, 7, p. 119. Cf. Etienne Gilson, *D'Aristote à Darwin et retour,* pp. 75–81, especially his reference to Cuvier's "Eloge de M. de Lamarck," cited p. 77, note 16.

28. Speaking of the further evolution of sea cows, Michelet relates their moral capacities directly to physical preconditions: "Voilà deux grandes choses qui pouvaient mener loin ces amphibies: Déjà chez eux, la main est née, l'organe d'industrie, l'essentiel instrument du travail à venir.... D'autre part, l'éducation est devenue possible" (*Mer,* pp. 254–55).

29. Loren Eiseley *Darwin's Century,* p. 30.

30. *Sea,* p. 196; *Mer,* p. 258.

31. *Bird,* pp. 95–96; *Oiseau,* p. 39. The following two quotations are from pp. 104–5 and 49–50 of the English and French versions respectively.

32. *Bird,* p. 157; *Oiseau,* p. 107. The following two quotations are from pp. 166, 84 and 117–18, 26 of the English and French versions respectively.

33. For this and other related insights, I owe a significant intellectual debt to Hans Jonas, *The Phenomenon of Life: Toward a Philosophical Biology* (Harper and Row, 1966), especially "To Move and To Feel: On the Animal Soul," pp. 99–107.

3 A Spiritual Interpretation of Evolutionary Theory

1. *Bird,* p. 205; *Oiseau,* p. 161.

2. *The Insect,* trans. W. H. Davenport Adams (London: T. Nelson and Sons, 1875); *L'Insecte,* 2nd edition, "revue et corrigée" (Hachette, 1858), p. 377.

3. *Mountain,* p. 163; *Montagne,* pp. 183–84.

4. *Mountain,* pp. 116–18; *Montagne,* pp. 124–26.

5. This and the next quotation are from Loren Eiseley, *Darwin's Century,* pp. 66–67. For a good account of this geological history see René Taton, ed. *Science in the Nineteenth Century,* pp. 327–46.

6. This and the next quotation are from Stephen Mason, *A History of the Sciences,* p. 407; see ibid., chap. 33, pp. 395–411 for the whole story of nineteenth-century geology.

7. Before summarizing Lyell's definitive refutation of Cuvier's geological theories, the *Larousse du XIXe siècle,* in an act of patriotism similar to that of Michelet, describes the work of Constant Prévost (1787–1856) who, since 1809 (cf. ibid., s.v. "Prévost"), opposed Cuvier's catastrophic theories: "M. Lyell a attaché son nom à la théorie de l'*évolution,* c'est-à-dire des causes actuelles, des causes lentes; mais il n'est que juste d'associer à ce nom celui de notre compatriote Constant Prévost. Longtemps avant l'apparition de l'ouvrage célèbre du géologue anglais, des *Principes de géologie,* M. Constant Prévost avait reconnu et déclaré dans ses écrits qu'on n'avait nul besoin d'invoquer des agents extraordinaires, des bouleversements subits pour expliquer ce que nous trouvons dans l'écorce terrestre...." (s.v. "Evolution").

8. Loren Eiseley, *Darwin's Century,* p. 160, and note 20: John W. Judd, *The Coming of Evolution* (Cambridge University Press, 1912), p. 73; previous information from Eiseley, p. 151.

9. *Mountain,* pp. 118–19; *Montagne,* pp. 126–28.

10. For an illuminating discussion of differences between Goethe and Robinet

see Alexander Gode-von Aesch, *Natural Science in German Romanticism*, pp. 144–48; quotation from p. 144.

11. René Taton, ed., *Science in the Nineteenth Century*, p. 430.

12. Stephen Mason, *A History of the Sciences*, p. 355. A specific consequence of this analogy of human with natural structure is the principle of autonomy, the keynote of Michelet's and Oken's system of spiritual evolution; Mason continues: "The nature philosophers recognized three main grades or levels of development in nature. Firstly, there were mechanical entities, like the sun and planets, which formed a system, though they possessed the lowest degree of self-determination; secondly, there were the chemical substances which had a greater individuality and self-activity, as many chemical processes were spontaneous and highly specific: and thirdly, there were living organisms which were self-developing individuals with self-contained structures" (ibid., p. 357).

13. The following story is traced in René Taton, *Science in the Nineteenth Century*, pp. 431–32, 458, 477–78.

14. For highly readable and broad surveys of this problem see Stephen Toulmin and June Goodfield, *The Discovery of Time* (Harper Torchbooks, 1965), especially chap. 3; and Loren Eiseley, *The Firmament of Time* (Atheneum, 1970).

15. *Sea*, pp. 52–53; *Mer*, pp. 55–56.

16. Biographical evidence suggests that Michelet's naturalist principles were deeply established before the preparation of his nature books led him to observations and detailed research. In an early notation to *Journal* II (8 August 1856), the historian anticipates the full theory elaborated over the next twelve years: "Interlaken. Comment l'amour accomplit la nature: 1. La formation du globe et la formation des espèces (voir carton *Physiologie*). 2. La formation et le progrès de la vie morale par échange d'êtres, augmentés l'un par l'autre" (p. 307). See the rest of this quotation (pp. 307–8) for a sketch of his entire theory.

17. *Mountain*, pp. 308–9; *Montagne*, pp. 378–79.

18. *Bird*, p. 171; *Oiseau*, pp. 123–24. Next quotation from *Bird*, pp. 81–82; *Oiseau*, pp. 23–24.

19 *Mountain*, p. 182; *Montague*, p. 210. Next passage from pp. 172–73; 195–96 of the English and French versions respectively.

20. *Mountain*, p. 114; *Montagne*, p. 210; next quotation from pp. 308 and 377 of the English and French versions respectively.

21. Speaking of volcanoes Michelet describes the earth's progress as a quest for fertility: "La Terre a-t-elle un cœur? un tout-puissant organe, où ses énergies se révèlent, où elle aspire, respire, palpite de ses transformations? Si cet organe existe, on doit moins le chercher aux foyers ténébreux de son noyau central, où elle est comprimée de sa masse elle-même. Il doit être plutôt là où son effort intérieur arrive enfin à la surface, à la libre expansion, là où son âme de désir rencontre la grande âme d'amour et de fécondation" (*Montagne*, p. 164). The "âme de désir" represents the inherent spiritual will of nature, expressed on a physically (and spiritually) higher level of love and fecundity, itself a form of evolutionary progress.

22. *Mountain*, p. 308; *Montagne*, p. 377.

23. *Sea*, p. 98; *Mer*, p. 120. Georges Poulet correctly emphasizes the male sexual rhythm which characterizes Michelet's vision of history: "D'un côté, l'histoire est progrès et mouvement. C'est une série d'ébauches à travers lesquelles il faut suivre l'organisation, plus ou moins lente, d'une idée, moins encore, d'un désir, à travers les générations. Mais l'histoire, c'est aussi la saisie de l'actualité en sa convulsion créatrice, moment de crise d'où, vertigineusement, jaillit l'avenir" ("Le Mo-

ment d'Eros," *Nouvelle Revue Française* [October 1967], p. 635). Cf. Roland Barthes, *Michelet par lui-même* (Le Seuil 1954; 1965), pp. 130–31.

24. *Mountain*, p. 306; *Montagne*, note, p. 373.

25. *Sea*, p. 177; *Mer*, p. 232.

26. *Mountain*, p. 224; *Montagne*, p. 262.

27. *Bird*, p. 87; *Oiseau*, p. 30.

4 The Inner Universe: Emergence of Creativity in Nature and Humanity

1. Henri Joly, *L'Homme et l'animal: Psychologie comparée.* Ouvrage couronné par l'Académie des Sciences morales et politiques. (Hachette, 1877), p. 6; the last chapter (pp. 323–433) contains a useful historical survey of discussions of the relation of animal instinct to human intelligence from primitive times to Darwin and Spencer. See also H. Joly, *L'Instinct, ses rapports avec la vie et l'intelligence* (1870).

2. Félix Ravaisson, *La Philosophie en France au XIXe siècle* (1867) (Hachette, 1889), p. 202: "Frédéric Cuvier; M. Flourens, dans plusieurs articles du *Journal des Savants* et dans son traité *De l'instinct et de l'intelligence des animaux* [1841; revised 1861]; M. de Quatrefages, dans un de ses articles sur *l'Unité de l'espèce humaine*[1] [1. *Revue des deux mondes*, 1861]; M. Maury, dans son *Traité du sommeil et des rêves* [1861]; M. Vulpian, dans la dernière de ses *Leçons sur la physiologie* [*générale et comparée du système nerveux*, 1866]; M. Michelet dans l'*Oiseau* et dans l'*Insecte;* M. Durand (de Gros), dans son *Electrodynamisme vital*, publié sous le pseudonyme de Philips, et dans ses *Essais de physiologie philosophique* (1861), ont cherché à déterminer . . . les différences et les ressemblances de l'instinct et de l'intelligence."

For a point of departure for a much needed history of the philosophy of this period see George Boas, *French Philosophies of the Romantic Period* (Baltimore: The Johns Hopkins Press, 1925); Joseph Dopp, *Félix Ravaisson, La Formation de sa pensée d'après des documents inédits* (Louvain: Editions de l'Institut supérieur de philosophie, 1933); F. Ravaisson, *Testament Philosophique et Fragments* (with Henri Bergson's 1904 mémoire to the Academy of Sciences) (Boivin et Cie., 1935); Jean Cazeneuve, *Ravaisson et les médecins animistes et vitalistes* (Presses Universitaires de France, 1957); and Dominique Janicaud, *Une Généalogie du spiritualisme français* (La Haye: Martinus Nijhoff, 1969).

3. *Bird*, p. 271; *Oiseau*, p. 237.

4. *Bird*, p. 266; *Oiseau*, p. 230.

5. Some examples of Michelet's use of the word *ingegno* to denote an instinct: "son talent naturel, son réel *ingegno*" (*Nos Fils*, p. 190); "la force entière d'une race toute nouvelle, l'étincelle de l'*ingegno*" (ibid., p. 333); also ibid., p. 335; as autonomous creativity: "le livre unique, su par cœur, est un récitatif qui soutient, qui anime, qui fait comme *la chaîne* du tissu des pensées, sur laquelle l'ingegno surajoute sa *trame* féconde" (ibid., p. 296). In the cited text of *L'Oiseau*, this element of personal freedom is stressed.

6. *Bird*, p. 336; *Oiseau*, pp. 323–24.

7. L.-F.-Alfred Maury, *Le Sommeil et les rêves*, 3rd ed., "revue et considérablement augmentée" (Didier, 1865), pp. 351–408. In *L'Insecte* Michelet continues his argument against the animal automatons of Buffon and Malebranche, pp. 336–39. Here is the essence of his argument: "C'est un monde *régulier*, mais qui prouve *libre* au besoin" (note, p. 372). The very possibility of freedom from determinism is the significance of animal "reason" for Michelet.

8. *Bird,* pp. 271–72; *Oiseau,* pp. 237–38.

9. Maurice Z. Shroder, *Icarus: The Image of the Artist in French Romanticism* (Cambridge, Mass.: Harvard University Press, 1961), p. 1.

10. Cf. Diderot's dialogue between the Cuckoo and the Nightingale who represent Method and Genius respectively, in *Lettres à Sophie Volland* (Gallimard, 1938), letter LXVII, pp. 150 ff. Jacques Barzun, in *Classic, Romantic and Modern* (Anchor Books, 1961), traces a short history of this image: "We saw above how Diderot, reporting Galiani, launched the nightingale as a critical symbol. Among the romanticists, Goethe gave the image its most precise significance. To him it represented the completeness of achievement through the power to transcend its own class. (*Elective Affinities,* chap. 11). In the modern period, it has come to represent an impossible dream, a beauty that cannot survive, or which is at least spoiled—as by Sweeney—through contact with sordidness. A French musician, Auric, has described Erik Satie's score, *Parade,* as 'submitting very humbly to reality, which drowns out the nightingale's song under the clanging of street-cars.' Eliot used the nightingale again in *The Wasteland,* 'And still she cried, and still the world pursues, "Jug Jug" to dirty ears.' (II, 102)" (p. 224). The *Larousse du XIXe siècle* (s.v. "Rossignol") writes about the natural history of the animal and in evoking its song quotes five long paragraphs from Michelet's *L'Oiseau* which describe the reality of this bird as artist.

11. *Bird,* p. 280; *Oiseau,* p. 248.

12. *Bird,* p. 282, *Oiseau,* p. 250.

13. See *Oiseau,* pp. 251–52, 257; also *Insecte,* p. 219.

14. *Bird,* p. 281; *Oiseau,* p. 249.

15. Michelet's description expands, at one point, into a phenomenology of the creation of abstract art, the basis of which is freedom from perception; creation then becomes pure and abstract. In another context, he speaks of beautiful insects as a point of departure for free imagination: "Est-ce à dire qu'il faille copier? Point du tout. Ces êtres vivants, et dans leur robe d'amour, par cela seul ont une grâce, je dirai une auréole animée, qu'on ne traduit pas. Il faut les aimer seulement, les contempler, s'en inspirer, et tirer des formes idéales, et des iris toutes nouvelles, de surprenants bouquets de fleurs. Ainsi transformés, ils seront, non pas tels que dans la nature, mais fantastiques et merveilleux, comme l'enfant qui les désire les vit en dormant, ou la fille amoureuse d'une belle parure, ou comme la jeune femme enceinte dans ses envies les a rêvés" (*Insecte,* pp. 196–97). Here we see *love* as the motivating force of creative imagination. The progression "il faut les *aimer* seulement, les *contempler, s'en inspirer,* en *tirer* des formes idéales" passes from a committed contemplation to the stimulation of one's own powers, leading, finally, to the actual creation. The absolute autonomy of this creation is expressed by the comparisons with dream, in which the dream is ontologically consubstantial with the dreamer; cf. ibid., p. 175: "comme un rêve mêlé à toute l'existence et qu'on n'en détache plus."

16. This and the next quotation are from *Bird,* pp. 283–84; *Oiseau,* p. 252.

17. *Bird,* p. 290, second paragraph omitted; *Oiseau,* p. 261. The next quotation is from p. 290 and p. 262 of the English and French versions respectively.

18. *Love,* trans. J. W. Palmer, M.D. (Rudd and Carleton, 1859), pp. 288–89; *Amour* (Calmann-Lévy, 1894), p. 376.

19. For a study of Michelet's social attitudes toward women see Anne R. Pugh, *Michelet and His Ideas on Social Reform* (Columbia University Press, 1923), pp. 107–220.

20. This and the following quotation are from *Woman,* trans. J. W. Palmer,

M.D. (Rudd and Carleton, 1860), pp. 114–15; *Femme*, 3rd edition (Hachette, 1860), pp. 175–77.

21. Ernst Cassirer, *Language and Myth*, trans. Susanne K. Langer (Dover Publications, 1953), pp. 25–26. See also Ernst Cassirer, *The Philosophy of Symbolic Forms* (Yale University Press, 1955), vol. 2.

22. Again I have been aided at a crucial point in my thinking by Hans Jonas, *The Phenomenon of Life*, esp. pp. 183–87.

23. *Love*, p. 331; *Amour*, pp. 434–35.

24. This and the following quotation are from *Woman*, p. 220; *Femme*, pp. 360–61.

25. Pierre Teilhard de Chardin, *La Place de l'homme dans la nature* (Le Seuil, 1956), p. 117. See also Teilhard de Chardin, *Le Phénomène humain* (Le Seuil, ed. Points, 1970), pp. 178 et seq. For an excellent catalogue of other nineteenth-century proponents of Humanity as a single organism see A. J. L. Busst, "The Image of the Androgyne in the Nineteenth Century," in *Romantic Mythologies*, ed. Ian Fletcher (London: Routledge and Kegan Paul, 1967), pp. 1–95.

26. For studies of Teilhard de Chardin's evolutionary thought see *Zygon: Journal of Religion and Science*, 3, 3 (September 1968), and 3, 4 (December 1968); and Madelaine Barthélemy-Madaule, *Bergson et Teilhard de Chardin* (Le Seuil, 1963) as background for what might prove to be a substantive study of the development of Ravaisson's (and Michelet's) spiritualism through Bergson, Teilhard and others.

27. "Entre Dieu et la Raison, est-il une différence? il serait impie de la croire. Et de toutes les formes de l'Amour éternel (beauté, fécondité, puissance) nul doute que la Raison ne soit la première, la plus haute. C'est par elle qu'il est harmonie, l'ordre qui fait prospérer tout, l'ordre bienfaisant, bienveillant. Dans la Raison qui paraît froide, il n'est pas moins l'Amour encore" (*Femme*, p. 179).

28. This and the next quotation are from *Insect*, p. 114; *Insecte*, pp. 74–75.

5 Nature's Message to a Declining Humanity

1. Maurice Shroder, *Icarus*, p. 68. The best study of the Orphic phenomenon is Paul Bénichou, *Le Sacre de l'écrivain*. 1750–1830 (José Corti, 1973), especially pp. 155–76 on Ballanche.

2. I have borrowed these terms from Paul Tillich, *The Courage to Be* (New Haven: Yale University Press, 1952), especially pp. 32–62 on different types of anxiety. Tillich's theology of culture approach should complement the Marxist view of Barbéris and the psychoanalytical analysis of Michelet's anxiety by Linda Orr.

3. *Journal* I, p. 433.

4. *Bird*, p. 84; *Oiseau*, p. 26. The human desire for transcendence can be described as an "Icarus syndrome" (see Maurice Z. Shroder, *Icarus: The Image of the Artist in French Romanticism*), in which the need to ascend, or to create like God, meets ultimate failure. Rimbaud employs the same structure of a return to the earth at the end of his *Saison en enfer*: "Moi! moi qui me suis dit mage ou ange, dispensé de toute morale, je suis rendu au sol, avec un devoir à chercher, et la réalité rugueuse à étreindre! Paysan!" ("Adieu")

"The fate of Icarus frightened no one. Wings! wings! wings! they cried from all sides, even if we should fall into the sea. To fall from the sky, one must climb there, even for but a moment, and that is more beautiful than to spend one's whole life crawling on the earth" (from Théophile Gautier, *Histoire du romantisme*, p. 153; cited by Shroder, p. 55). Cf. chapter 6, note 20.

5. *Bird*, p. 84; *Oiseau*, p. 26. Cf. our quotation from Rimbaud in note 4. Did *L'Oiseau* inspire that part of *Une Saison en enfer?*

The same problem is expressed by Victor Hugo in "Sur un portrait de sainte" (1855):

> Sans quitter le réel, conquérons l'idéal;
> Restons homme, en montant vers le sépulcre austère.
> Il faut aller au ciel en marchant sur la terre.

From *Les Quatre Vents de l'esprit* in *Poésie*, vol. II ("Edition L'Intégrale," Le Seuil, 1972), p. 684.

Théophile Gautier wrote a poem "Des Ailes" inspired by Rückert.

6. *Bird*, p. 84; *Oiseau*, p. 27.

7. *Bird*, p. 108; *Oiseau*, p. 53.

8. *The Insect*, trans. W. H. Davenport Adams (London: T. Nelson and Sons, 1875), p. 21; *L'Insecte*, 2nd edition, "revue et corrigée" (Hachette, 1858), p. viii.

9. This and the next quotation are from *Insect*, pp. 342–43; *Insecte*, pp. 369–71.

10. *Insect*, p. 110; *Insecte*, p. 69.

11. *Insect*, p. 115; *Insecte*, pp. 75–76.

12. *La Femme*, 3rd edition (Hachette, 1860), p. 434.

13. *Journal* I, p. 356; ibid., note p. 809; "Au même moment [1840, the year of publication of Reynaud's article *"Terre"* in the *Encyclopédie nouvelle*], Michelet, méditant sur la mort de Pauline [his first wife] et sur le pouvoir de résurrection dont il lui semblait que disposait l'historien, n'était pas éloigné d'adopter une pareille croyance [in metempsychosis]. C'est pourquoi il lut Reynaud avec sympathie, comme l'atteste une lettre [unpublished] adressée par Alfred Dumesnil à sa mère, le 7 janvier 1841: 'M. Michelet vint à parler de l'*Encyclopédie nouvelle* publiée par MM. Leroux et Reynaud, rapporte le jeune homme, racontant une soirée passée chez son maître; il nous a parlé des articles *terre* et *ciel* comme de morceaux éminemment remarquables... Je n'analyserais point malheureusement les considérations sur l'immortalité de l'âme et la destinée de l'homme que suggéra à M. Michelet tout naturellement la discussion de quelques-unes des opinions de M. Reynaud qu'il ne partage pas toujours ...' (Bibliothèque historique de la Ville de Paris; fonds Dumesnil-Baudouin.)."

14. *La Sorcière* (Garnier-Flammarion, 1966), p. 94, note 1. See also *Bible de l'humanité* (Chamerot, 1864), pp. 96, 107 note 1, 153–54.

15. The history of the problem of immortality in nineteenth-century France has yet to be written. For a start see the following book reviews: E. de Fontette, *"Terre et ciel; La Vie future,"* in *Le Correspondant*, vol. I, n.s. (December 1855), 374–97; H. Taine on *Terre et ciel*, "Philosophie religieuse," in *Nouveaux essais de critique et d'histoire*, 5th ed. (Hachette, 1892), pp. 1–33; E. Caro on *La Vie future* in *Revue de l'instruction publique* (21 February 1856), pp. 630–32. For broader views: E. Caro, *L'Idée de Dieu et ses nouveaux critiques* (Hachette, 1864); Guizot, *Méditations sur l'état actuel de la religion chrétienne en France* (Michel Lévy frères, 1866), and Paul Janet, *Les Problèmes du XIXe siècle* (Michel Lévy frères, 1872) which contains a critique of the preceding book.

16. This and the next quotation are from *Insect*, pp. 294–95; *Insecte*, pp. 306–07.

17. This account, dated 28 October 1856, shows how Michelet translated his own life into symbols: "J'avais cru voir sur son visage [de son fils] comme une lueur des pensées fortes et tendres qui me remplissaient le cœur à ce dernier moment de mon enseignement. Vanité de nos espérances! Cette fleur de mon automne, que

j'aurais voulu animer de la vitalité puissante qui a commencé tard pour moi, elle disparut presque en naissant" (*Insecte*, p. 307). The Lazarus theme in Michelet's life is of course part of his conception of history as an "integral resurrection of the past." Cf. Gabriel Monod, "Yves-Jean-Lazare Michelet," in *Jules Michelet, Etudes sur sa vie et ses œuvres* (Hachette, 1905), pp. 237–96.

18. *Insect*, p. 259;; *Insecte*, pp. 259–60.

19. *Insect*, p. 263; *Insecte*, p. 265.

20. This and the next quotation are from *Insect*, pp. 267–68; *Insecte*, pp. 270–72.

21. *Insect*, p. 311; *Insecte*, p. 329.

22. This and the next quotation are from *Insect*, pp. 329, 342; *Insecte*, pp. 354, 369.

23. This and the next quotation are from *Sea*, pp. 42, 44, 41; *Mer*, pp. 39, 41, 39.

24. *Sea*, p. 53; *Mer*, p. 55.

25. In the general summary of *La Mer*, Michelet evokes "des rêves allemands" —probably those of Ritter—to support his premise that the earth is a single organism ("le gros animal, la Terre") and the sea its womb ("son organe principal de fécondité"), p. 419.

26. This and the next two quotations are from *Sea*, pp. 91, 120; *Mer*, pp. 110, 152.

27. *The Women of the French Revolution*, trans. Meta Roberts Pennington (Philadelphia: H. C. Baird, 1855), p. 122; *Les Femmes de la Révolution* (Adolphe Delahays, 1855), p. 100. This passage was originally published by Michelet in his *Histoire de la Révolution française*, vol. II (Gallimard, 1952), p. 819.

28. *Mer*, p. 326.

29. He hopes to pave the way for a nineteenth-century renaissance: "Entre deux âges de force, la force de la Renaissance, la force de la Révolution, il y eut un temps d'affaissement, où des signes graves accusèrent une énervation morale et physique" (*Mer*, p. 347).

30. In *Charles Demailly*, a novel by the Goncourt brothers published one year before *The Sea*, the hero is suffering from anemia, which his doctor characterizes as the sickness of the century, a "degeneration of the human species." Cited by Maurice Z. Shroder, *Icarus*, pp. 220–21.

31. *Sea*, pp. 309–10; *Mer*, p. 413.

32. This and the next quotation are from *Sea*, pp. 307, 320; *Mer*, pp. 409, 425–26.

33. *Mountain*, p. 112; *Montagne*, p. 115.

34. *Mountain*, p. 239; *Montagne*, p. 279.

35. *Mountain*, p. 121; *Montagne*, p. 131.

36. *Mountain*, pp. 177–78; *Montagne*, p. 202.

37. The *Larousse du XIXe siècle* (s.v. "Rameau") gives the general interpretation of the golden bough: "Dans l'application, le rameau d'or d'Enée est la puissance secrète, le talisman qui fait céder toutes les volontés contraires." Michelet's golden bough enabled him to understand the dead (by empathy) so that he could rescue them from oblivion: "C'est le prix de ma vie d'avoir ressuscité tant d'hommes oubliés, méconnus, d'avoir été pour eux l'instrument de justice et le réparateur du sort" (*Montagne*, p. 202).

Defending his compassion for the dead as a valid research method, Michelet describes his mission as historian in terms of Virgilian symbolism: "Des sages me disaient: 'Ce n'est pas sans danger de vivre à ce point-là dans cette intimité de l'autre monde. . . . Faites au moins comme Enée, qui ne s'y aventure que l'épée à la main pour chasser ces images, ne pas être pris de trop près (*Ferro diverberat umbras*).'

"L'épée! triste conseil. Quoi! j'aurais durement, quand ces images aimées venaient à moi pour vivre, moi je les aurais ècartèes! Quelle funeste sagesse!... Oh! que les philosophes ignorent parfaitement le vrai fond de l'artiste, le talisman secret qui fait la force de l'histoire, lui permet de passer, de repasser à travers les morts!

"Sachez donc, ignorants, que, sans épée, sans armes, sans quereller ces âmes confiantes qui réclament la résurrection, l'art, en les accueillant, en leur rendant le souffle, l'art pourtant garde en lui sa lucidité tout entière. Je ne dis nullement l'*ironie* où beaucoup ont mis le fond de l'art, mais la forte dualité qui fait qu'en les aimant il n'en voit pas moins ce qu'elles sont, que ce sont des morts' " *(Préface de 1869 à l'Histoire de France*, p. 175).

38. This and the next three quotations are from *Mountain*, p. 239; *Montagne*, pp. 279–80.

39. "Lapiaz ou lapié, n.m. (1895, dial.; du lat. *lapis* "pierre"). Géogr. Ciselure superficielle de formes variées, creusée par les eaux en terrain calcaire" (*Petit Robert*). The rare and specialized use of the term in Michelet's time (it does not appear either in Littré or in the *Larousse du XIXe siècle*) underlines the close connection between Michelet's technical knowledge of nature and his personal use of symbolism.

40. *Mountain*, p. 301; *Montagne*, p. 365.

6 *Michelet's Mysticism: Nature as Symbol of Spirit*

1. The most penetrating study of Michelet's religious thought (with an excellent selection of texts) is Jean Gaulmier, *Michelet devant Dieu* (Desclée de Brouwer, 1968); cf. Frank Paul Bowman, "Michelet et les métamorphoses du Christ," *Revue d'histoire littéraire de la France* 74 (September–October 1974), 824–51; Jean-Louis Cornuz, *Jules Michelet: Un aspect de la pensée religieuse au XIXe siècle* (Geneva: Droz, 1955). See also the important study of Raymond Schwab, *La Renaissance orientale* (Payot, 1950); his chapter on Michelet, pp. 410–26 needs to be continued.

2. *Journal* II, p. 224; 24 December 1853.

3. See preface to the *Histoire de la Révolution française*, vol. 1, (Pléiade edition, 1952): "[Le Christianisme] est la religion de la Grâce, du salut gratuit, arbitraire, et du bon plaisir de Dieu. . . . Si l'on restait fidèle au principe que le salut est un don, et non le prix de la Justice, l'homme se croisait les bras, s'asseyait et attendait; il savait bien que ses œuvres ne pouvaient rien pour son sort. Toute activité morale cessait en ce monde" (p. 28).

4. It is a pity that the only full length study of Michelet's natural histories— Robert Van der Elst, *Michelet naturaliste: Esquisse de son système de philosophie* (Delagrave, 1914)—was written as a refutation of the historian's "pantheism": "de tendance et même d'intention, [Michelet] a été sincèrement spiritualiste, mais que, étant donné la méthode [subjective] choisie par lui pour y parvenir, il devait fatalement dévier dans le monisme panthéistique" (pp. 151–52). Cf. Henri Hauser, "Michelet naturaliste et l'âme française d'aujourd'hui," *Revue du Mois*, XIX (10 February 1915), 151–71, in which the author reveals the distortions of Van der Elst's thesis, and accuses his Catholic conservatism as the deforming influence. For a materialist

critique of Michelet see that of Hippolyte Taine cited at the end of this chapter (and note 24); also below note 15.

5. This and the next quotation are from *Bird*, pp. 91–92; *Oiseau*, pp. 35–36.

6. This polarity of admiration and terror is described by Rudolf Otto in his classic work, *The Idea of the Holy* (Galaxy Books, 1958; German original, 1917). A modern religious philosopher, Abraham J. Heschel, in *Man Is Not Alone* (Harper Torchbooks, 1951), considers emotional experiences of the sublime—such as amazement, surprise, awe, reverence and a sense of the ineffable—as genuine "cognitive insights" into the spiritual. Pascal's *pensée* on man's disproportion (number 72 of the Brunschvicg edition) has the same purpose as Michelet's paradigm.

7. This and the following eight passages are from *Sea*, pp. 299–301; *Mer*, pp. 399–401.

8. An in-depth study of this type of imaginative action can be guided by Gaston Bachelard, *L'Air et les songes* (Corti, 1943). Reveries stimulated by the earth are discussed by Gaston Bachelard, in *La Terre et les rêveries de la volonté*, and *La Terre et les rêveries du repos* (both Corti, 1948). Bachelard was probably the first to understand Michelet as an imaginative writer, influencing, in turn, the pioneer work of Roland Barthes, *Michelet par lui-même* (Le Seuil, 1954).

9. Michelet's use of this traditional symbol takes its place in a long Western tradition; cf. Ernst Robert Curtius, *European Literature in the Latin Middle Ages* (New York: Harper Torchbooks, 1963), pp. 319–26. The Book of Nature is also prominent in the poetry of Victor Hugo: "Cette image n'est pas neuve: elle est chez Voltaire, on la trouve au XVIIe siècle, et déjà dans la Bible. Mais Hugo en a fait un tel usage qu'il s'est acquis presque un droit sur elle" (J.-B. Barrère, *La Fantaisie de Victor Hugo*, vol. III [Corti, 1950], p. 127); cf. ibid., pp. 127–30 for examples from Hugo's works.

10. For the clearest analysis of this type of prescientific thought see Gaston Bachelard, *La Formation de l'esprit scientifique: Contribution à une psychanalyse de la connaissance objective* (Vrin, 1938), and G. Bachelard, *La Psychanalyse du feu* (Gallimard, 1938). In addition to Bachelard, my analysis was guided by the seminal book of Michael Polanyi, *Personal Knowledge: Towards a Post-Critical Philosophy* (Harper Torchbooks, 1964).

11. Gaston Bachelard analyzes the following passage in *L'Eau et les rêves* (Corti, 1942), p. 143. For up to date discussions of the composition of sea water see Thompson King, *Water: Miracle of Nature* (Collier Books, 1961), chap. 9; K. S. Davis and J. A. Day, *Water: Mirror of Science* (Anchor Books, 1969), chap. 6; Raymond Furon, *The Problem of Water* (American Elsevier Pub. Co., 1967), chap. 3 on salt water. (These references were given to me by Dr. Sidney Sussman of Water Service Laboratories, Inc., New York City.)

12. This and the next two passages are from *Sea*, pp. 92–94; *Mer*, pp. 111–14.

13. "Tout le programme de *L'eau de mer,* assimilé au mucus du... vagin" (*Journal* II, pp. 529–30); cf. ibid., p. 535, entry of 26 June. The books of Roland Barthes, Jeanne Calo, and Linda Orr (all cited in the Bibliography) explore directly this aspect of Michelet's imagination.

14. Michelet supports this intuition (now justified by modern science) by another scientific consultation, made immediately after the one to the Chemist: "En le quittant, j'allai tout droit chez un grand physiologiste dont l'opinion n'a pas moins d'autorité sur mon esprit [probably Robin]. Je lui pose la même question. Sa réponse fut très-longue, très-belle" (*Mer*, p. 114). Again, an authoritative savant seems to be

personally excited by the problem, and Michelet reacts according to the esthetic, or emotive, aspect of the answer that sea water is primarily organic. The stubbornness of intuitive knowledge is shown as the scientist expresses his awareness of the fragility of his own explanations: " 'C'est, de toutes les hypothèses, la plus vraisemblable; en sortir, c'est se jeter dans d'extrêmes difficultés' " (ibid., p. 115). The security of personal knowledge is greater than objective, cautious science in this example.

15. The main purpose of Van der Elst's *Michelet naturaliste* is to show that Michelet's spiritualism (well documented but poorly understood) is ultimately canceled by his divinization of physical nature, his pantheism: "On a beau dire avec M. Monod que Michelet spiritualisa la matière, il n'en est pas moins vrai que le néophyte matérialiste y verrait aussi bien un prétexte à matérialiser l'esprit; car le véritable spiritualiste ne nie pas la matière, c'est le panthéiste qui la nie quand il identifie la matière et l'esprit" (p. 152).

The Protestant Anthony Vincent, less defensive and more astute, accepts the premise of Michelet's evolutionism and correctly sees that his God is both transcendent and immanent: "Mais ce panthéisme est plus poétique que philosophique: il n'y a point là un système.... Non, Dieu ne se *perd* point dans la Nature, il s'y *manifeste* seulement comme Bonté toujours agissante comme source de vie et de progrès" (*Michelet et une nouvelle forme de religion naturelle* [thèse, Montauban, 1899], p. 22).

16. For a good analysis of this distinction see R. C. Zaehner, *Mysticism Sacred and Profane* (Galaxy Books, 1951), esp. pp. 28 sqq. Jean-Louis Cornuz, in *Jules Michelet: Un aspect de la pensée religieuse au XIXᵉ siècle*, uses biographical data and a perceptive study of Michelet's *Histoire de France* to arrive at the same formulation of his religion (which he does not, unfortunately, apply to the nature books): "Dieu est peut-être créateur de ce monde. Et nous voyons que plus probablement, il est l'esprit de ce monde qui s'est créé lui-même.[25] Il est Justice, et par là tenu de respecter la Justice telle que les hommes la conçoivent. Jamais Michelet ne distingue entre Justice divine et justice humaine. Dieu est encore *action*, lutte pour le progrès et la liberté, non pas acteur transcendant, à la façon des Dieux antiques, mais immanent, habitant le cœur de l'homme et dirigeant son bras, sans pouvoir toutefois détourner les coups qu'il reçoit, ni même le préserver des tentations.... Note 25: On pourrait dire peut-être que Michelet n'est pas panthéiste (identification de Dieu et du monde), mais panenthéiste: Dieu est à la fois immanent et transcendant; sans être tout, il est dans tout" (ibid., p. 336).

17. *Journal* II, pp. 263-74.

18. *Larousse du XIXᵉ siècle:* "Les anciens prenaient la Terre pour la Nature ou la mère universelle de tous les êtres. C'est pourquoi on l'appelait communément la grande mère, *magna mater*" (s.v. *Terre* [*Tellus*]), "*Poét. Mère commune*, la terre, parce que le premier homme a été fait de terre, d'après le récit de Moïse" (s.v. *Mère*). For Michelet, the earth is the primordial woman just as the woman is Nature itself. For a more analytical treatment of this image see Gilbert Durand, *Les Structures anthropologiques de l'imaginaire* (Presses Universitaires de France, 1963), pp. 243-46; see above, chap. 2, note 16. For a discussion of the following episode see Gaston Bachelard, *La Terre et les rêveries du repos.*

19. This and the following three passages are from *Mountain*, pp. 109-12; *Montagne*, pp. 112-15.

20. The polarity characteristic of Michelet's imagination is described by Louis Reybaud, in the article *Antée* of the *Larousse du XIXᵉ siècle*, as a general tendency of the period: "Toute science relative à l'homme est double comme lui: elle ne peut pas intéresser la chair qu'elle n'intéresse pas aussi l'esprit. C'est la condition de notre

existence. Comme le *géant* de la Fable, l'homme doit, de temps à autre, toucher à la terre pour se fortifier dans son élan vers le ciel, et cette oscillation incessante entre un spiritualisme et un sensualisme toujours perfectibles et toujours progressifs, constitue la vie du monde comme elle est la vie de chaque individu."

21. According to Goethe, symbolism expresses a direct relation between natural phenomena and the realm of ideas (or spirit): "True symbolism is where the particular represents the more general, not as a dream or shadow, but as a living momentary revelation of the Inscrutable" (cited by René Wellek, *A History of Modern Criticism: 1750–1950, The Later Eighteenth Century* [New Haven: Yale University Press, 1955] p. 211).

Michelet's vision of reality resembles this and the medieval conception of symbolism which presupposed a mystical connection between a physical object and its divine essence. Medieval "realism" (as the Scholastics called it) equates knowledge of the symbol with spiritual experience; see J. Huizinga, *The Waning of the Middle Ages* (Doubleday Anchor Books, 1954), pp. 200–14. Another valuable approach to Michelet in this respect can be derived from Lucien Lévy-Bruhl's "catégorie affective du surnaturel," elaborated in *L'Expérience mystique et les symboles chez les primitifs* (Félix Alcan, 1938).

22. See *Journal* II, entry of 26 June 1854: "Je reste longtemps aux boues; j'y suis trè bien d'abord. Quiétude singulière, ce que les mystiques auraient appelé un état propre à l'oraison" (p. 272). An extended comparison of Michelet's own expressed religious experiences (as distinguished from his anticlerical ideology) with those in the traditional Christian literature would demonstrate a deep affinity of the historian with the mysticism he takes such pains to attack in *Le Prêtre, la Femme et la Famille*, for example. See St. Teresa of Avila, *Interior Castle*, and Louis Oeschslin, *L'Intuition mystique de sainte Thérèse* (Presses Universitaires de France, 1946).

23. This and the next passage are from *Bird*, pp. 290–91; *Oiseau*, pp. 262–63.

24. H. Taine, *Essais de critique et d'histoire*, 6th ed. (1892), pp. 143–44; article originally published in the *Revue de l'instruction publique*, 27 March 1856.

7   *The Two Sexes of the Mind: Michelet's Analysis of Creative and Moral Thought*

1. *Mountain*, p. 287; *Montagne*, p. 351.

2. See the indispensable article of A. J. L. Busst, which, however, does not mention Michelet: "The Image of the Androgyne in the Nineteenth Century," in *Romantic Mythologies*, ed. Ian Fletcher (London: Routledge and Kegan Paul, 1967), pp. 1–95, with its generous bibliography. A path of further inquiry could be guided by the Jungian symbolism of *animus-anima*: see C.-G. Jung, *Psyche and Symbol* (Doubleday Anchor Books, 1958); also David Bakan, *Sigmund Freud and the Jewish Mystical Tradition* (Schocken Books, 1969); Gaston Bachelard, *La Poétique de la rêverie* (Presses Universitaires de France, 1960); Albert Béguin, *Balzac visionnaire* (Le Seuil, 1965), pp. 67–72; Mircea Eliade, *Mephistopheles and the Androgyne* (Sheed and Ward, 1965); and Carolyn G. Heilbrun, *Towards Androgyny: Aspects of Male and Female in Literature* (London: Victor Gollancz, 1973).

3. *Woman*, pp. 222–23; *Femme*, pp. 364–65.

4. This and the next quotation are from *People*, pp. 137–39; *Peuple*, pp. 190–94; McKay translation, pp. 143–46.

5. *Peuple,* p. 194: "Cette science est à créer. La philosophie qui depuis des siècles tourne sur les mêmes idées, n'y a pas touché encore. Les mystiques qui ont tant regardé dans l'âme humaine, s'aveuglaient à y chercher Dieu, qui y est sans nul doute, mais qu'on y distingue bien mieux quand on l'y voit en son image qu'il y déposa, la Cité humaine et divine."

6. The analysis in this section was enhanced by reflection on Hans Jonas, "The Nobility of Sight: A Study in the Phenomenology of the Senses," in *The Phenomenon of Life,* pp. 135–52; and his "Image Making and the Freedom of Man," ibid., pp. 157–75.

7. In "Ce qu'on entend sur la montagne," Hugo views the totality of nature and humanity from a mountain top, arriving at the opposition which Michelet had overcome: "Et pourquoi le Seigneur, qui seul lit à son livre / Mêle éternellement dans un fatal hymen / Le chant de la nature au cri du genre humain?" (*Les Feuilles d'automne,* v [*Oeuvres poétiques,* vol. I (Bibliothèque de la Pléiade, 1964), p. 728]).

Michelet uses a mountain top perspective to illustrate his spiritual interpretation of the French Revolution, as he describes its adversary: "Le Vendéen, enfermé, aveuglé dans son fourré sauvage, ne voyait nullement le mouvement qui se passait autour de lui. S'il eût vu un moment, il eût été découragé et n'eût pas combattu. Il eût fallu qu'on le menât bien haut, au haut d'une montagne, et que là, donnant à sa vue une portée lointaine, on lui fît voir ce spectacle prodigieux [la Révolution]. Il se fût signé, se fût cru au Jugement dernier, il eût dit: Ceci est de Dieu" (*Histoire de la Révolution française,* vol. I, pp. 1165–66).

8. This and the next quotation are from *Mountain,* pp. 287–89; *Montagne,* pp. 351–53.

9. Littré, s.v. *Imagination:* "1° Faculté que nous avons de nous rappeler vivement et de voir en quelque sorte les objets qui ne sont plus sous nos yeux. Cf. Volt. *Dict. Phil., Imagination.*" This is the traditional definition of imagination, which derives from previous perceptions an imitation of reality. For Michelet, however, the Romantic imagination is a positive function, a free and creative force. This is also true of the author of the article *Imagination* in the *Larousse du XIXe siècle:* "Si enfin [l'homme] les [faits] rappelle volontairement, en cherchant à les combiner, à les ordonner, non comme ils furent ordonnés en fait, mais comme l'esprit veut qu'ils soient pour réaliser un type idéal, un tableau préconçu, alors on dit que c'est de l'imagination active." Here the passage from passive imagination as a *reproduction* of reality to active imagination which creates an *idealization* describes the development of creative and abstract thought. Cf. below note 12.

For the evolution of the concept of imagination in French literature see Margaret Gilman, *The Idea of Poetry in France, from Houdar de La Mothe to Baudelaire* (Cambridge, Mass.: Harvard University Press, 1958); François Germain, *L'Imagination d'Alfred de Vigny* (Corti, 1961), especially pp. 20–88; Jean Starobinski, "Jalons pour une histoire du concept d'imagination," in *Relation critique* (Gallimard, 1970), pp. 174–95; and a fascinating theological work by Ray L. Hart, *Unfinished Man and the Imagination* (Herder and Herder, 1968).

10. Cf. *Critique de la raison pure,* 3rd French edition, trans. J. Tissot (Librairie Philosophique de Ladrange, 1864): "[The three sources of all experience are] le *sens,* l'*imagination* et l'*aperception.* Elles sont le fondement: 1° de la *synopsis* de la diversité *a priori* fournie par le sens; 2° de la *synthèse* de la diversité fournie par l'imagination; 3° enfin de l'*unité* de cette synthèse par une aperception primitive" (Appendix IX, p. 345); see also Analytique des Concepts, XV–XVII, and appendices IX–X.

Without entering into too many details, may I suggest, if not a direct influence of Kant on Michelet, at least a striking parallel. For the possible influence of Kant on Michelet see Gabriel Monod, *La Vie et la pensée de Jules Michelet*, 1798–1852 (Champion, 1923), p. 19, n. 2, pp. 131, 137, 148, 192; M. Vallois, *La Formation de l'influence kantienne en France* (Felix Alcan, 1924), and especially Oscar A. Haac, *Michelet et l'histoire allemande* (Unpublished doctoral dissertation, Yale University, 1948). For Michelet himself on Kant see *Histoire de la Révolution française*, vol. I, pp. 58–59, 415–16; and *Nos Fils*.

11. *Mountain*, pp. 122–23; *Montagne*, pp. 135–36.

12. *Larousse du XIXᵉ siècle*, s.v. *Représentation:* "Image représentant un fait ou un objet. Philos. Acte par lequel les objets extérieurs sont représentés à l'esprit." The encyclopedic explanation of the term suggests, in its general outlines, Michelet's theories of animal evolution as well as of human thought: "La classification des *représentations* a été faite par Kant dans sa *Critique de la raison pure*.... Kant laisse d'abord au plus bas de l'échelle les *représentations* telles qu'on peut les supposer chez les animaux, accompagnées de peu ou point de conscience. Puis viennent celles que fournissent les sens exclusivement, et qu'on peut nommer perceptions, plutôt que *représentations* sensibles ou sensations représentatives. Au-dessus, et comme pour coordonner ces *représentations* de premier degré, on peut mentionner les *représentations* de l'entendement, les concepts (*Begriff*), c'est-à-dire toutes les idées abstraites et générales qui servent à constituer une hiérarchie logique des *représentations* sous les trois chefs superposés: individu, espèce et genre. Enfin, et sans sortir de l'intelligence, au-dessus des catégories elles-mêmes qui, selon Kant, sont des *représentations* de *représentations*, on trouve les *représentations* des idées transcendentales, des principes *a priori*, des jugements absolus de la raison. Ici, la *représentation* n'a plus d'objet, de matière empruntée à l'expérience; elle est purement nécessaire de la pensée humaine." Michelet's fundamental difference from Kantian philosophy is his intuition of the immanence of the "categories" in nature and mankind. For Michelet, however, there is an essential—though not a functional—distinction between the spiritual and the natural worlds.

13. *Le Prêtre, la Femme et la Famille* (Calmann-Lévy, 1881), p. 276. This, incidentally, was the book that had first attracted Athénaïs Mialaret to Michelet. One English translation (with a violently anti-Catholic introduction by the anonymous translator) exists: *Spiritual Direction, and Auricular Confession* (Philadelphia: James M. Campbell, 1845).

14. See the excellent pioneer study by Roland Barthes, *Michelet par lui-même* (Le Seuil, 1954; 1965), extremely perspicacious, but inexact when analyzing Michelet's view of orgasm; cf. Georges Poulet, "Le Moment d'Eros," *Nouvelle Revue Française* (October 1967), pp. 610–35; and Michelet's journals; also Claude Digeon, "Note sur le *Journal* de Michelet (1860–74)," *Annales Universitatis Saraviensis*, Série Philosophie, I (1959). For a psychological profile of Michelet worthy of Krafft-Ebing see Jeanne Calo, *La Création de la femme chez Michelet* (Nizet, 1975).

15. This and the next passage are from *Love*, pp. 138–39; 156; *Amour*, pp. 181–82; 206.

16. *The Women of the French Revolution*, trans. by Meta Roberts Pennington (Philadelphia: Henry Carey Baird, 1855), pp. 18–19; *Les Femmes de la Révolution* (Delahays, 1855), pp. 10–11.

17. *Woman*, pp. 187–88; *Femme*, pp. 303–4.

18. *Love*, p. 155; *Amour*, p. 204.

19. Much of the disrepute of Michelet's work after 1850 can be attributed to

the evolution of literary taste, as suggested by the judgment of Charles Bruneau: "Michelet, que j'ai déjà étudié dans le vol. XII de cette *Histoire,* exagère encore sa manière. Il achève son *Histoire de France* et publie une série d'essais dans son style tendu et passionné. Il est nécessaire de considérer à part ces deux séries d'ouvrages, de caractère essentiellement différent et souvent opposé" (F. Brunot and C. Bruneau, *Histoire de la langue française des origines à nos jours,* vol. XIII, part 1 [Armand Colin, 1953], p. 175), and his final condemnation: "Quoi qu'il en soit, ses 'Essais' sont difficilement lisibles aujourd'hui" (ibid., p. 197).

Another subjective reaction is illustrated by the intense distrust of the second Mme. Michelet, Athénaïs Mialaret, expressed pungently by Elie Faure: "Sa femme est désormais sa collaboratrice active.... Pendant les dix ans qui suivirent, bien que, de temps à autre, un nouveau volume de l'*Histoire de France* reprise crevât, comme un cri de révolte, l'entassement nuageux des déclamations sentimentales où s'abêtissait sa pensée, Michelet ne fut plus lui-même.... C'est presque toujours l'écoulement diffus d'une diarrhée sentimentale.... Ces œuvres doivent disparaître" (*Les Constructeurs* [Plon, 1950], p. 62).

20. *Women of the French Revolution,* p. 367, note; *Femmes de la Révolution,* pp. 324–25, note 1.

21. "L'homme moderne, victime de la division du travail, condamné souvent à une spécialité étroite où il perd le sentiment de la vie générale et où il s'atrophie lui-même, aurait besoin de trouver chez lui un esprit jeune et serein, moins spécialisé, mieux équilibré, qui le sortît de son métier, et lui rendît le sentiment de la grande et douce harmonie" (*Le Prêtre, la Femme et la Famille* [Calmann-Lévy, 1881], p. 277).

22. For some background on these still innovative approaches to sex roles see: Alice Rossi, "Equality between the Sexes: An Immodest Proposal," *Daedalus* 93, no. 2 (1964), reprinted in Garskof, ed., *Roles Women Play: Readings Toward Women's Liberation* (Belmont, California: Wadsworth Publishing Co., 1971), pp. 145 et seq.; Sandra Bem and Daryl Bem, "Training the Woman to Know Her Place: The Power of an Unconscious Ideology," in Garskof, pp. 84–96; Ruth Hartley, "Some Implications of Current Changes in Sex Role Patterns," *Merrill-Palmer Quarterly* 3, no. 6 (April 1960), 153–64. The most recent and comprehensive examination of this problem is the critical anthology of Alexandra G. Kaplan and Joan Bean, *Beyond Sex Role Stereotypes: Toward a Theory of Androgyny* (Boston: Little Brown and Co., 1976).

23. This and the final quotation are from *Love,* pp. 74–75; 305–6; *Amour,* pp. 94–95; 399.

8 Michelet the Poet of History: Conclusion

1. "Le juge du vrai est *la conscience*. Mais il lui faut des contrôles, *l'histoire,* conscience du genre humain, et *l'histoire naturelle,* conscience instinctive de la nature.... Quand les trois s'accordent, croyez" (*La Femme,* p. 456).

2. *Préface de 1869 à l'Histoire de France,* ed. Charles Morazé (Armand Colin, 1962), p. 175. See Appendix, p. 157.

3. Ernst Cassirer, *An Essay on Man,* pp. 204–5. Cassirer's entire chapter on history (pp. 171–206) suggests many parallels between Herder and Michelet (without mentioning the latter). Cf. Ernst Cassirer, *The Problem of Knowledge,* trans. W. H. Woglom and C. W. Hendel (New Haven: Yale University Press, 1950),

especially parts 2, "The Ideal of Knowledge and its Transformations in Biology," and 3, "Fundamental Forms and Tendencies of Historical Knowledge."

4. *Sea*, p. 34; *Mer*, pp. 25–26.

5. Preface to *The Bird*, pp. 46–47; *Oiseau*, p. xlii.

6. *Mountain*, pp. 300–301; *Montagne*, p. 365.

7. *Love*, pp. 308–9; *Amour*, pp. 403–4.

8. All forms of the simple person are synonyms of the People, itself an aspect of genius, the ideal man: "L'enfant est l'interprète du peuple. Que dis-je? il est le peuple même, dans sa vérité native, avant qu'il ne soit déformé, le peuple sans vulgarité, sans rudesse, sans envie, n'inspirant ni défiance, ni répulsion" (*Peuple*, p. 158). The poor person, too, by his closeness to nature, represents another idealization of the common People: "Par bonheur, la nature, dans la famille pauvre, (le pauvre, c'est le peuple, c'est presque tout le monde) domine et écarte le dogme" (*Fils*, p. 113). Finally, the People itself is not essentially an historical or sociological reality, but an abstraction ("sa plus haute idée") based on some faculties of genius, the essence of mankind: "Le peuple, en sa plus haute idée, se trouve difficilement dans le peuple. Que j'observe ici ou là, ce n'est pas lui, c'est telle classe, telle forme partielle du peuple, altérée et éphémère. Il n'est dans sa vérité, à sa plus haute puissance, que dans l'homme de génie; en lui réside la grande âme..." (*Peuple*, p. 187). Genius subsumes all forms of ideal simplicity: "C'est le simple par excellence, l'enfant des enfants, il est le peuple, plus que le peuple même" (ibid., p. 186). Cf. also *Fils*, p. 310. Michelet's philosophy of "the People" should thus, with respect to the reality behind the symbol, be called a philosophy of the man of genius.

9. For the Romantics, the man of genius, usually a symbol of the artist, was alienated from society because of his extraordinary sensitivity and creative passion. Cf. Gretchen Besser, *Balzac's Concept of Genius: The Theme of Superiority in the "Comédie Humaine"* (Geneva: Droz, 1969), especially chap. I, pp. 15–60 in which she compares Balzac's themes with those of his contemporaries; also Ernst Cassirer, "Intuitional Aesthetics and the Problem of Genius," in *The Philosophy of the Enlightenment*, pp. 312–31; Herbert Dieckmann, "Diderot's Conception of Genius," *Journal of the History of Ideas*, II (1941), 151–82. Michelet's stress is on the characteristics of the man of genius which bind him to humanity, those aspects of genius which most people can develop.

10. This and the next passage are from *People*, pp. 112, 132–33; *Peuple*, pp. 147–48; 183; McKay, pp. 113; 138–39.

11. The passage from *Le Peuple* which follows in my text reappeared nineteen years later in *La Bible de l'humanité* (Chamerot, 1864), p. 63: "La pitié a eu dans l'Inde les effets de sagesse. Elle a fait de la conservation, du salut de tous les êtres un devoir religieux. Et elle en a été payée. Elle y a gagné l'éternelle jeunesse. A travers tous les désastres, la vie animale respectée, chérie, multipliée, surabondante, lui donne les renouvellements d'une intarissable fécondité." See note 1.

12. This and the following passage are from *People*, pp. 127–28; *Peuple*, pp. 173–75; McKay, pp. 131–33.

Selected Bibliography

The most complete bibliography on Michelet is the *Bibliographie des auteurs modernes de langue française* of H. Talvert and J. Place, XV (Paris: Editions de la Chronique des lettres françaises, 1963), 37–105, which, though abundant, is often incorrect, repetitive, and disorderly. Also useful is Hugo Thieme, *Bibliographie de la littérature française de 1800 à 1930*, II (Paris: Droz, 1933), 314–320, and the supplements of 1948 by Dreher and Rolli and 1954 by Drevet. The most practical working bibliography is that of Paul Viallaneix, *La Voie royale* (Paris: Flammarion, 1971), pp. 495–520, which includes all of Michelet's publications, manuscripts, correspondence, plus comments by Viallaneix on the most important criticism on Michelet. Chabaud, in his *Jules Michelet* (Paris: Editions de la Nouvelle Revue Critique, 1929) gives general accounts of the composition of Michelet's books and cites some of their contemporary critics (pp. 57–84). Contemporary press reviews of all Michelet's books will be printed in the superb critical edition of his *Oeuvres complètes* now being published by Flammarion under the direction of Paul Viallaneix. Included in the following list of secondary sources, therefore, are only works relevant to *Michelet's Poetic Vision*.

1. Chronological List of Michelet's Books

1825. *Tableau chronologique de l'histoire moderne* (1453–1789). Paris: L. Colas.

1826. *Tableaux synchroniques de l'histoire moderne.* Paris: L. Colas.

1827. *Principes de la philosophie de l'histoire*, translation from Vico and preceded by a *Discours sur le système et la vie de l'auteur*. Paris: J. Renouard.
Précis de l'histoire moderne. Paris: L. Colas, L. Hachette.

1831. *Introduction à l'histoire universelle.* Paris: Hachette. I have quoted from the 1962 Armand Colin Edition, edited by Charles Morazé. Michelet adds to the second edition (1834) a *Discours d'ouverture* delivered 9 January 1834, at the Faculté des Lettres de Paris, adding to the third edition (1843) a fragment on the *Education des femmes au Moyen Age*.
Histoire de la République romaine. Paris: Hachette; 2 volumes.

1833. *Précis de l'histoire de France jusqu'à la Révolution française.* Paris: Hachette.
Histoire de France, vols. 1 and 2. Paris: Hachette; 2 volumes.

1835. *Mémoires de Luther, écrits par lui-même*, etc. Paris: Hachette.

1837.   *Histoire de France*, vol. 3. Paris: Hachette.
        Origines du droit français cherchées dans les symboles et les formules du droit universel. Paris: Hachette.
1840.   *Histoire de France*, vol. 4. Paris: Hachette.
1841.   *Procès des Templiers*, vol. 1. Paris: Imprimerie Royale; collection des documents inédits relatifs à l'histoire de France.
        Histoire de France, vol. 5. Paris: Hachette.
1843.   *Des Jésuites.* Paris: Hachette et Paulin; published in the second half of the volume is the course of Edgar Quinet delivered at the Collège de France at the same time as Michelet.
1844.   *Histoire de France*, vol. 6. Paris: Hachette.
1845.   *Du Prêtre, de la Femme, de la Famille.* Paris: Imprimeurs réunis, Hachette, Paulin. I have used the Calmann-Lévy edition of 1881.
1846.   *Le Peuple.* Paris: Hachette et Paulin. I have used the critical edition of Lucien Refort: Paris: Didier, Société des textes français modernes, 1946; and translations by G. H. Smith (New York: D. Appleton and Co., 1846), and *The People,* translated by John P. McKay. Urbana: University of Illinois Press, 1973.
1847.   *Histoire de la Révolution française*, vols. 1 and 2. Paris: Chamerot. I have used the edition of Gérard Walter, Paris: N.R.F., Bibliothèque de la Pléiade, 1939; 1952. 2 volumes.
1848.   *Cours professé au Collège de France* (1847–1848). Paris: Chamerot. This course was republished in 1877 under the title *L'Etudiant.* Paris: C. Lévy.
1849.   *Histoire de la Révolution française*, vol. 3. Paris: Chamerot.
1850.   *Histoire de la Révolution française*, vol. 4. Paris: Chamerot.
1851.   *Histoire de la Révolution française*, vol. 5. Paris: Chamerot.
        Pologne et Russie, Légende de Kosciusko. Paris, Librairie Nouvelle.
1853.   *Histoire de la Révolution française*, vols. 6 and 7. Paris: Chamerot.
        Principautés danubiennes, Madame Rosetti. Paris: Bry aîné.
1854.   *Légendes démocratiques du Nord.* Paris: Garnier. This volume brings together *Pologne et Russie, Légende de Kosciusko, Principautés danubiennes* and *Madame Rosetti.*
        Les Femmes de la Révolution. Paris: Delahays. I have quoted from the 1855 edition and from *The Women of the French Revolution,* translated by Meta Roberts Pennington. Philadelphia: Henry Carey Baird, 1855.
1855.   *Histoire de France*, vols. 7 and 8. Paris: Chamerot. Complete title: *Histoire de France au XVIème siècle.*
1856.   *Histoire de France*, vols. 9 and 10. Paris: Chamerot. Complete title: *Histoire de France au XVIème siècle.*
        L'Oiseau. Paris: Hachette. I have used the sixth edition: Paris: Hachette, 1859. The translation of *The Bird* quoted is that of A. E. [W. H. Davenport Adams], with 210 illustrations by Giacomelli. London: T. Nelson and Sons, 1869.
1857.   *Histoire de France*, vol. 11. Paris: Chamerot. Complete title: *Histoire de France au XVIIème siècle.*
        L'Insecte. Paris: Hachette. I have used the second edition, "revue et corrigée": Paris: Hachette, 1858. The translation of *The Insect* quoted is that of W. H. Davenport Adams, with 140 illustrations by Giacomelli. London: T. Nelson and Sons, 1875.
1858.   *Histoire de France*, vol. 12. Paris: Chamerot. Complete title: *Histoire de France au XVIIème siècle.*

L'Amour. Paris: Hachette. I have used the 1894 Calmann-Lévy edition. The translation of *Love* quoted is that of J. W. Palmer, M.D. New York: Rudd and Carleton, 1859.

1860. *La Femme.* Paris: Hachette. Although it carries the date 1860, the original edition was put on sale 21 November 1859. I have used the third edition, 1860. The translation of *Woman* quoted is that of J. W. Palmer, M.D. New York: Rudd and Carleton, 1860.
  Histoire de France, vol. 13. Paris: Chamerot. Complete title: *Histoire de France au XVIIème siècle.*

1861. *La Mer.* Paris: Hachette. I have used the first and second editions, both 1861. The translation of *The Sea* quoted is that of W. H. Davenport Adams. London: T. Nelson and Sons, 1875.

1862. *Histoire de France,* vol. 14. Paris: Chamerot. Complete title: *Histoire de France au XVIIème siècle.*
  La Sorcière. Paris: Dentu et Hetzel. I have used the Garnier-Flammarion edition, 1966.

1863. *La Pologne martyr (sic). Russie, Danube.* Paris: Dentu; Brussels: Lacroix et Verboeckhoven. Under a new title this is practically a reissue, with a new preface, of *Légendes démocratiques du Nord.*
  Histoire de France, vol. 15. Paris: Chamerot. Complete title: *Histoire de France au XVIIIème siècle.*

1864. *Bible de l'humanité.* Paris: Chamerot. I have used the first edition.

1866. *Histoire de France,* vol. 16. Paris: Chamerot. Complete title: *Histoire de France au XVIIIème siècle.*

1867. *Histoire de France,* vol. 17. Paris: Chamerot. Complete title: *Histoire de France au XVIIIème siècle.*

1868. *La Montagne.* Paris: Librairie Internationale. Lacroix et Verboeckhoven. I have used the first edition. The translation of *The Mountain* quoted is that of W. H. Davenport Adams, with 54 illustrations by Percival Skelton. London: T. Nelson and Sons, 1872.

1869. *Nos Fils.* Paris: Librairie Internationale. Lacroix et Verboeckhoven. I have used the 1903 Calmann-Lévy edition.

1871. *La France devant l'Europe.* Florence: Le Monnier; Lyons: A. Faure; Bordeaux: Ch. Lévy.

1872. *Histoire du XIXème siècle,* vol. 1. Paris: Lévy frères.

1873. *Histoire du XIXème siècle,* vol. 2. Paris: Lévy frères.

Posthumous Publications

1875. *Histoire du XIXème siècle,* vol. 3. Paris: Lévy frères.

1878. *Les Soldats de la Révolution.* Paris: Marpon.

1879. *Le Banquet* (written in 1854), contained in *Un Hiver en Italie: Papiers intimes.* Paris: Marpon et Flammarion.

1884. *Ma Jeunesse* (1798–1820). Paris: Marpon et Flammarion.

1888. *Mon Journal* (1820–1823). Paris: Marpon et Flammarion.

1891. *Rome.* Paris: Marpon et Flammarion.

1893. *Sur les chemins de l'Europe.* Paris: Marpon et Flammarion.

1898. *Précis de l'histoire de France au Moyen Age.* Paris: Calmann-Lévy.

1898–1903. *Oeuvres complètes.* 46 volumes. Paris: Calmann-Lévy.

1924. *Lettres inédites à Alfred Dumesnil et à Eugène Noel* (1841–1871). Ed. Paul Sirven. Paris: Presses Universitaires de France.

1955. *Nouvelles lettres inédites de Michelet* [and Mme. Michelet]. To Charles Alexandre. Ed. Paul Desachy. Monaco: Editions de l'Acanthe.

1959. *Journal,* vol. 1 (1828–1848), first complete edition prepared by Paul Viallaneix. Paris: Gallimard.

  Ecrits de jeunesse (*Journal* 1820–1823, *Mémorial, Journal des idées*), first complete and critical edition prepared by Paul Viallaneix. Paris: Gallimard.

1962. *Journal,* vol. 2 (1849–1860). Ed. Paul Viallaneix. Paris: Gallimard.

1971–. *Oeuvres complètes.* Ed. Paul Viallaneix. Paris: Flammarion. 20 volumes to appear.

2. *Secondary Sources*

Albalat, Antoine. "Michelet artiste," *Nouvelle Revue,* CXVII (March–April 1899), 276–85.

Albouy, Pierre. *Mythes et mythologies dans la littérature française.* Paris: Armand Colin, 1969.

Annales des sciences naturelles, vols. 19, 22, and 23. Paris: Crochard, 1830–1831.

Atherton, John. "Michelet: Three Conceptions of Historical Becoming," *Studies in Romanticism* IV, 1 (Autumn 1964), 220–39.

Bachelard, Gaston. *L'Air et les songes: Essai sur l'imagination du mouvement.* Paris: José Corti, 1943.

———. *L'Eau et les rêves: Essai sur l'imagination de la matière.* Paris: Corti, 1942.

———. *La Formation de l'esprit scientifique: Essai d'une psychanalyse de la connaissance objective.* Paris: Vrin, 1960.

Barbéris, Pierre. *Balzac et le mal du siècle.* Contribution à une physiologie du monde moderne. Paris: Gallimard, 1970.

Barthes, Roland. "Aujourd'hui, Michelet," *L'Arc* 52 (1973), pp. 19–27.

———. *Michelet par lui-même.* Paris: Le Seuil, 1954, 1965. (Cf. Jean Pommier. "Baudelaire et Michelet devant la jeune critique," *Revue d'histoire littéraire de la France* [1957], pp. 544–47.)

Barzun, Jacques. *Classic, Romantic and Modern.* New York: Anchor Books, 1961.

Bellet, Roger. *Presse et journalisme sous le Second Empire.* Paris: Armand Colin, 1967.

Bénichou, Paul. *Le Sacre de l'écrivain, 1750–1830.* Essai sur l'avènement d'un pouvoir spirituel laïque dans la France moderne. Paris: José Corti, 1973.

Berthelot, M[arcelin]. "Etude de *l'Insecte,*" in *L'Insecte* of Jules Michelet. Paris: Calmann-Lévy, 1903, pp. 3–39.

Boas, George. *French Philosophies of the Romantic Period.* Baltimore: The Johns Hopkins University Press, 1925.

Borzeix, Jean-Marie. "L'Unité et l'Union, du *Peuple* à la *Bible de l'humanité,*" *Romantisme,* nos. 1–2 (1971), 111–16.

Bowman, Frank Paul. *Le Christ romantique.* Geneva: Droz, 1974.

———. "Michelet et les métamorphoses du Christ," *Revue d'histoire littéraire de la France* 74 (September–October 1974), 824–51.

Brunot, Ferdinand and Charles Bruneau. *Histoire de la langue française des origines à nos jours.* Vol. XIII, part 1. Paris: Armand Colin, 1953.

Bury, J. B. *The Idea of Progress.* London: Macmillan and Co., 1920.

Busst, A. J. L. "The Image of the Androgyne in the Nineteenth Century," in *Romantic Mythologies,* edited by Ian Fletcher. London: Routledge and Kegan Paul, 1967.

Cahn, Théophile. *La Vie et l'œuvre d'Etienne Geoffroy Saint-Hilaire.* Paris: Presses Universitaires de France, 1962.

Calo, Jeanne. *La Création de la femme chez Michelet.* Paris: Nizet, 1975.

Carré, Jean-Marie. *Michelet et son temps* ("avec de nombreux documents inédits"). Paris: Perrin et Cie., 1926.

Caro, Edme. *L'Idée de Dieu et ses nouveaux critiques.* Paris: Hachette, 1864.

Cassirer, Ernst. *An Essay on Man: An Introduction to the Philosophy of Human Culture.* New Haven and London: Yale University Press, 1962. [1st ed. 1944.]

———. *Language and Myth.* Trans. Susanne K. Langer. New York: Dover Publications, 1953.

———. *The Philosophy of the Enlightenment.* Trans. Fritz Koelln and James Pettegrove. Boston: Beacon Press, 1966. [1st German ed. 1932.]

———. *The Problem of Knowledge.* Trans. W. H. Woglom and C. W. Hendel. New Haven: Yale University Press, 1950.

———. *Rousseau, Kant and Goethe.* Trans. James Gutmann, Paul O. Kristeller, and John H. Randall, Jr. New York: Harper Torchbooks, 1963.

Chabaud, Alfred. *Jules Michelet, son œuvre.* Paris: Editions de la Nouvelle Revue Critique, 1929.

Clarke, Margaret I. "Rimbaud—Michelet—Vico," *Modern Language Review,* XXXVII (1942), 50–55.

Collingwood, R. G. *The Idea of History.* London, Oxford, New York: Oxford University Press, 1956.

———. *The Idea of Nature.* London, Oxford, New York: Oxford University Press, 1960.

Cornuz, Jean-Louis. *Jules Michelet: Un aspect de la pensée religieuse au XIXe siècle.* Geneva: Droz, 1955.

Crouzet, Michel. "Michelet, les morts et l'année 1842." *Annales* (January–February 1976), 182–196.

Dictionnaire universelle d'histoire naturelle, edited by Charles d'Orbigny. 13 volumes. Paris: L. Houssiaux et Cie., 1861. [1st ed. 1841–1849.]

Dieckmann, Herbert. "Diderot's Conception of Genius," *Journal of the History of Ideas,* II (1941), 151–82.

Digeon, Claude. "Note sur le 'Journal' de Michelet (années 1860–1874)," *Annales Universitatis Saraviensis,* Série Philosophie, Fasc. 1 (1959). 48 pp.

Durand, Gilbert. *Les Structures anthropologiques de l'imaginaire: Introduction à l'archétypologie générale.* Paris: Presses Universitaires de France, 1963.

Eichner, Hans, editor. *'Romantic' and Its Cognates: The European History of a Word.* Toronto: University of Toronto Press, 1972.

Eiseley, Loren. *Darwin's Century: Evolution and the Men Who Discovered It.* New York: Doubleday and Co., 1958.

———. *The Firmament of Time.* New York: Atheneum, 1970.

Encyclopédie nouvelle, edited by Pierre Leroux and Jean Reynaud, 8 volumes. Paris: Gosselin, 1831–1841.

Faure, Elie. *Les Constructeurs.* Paris: Plon, 1950. [1st ed. Paris: Crès, 1914.]

Febvre, Lucien. *Jules Michelet ou la liberté morale.* Geneva-Paris: Editions des Trois Collines, 1946.

Foucault, Michel. *Les Mots et les choses.* Paris: Gallimard, 1966.

Fouillée, Alfred. "La Psychologie religieuse dans Michelet," *Revue Philosophique de la France et de l'étranger,* XLVII (1899), 259–75.

France, Archives de. *Michelet, sa vie, son œuvre.* Paris: Hôtel de Rohan, 1961.

Gaulmier, Jean. Introduction to André Breton, *Ode à Charles Fourier*. Paris: C. Klincksieck, 1961, pp. 12–59.

――――. *Michelet devant Dieu*. Paris: Desclée de Brouwer, 1968. (Cf. the review of Paul Viallaneix in *Revue d'histoire littéraire de la France* [July–August 1970], pp. 667–73.)

Geoffroy Saint-Hilaire, Isidore. *Histoire naturelle des règnes organiques, principalement étudiée chez l'homme et les animaux*, vol. 1. Paris: Victor Masson, 1854.

Gillispie, Charles Coulton. *Genesis and Geology: The Impact of Scientific Discoveries upon Religious Beliefs in the Decades before Darwin*. New York: Harper Torchbooks, 1959.

Gilson, Etienne. *D'Aristote à Darwin et retour*. Paris: Vrin, 1970.

Gilman, Margaret. *The Idea of Poetry in France from Houdar de La Motte to Baudelaire*. Cambridge, Mass.: Harvard University Press, 1958. (Cf. Michael Riffaterre. *Romanic Review*, LI [1960], 115–22.)

Giraud, Victor. "L'Evolution spirituelle de Michelet," *Revue des Deux Mondes*, XLI (1927), 218–29.

Glass, Bentley, O. Temkin, and W. L. Straus, Jr., editors. *Forerunners of Darwin*. Baltimore: The Johns Hopkins University Press, 1959.

Gleckner, Robert and Gerald Enscoe, editors. *Romanticism: Points of View*. Second edition. New Jersey: Prentice-Hall, 1970.

Gode-von Aesch, Alexander. *Natural Science in German Romanticism*. New York, AMA Press, 1966. [1st ed., Columbia University Press, 1941.]

Gossman, Lionel. "The Go-Between: Jules Michelet, 1798–1874," *MLN* 89 (1974), 503–41.

Grand Dictionnaire Universal du XIXᵉ siècle. Ed. Pierre Larousse. 16 vols. and 2 supplements. Paris: Administration du Grand Dictionnaire Universel, 1866–1876.

Groethuysen, Bernard. *Anthropologie Philosophique*. Paris: Gallimard, 1952.

Guéhenno, Jean. *L'Evangile éternel, étude sur Michelet*. Paris: Grasset, 1962. [1st ed. 1927.]

Guérard, Albert Leon. *French Prophets of Yesterday: A Study of Religious Thought Under the Second Empire*. New York: D. Appleton and Co., 1913.

Guizot, François. *Méditations sur l'état actuel de la religion chrétienne en France*. Paris: Michel Lévy frères, 1866.

Haac, Oscar. *Les Principes inspirateurs de Michelet*. New Haven: Yale University Press; Paris: P.U.F., 1951.

――――. *Michelet et l'histoire allemande*. New Haven: unpublished dissertation, Yale University, 1948.

Habert, J. "Jules Michelet et la mer," *Revue Universelle*, XXVIII (1 Sept. 1929), 565–84. (Cf. Pierre Guéguen. "J. Habert, Jules Michelet de la Mer," *Nouvelles Littéraires* [28 Sept. 1929], p. 8.)

Heschel, Abraham Joshua. *Man Is Not Alone*. New York: Harper Torchbooks, 1951.

Janicaud, Dominique. *Une Généalogie du spiritualisme français*. La Haye: Martinus Nijhoff, 1969.

Johnson, Mary-Elisabeth. *Michelet et le christianisme*. Paris: Nizet, 1955.

Joly, Henri. *L'Homme et l'animal*. Paris: Hachette, 1877.

Jonas, Hans. *The Phenomenon of Life: Toward a Philosophical Biology*. New York: Harper and Row, 1966.

Kaplan, Edward K. "Les Deux Sexes de l'esprit: Michelet phénoménologue de la pensée créatrice et morale," *Europe,* nos. 535–536 (November–December 1973), 97–111.

————. "Gaston Bachelard's Philosophy of Imagination: An Introduction," *Philosophy and Phenomenological Research,* XXXIII, 1 (September 1972), 1–24.

————. "Michelet évolutionniste," *Michelet Cent Ans Après,* ed. Paul Viallaneix. Grenoble: Presses Universitaires de Grenoble, 1975, pp. 111–28.

————. "Michelet's Revolutionary Symbolism: From Hermeneutics to Politics," *The French Review,* Vol. 50, no. 5 (April 1977).

————. "Le Symbolisme de la nature chez Michelet: Introduction littéraire à son spiritualisme," *Nineteenth-Century French Studies,* III, nos. 3 and 4 (Spring–Summer 1975), 141–64.

Lamarck, Jean Baptiste Monet de. *Zoological Philosophy,* trans. Hugh Elliot. New York: Hafner Publishing Co., 1963.

Lanson, Gustave. "La Formation de la méthode historique de Michelet," *Revue d'Histoire moderne et contemporaine,* VII (1905), 5–31.

Leroy, Maxime. *Histoire des idées sociales en France.* Vol. 3, *D'Auguste Comte à P.-J. Proudhon.* Paris: Gallimard, 1954.

Lovejoy, Arthur O. *Essays in the History of Ideas.* Baltimore: The Johns Hopkins University Press, 1948.

————. *The Great Chain of Being.* New York: Harper Torchbooks, 1960. [1st ed. 1936.]

Ludlow, J. M. "Spiritualistic Materialism, Michelet," *Macmillan's Magazine,* II (1860), 41–51.

Manuel, Frank E. *The Prophets of Paris.* New York: Harper Torchbooks, 1962.

Mason, Stephen F. *A History of the Sciences.* New York: Collier Books, 1962.

Maury, L.-F.-Alfred. *Le Sommeil et les rêves.* 3rd ed., "revue et considérablement augmentée." Paris: Didier, 1865.

Mayer, Ernest. "Lamarck Revisited," *Journal of the History of Biology,* V, 1 (Spring 1972), 55–94.

Mazzeo, Joseph A. *The Design of Life; Major Themes in the Development of Biological Thought.* New York: Pantheon Books, 1967.

Michelet, Athénaïs Mialaret (Mme. Jules). *Les Chats.* Ed. Gabriel Monod. Paris: E. Flammarion, [1904].

————. *Mémoires d'une enfant.* 1st ed. Paris: Hachette, 1867.

————. *Nature; or, The Poetry of Earth and Sea.* Trans. W. H. Davenport Adams. London: T. Nelson and Sons, 1877.

"Michelet a Naturalist," *Dublin University Magazine,* L (1857), 564–68.

Mignot, Henri. *Michelet éducateur.* Paris: Armand Colin, 1930.

Milne-Edwards, Henri. *Rapport sur les progrès récents des sciences zoologiques en France.* Paris: L'Imprimerie impériale, Hachette, 1867.

Monod, Gabriel. "Isidore Geoffroy Saint-Hilaire et Michelet," *Revue politique et littéraire. Revue Bleue* (14 octobre 1911), pp. 481–84.

————. *Jules Michelet: Etudes sur sa vie et ses œuvres.* Paris: Hachette, 1905.

————. *Les Maîtres de l'Histoire: Renan, Taine, Michelet.* Paris: Calmann-Lévy, 1894.

————. "Michelet dans l'histoire de son temps," *Bibliothèque universelle et Revue suisse,* Series 4, vol. 60 (June 1911), 449–70.

————. *La Vie et la pensée de Jules Michelet, 1798–1852.* 2 vols. Cours professé au Collège de France. Paris: Champion, 1923.

Montégut, Emile. "De l'amour et du mariage," *Revue des Deux Mondes*, XVIII (15 December 1858), 931–50.

———. "Les Fantaisies d'histoire naturelle de M. Michelet," *Revue des Deux Mondes*, XXXI (1 February 1861), 719–41.

———. "La Poésie des montagnes," *Revue des Deux Mondes*, LXXIV (1 March 1868), 217–33.

Morgan, Elaine. *The Descent of Woman*. New York: Stein and Day, 1972.

Neff, Emery. *The Poetry of History*. New York: Columbia University Press, 1947.

Nettement, Alfred. *Histoire de la littérature française sous le gouvernement de juillet*. Vol. II. Paris: J. Lecoffre et Cie., 1854.

Noël, Eugène. *Jules Michelet et ses enfants*. Paris: M. Dreyfous, 1878.

Orr, Linda. *Jules Michelet: Nature, History and Language*. Ithaca, New York: Cornell University Press, 1976.

———. "Les Alternatives bizarres de Michelet," *Europe*, nos. 535–536 (November–December 1973), 117–31.

———. "L'Eternel Entr'acte: le temps de l'histoire naturelle," *Revue d'histoire littéraire de la France* 74 (September–October 1974), 775–86.

———. *Michelet the Naturalist: Dialectics and Stylistics of Metamorphosis*. New Haven: Unpublished dissertation at Yale University, September 1971.

Otto, Rudolph. *The Idea of the Holy*. Trans. John W. Harvey. New York: Galaxy Books, 1958. [1st German ed. 1917.]

Papillard, François. *Michelet et Vascoeuil*. Catalog of the Centenary of Michelet's Death. Paris, 1974.

Pelletan, Eugène. *Profession de foi du XIXème siècle*. Paris: Pagnerre, 1852.

Perrier, Edmond. *La Philosophie zoologique avant Darwin*, 3rd ed. Paris: Felix Alcan, 1896.

Peyre, Henri. *Historical and Critical Essays*. Lincoln: University of Nebraska Press, 1968.

———. *Qu'est-ce que le romantisme?* Paris: Presses Universitaires de France, 1971.

Plessis, Alain. *De la fête impériale au mur des fédérés, 1852–1871*. Paris: Le Seuil, 1973.

Polanyi, Michael. *Personal Knowledge: Towards a Post-Critical Philosophy*. New York: Harper Torchbooks, 1964.

Poulet, Georges. "Le Moment d'Eros," *Nouvelle Revue Française* (October 1967), pp. 610–35.

Pugh, Anne R. *Michelet and His Ideas on Social Reform*. New York: Columbia University Press, 1923.

Quatrefages, A. de. *Charles Darwin et ses précurseurs français: Etude sur le transformisme*. Paris: Germer Baillière, 1870.

Quinet, Mme. Edgar. *Cinquante ans d'amitié, Michelet et Quinet*. Paris: A. Colin, 1899.

Rambaud, Eugène. "Les Derniers Ouvrages de Michelet: *L'Oiseau, L'Insecte, L'Amour*," *Bibliothèque universelle et Revue suisse*, IV (1859), 521–56.

Ravaisson, Félix. *La Philosophie en France au dix-neuvième siècle (1867)*. 3rd ed. Paris: Hachette, 1889.

Rearick, Charles. *Beyond the Enlightenment: Historians and Folklore in Nineteenth-Century France*. Bloomington: Indiana University Press, 1974.

Refort, Lucien. *L'Art de Michelet dans son œuvre historique jusqu'en 1867*. Paris: Champion, 1923.

————. *Essai d'introduction à une étude lexicologique de Michelet.* Paris: Champion, 1923.

Riffaterre, Michael. *Essais de stylistique structurale.* Paris: Flammarion, 1971.

————. "Système d'un genre descriptif," *Poétique* 9 (1972), 15–30.

Roger, Jacques. *Les Sciences de la vie dans la pensée française du XVIIIe siècle.* Paris: Armand Colin, 1963.

Scherer, Edmond. *Etudes sur la littérature contemporaine.* Vol. 1. 1st ed. Paris: Michel Lévy, 1863.

Schlanger, Judith. *Les Métamorphoses de l'organisme.* Paris: Vrin, 1971.

Seebacher, Jacques. "L'Attitude politique de Michelet," *Revue des travaux de l'Académie des sciences morales* (1967), pp. 107–27.

————. "Le Côté de la mort, ou l'histoire comme clinique," *Revue d'histoire littéraire de la France* 74 (September–October 1974), 810–23.

————. "L'Education ou la fin de Michelet," *Europe,* nos. 535–536 (November–December 1973), 132–45.

Serres, Michel. "Michelet, la soupe," *Revue d'histoire littéraire de la France* 74 (September–October 1974), 787–802.

Shroder, Maurice Z. *Icarus: The Image of the Artist in French Romanticism.* Cambridge, Mass.: Harvard University Press, 1961.

Starobinski, Jean. *La Relation critique.* Paris: Gallimard, 1970.

Taine, Hippolyte. *Essais de critique et d'histoire.* 12th ed. Paris: Hachette, 1913.

Taton, René, ed. *Science in the Nineteenth Century,* trans. A. J. Pomerans, London: Thames and Hudson, 1965; *La Science Contemporaine.* Vol. III, part 1, "le XIXe siècle." Paris: P.U.F., 1961.

Teilhard de Chardin, Pierre. *Le Phénomène humain.* Paris: Le Seuil, 1970. [1st ed. 1955.]

————. *La Place de l'homme dans la nature: Le groupe zoologique humain.* Paris: Le Seuil, 1956.

Theuriet, André. "Une Étude de *La Montagne,*" in *La Montagne* of Michelet. Paris: Calmann-Lévy, 1899, pp. i–xiii.

Toulmin, Stephen and June Goodfield. *The Discovery of Time.* New York: Harper Torchbooks, 1965.

Van der Elst, Robert. *Michelet Naturaliste: Esquisse de son système de philosophie.* Paris: Delgrave, 1914. (Cf. Henri Hauser, "Michelet naturaliste et l'âme française d'aujourd'hui," *Revue du Mois,* XIX [10 February 1915], 151–71.)

Viallaneix, Paul. "A l'école buissonnière," *L'Arc,* no. 52, 1973.

————. "Michelet et la Révolution vivante," *Europe,* nos. 535–536 (November–December 1973), 3–15.

————.*La Voie royale: Essai sur l'idée de Peuple dans l'œuvre de Michelet.* Paris: Delagrave, 1959; Flammarion, 1971.

Vianey, Joseph. "Les grands poètes de la nature en France": "Ronsard, La Fontaine," *Revue des cours et conférences,* I (15 December 1925), 3–19; "J.-J. Rousseau, Bernardin de Saint-Pierre, Chateaubriand," ibid., III (15 January 1926), 203–20; "Lamartine," ibid., V (15 February 1926), 432–40; "Victor Hugo," ibid., VII (15 March 1926), 628–44; "George Sand, Michelet," ibid., X (30 April 1926), 149–63; "Leconte de Lisle, Pierre Loti," ibid., XII (30 May 1926), 334–51.

Vico, Jean-Baptiste. *Principes de la philosophie de l'histoire,* "traduits de la *Scienza Nuova* et précédés d'un discours sur le système et la vie de l'auteur par Jules Michelet." Bibliothèque de Cluny. Paris: Armand Colin, 1963. [1st ed. Paris: Jules Renouard, 1827.]

Vincent, Anthony. *Michelet et une nouvelle forme de religion naturelle.* Thesis: University of Toulouse, Faculté de théologie protestante de Montauban. Montauban: Imprimerie J. Granié, 1899.

Wellek, René. *A History of Modern Criticism: 1750–1950. Vol. 1, The Later Eighteenth Century.* New Haven: Yale University Press, 1955.

White, Hayden. *Metahistory: The Historical Imagination in Nineteenth-Century Europe.* Baltimore: The Johns Hopkins University Press, 1973.

Wilson, Edmund. *To the Finland Station.* New York: Harcourt, Brace and Co., 1940.

Windelband, Wilhelm. *A History of Philosophy,* vol. 1. New York: Harper Torchbooks, 1958.

Index

Michelet's works are noted under their English titles.

Education. *See* Michelet, Jules: as moral educator

Egypt, 155–56

Ehrenberg, Christian Gottfried, 44

Eichthal, Gustave d', 153 n

Eighteenth century, period of Enlightenment, xiv, xvi, 11–12, 90, 132. *See also* Progress

Eiseley, Loren, 45, 46, 173 n.21, 175 n.5, 177 n.5, 178 n.14

Empathy, xii, 4, 20, 64, 76, 95, 134–36, 140–41, 145, 146, 155, 156–57, 162. *See also* History: historical knowing; as resurrection

England, xxii, 43–46, 161

Epistemology, 103–7, 119-22. *See also* Thought

Ethics, Michelet's system of, 11, 128–30, 134–35, 142. *See also* Androgyne; Empathy; Michelet, Jules: as moral educator

Evolution: of "amphibians," 33–38; of birds, 38–40; geological, 25–28, 43–49; of hands, 37–38, 66; history as evolutionary force, 70–73 (*see also* Angelism; Darwin; Geoffroy Saint-Hilaire, Etienne; History; Immortality; Lamarck; Mother; Progress; Vitalism; Will); of humanity, 38, 50, 70, 75; of individuality, 34–35, 178 n.12; of love, 36, 51–57; marine, 28–33; of mind, 21, 31–32, 40, 67–73, 76, 189 n.12 (*see also* Dream; Thought); of moral values, 28, 34–40, 56, 57, 84; of plants, 31; theories of, 20, 22–25, 41–57, 102, 107, 118 (*see also* Debate of 1830); use of word, xviii, 24–25, 46, 47, 49, 175 n.7 (*see also* Metamorphosis)

Family, xv, 37, 55–56, 91, 132, 138. *See also* Mother

Faure, Elie, 190 n.19

Female. *See* Woman

Feminism. *See* Sexism

Ferguson, Adam, 86

Fish, 34–35, 55–56. *See also* Evolution: marine

Flaubert, Gustave, xiii, xvii, 170 n.10

Flores, Joachim de. *See* Joachim de Flores

Flourens, Pierre, 60

Foucault, Michel, 104

Fourier, Charles, xiv, 7 n

Freedom: in artistic creation, 64, 179 n.7, 180 n.15 (*see also* Evolution; Progress); human, 10–13, 69; in nature and history, 20, 21, 24, 33, 38, 39, 50, 53, 60, 62, 82, 107, 121, 132, 152; as philosophical principle vs. determinism, 10, 11, 20, 21, 33, 36, 58, 59–60, 64, 76, 83, 150 (*see also* Instinct); of will, 18, 53, 68, 82

Frigate Bird, the, 39, 83

Froissart, Jean, 151, 160, 165

Gasparin, Adrien-Etienne-Pierre de, xiii, 134

Gaulmier, Jean, 184 n.1

Gautier, Théophile, 181 n.4, 182 n.5

Genius, mind of, xix, 3, 65 n, 117–18, 126–28, 137–42, 191 nn.8, 9. *See also* Androgyne; Michelet, Jules: the "artist-historian"

Geoffroy Saint-Hilaire, Etienne, 9–10, 13–17, 19, 20, 22–25, 47, 48, 54

Geoffroy Saint-Hilaire, Isidore (son of Etienne), 17–19, 48, 174 n.28

Geography (Tableau de la France). See *Tableau of France*

Geology. *See* Evolution: geological

Georama, 121. *See also* Thought

Géricault, Théodore, 148

Germany, xxii, xxiii, 81–82. *See also* Romanticism; Rückert

God: accessible within the world (immanent), 4, 50–52, 60–63, 67, 73, 90, 98, 100, 107–13, 116, 118; and faith, 3–4, 94, 98, 99–103, 107–13; human invention as analogous to, 11–13, 52, 65; male and female, 73 (*see also* Creation); Michelet identifies with, 36, 65–66; natural evolution as analogous to, 18–19, 23–24, 51, 56–57, 66, 90, 102–3, 116; supernatural (transcendent), 25, 50, 67, 98–99, 101, 103, 107–13. *See also* Christianity; Mother; Pantheism

Gode-von Aesch, Alexander, 174 n.30, 178 n.10

Goethe, Wolfgang, 16, 22, 47, 48, 52, 111, 187 n.21

Library of Congress Cataloging in Publication Data
Kaplan, Edward K   1942–
   Michelet's poetic vision.
   Bibliography: p.
   Includes index.
      1. Michelet, Jules, 1798–1874.   2. Man.
3. Philosophy of nature.   I. Title.
B2331.M54K36   128'.092'4   76-45050
ISBN 0-87023-236-3